The Encyclopedia of
North American Indians

Volume III

Cheyenne–Delaware

General Editor
D. L. Birchfield

Marshall Cavendish
New York • London • Toronto

Published in 1997 by
Marshall Cavendish Corporation
99 White Plains Road
Tarrytown, NY 10591-9001
U.S.A.

© 1997 by Marshall Cavendish Corporation

Developed, designed, and produced by Water Buffalo Books, Milwaukee

Project director: Mark J. Sachner
General editor: D. L. Birchfield·
Art director: Sabine Beaupré
Photo researcher: Diane Laska
Project editor: Valerie J. Weber

Editors: Elizabeth Kaplan, MaryLee Knowlton, Judith Plumb, Carolyn Kott Washburne

Consulting editors: Donna Beckstrom, Jack D. Forbes, Annette Reed Crum, John Bierhorst.

Picture credits: © 1995 Paul Abdoo: 388 (top); © B. & C. Alexander: 382, 383, 400; © Archive Photos: 327 (bottom), 329, 344, 345, 348, 365, 376 (bottom), 412, 416, 432; © 1995 Noella Ballenger: title, 331, 332, 421; Sabine Beaupré 1996: 399; © 1994 Kenny Blackbird: 362; © Steve Bly: 294, 307, 379, 402, 415, 417, 420, 422; © Kit Breen: Cover, 340, 346, 376 (top), 404; © Brown Brothers, Sterling, PA: 304, 336; Courtesy of the Bureau of Indian Affairs, U. S. Department of the Interior: 429; © Corbis-Bettmann: 293, 296, 302, 324, 327 (top), 328, 353, 359, 361, 367, 368, 385, 413, 423, 425; Courtesy of Carter Blue Clark: 330; © Culver Pictures: 363 (both); © Susan Dirks Photography: 320 (top); © Eugene Fisher: 306, 308, 309, 313; © William B. Folsom 1987: 431; © Robert Frerck, Odyssey Productions: 297, 349, 350; © Hazel Hankin: 326; Courtesy of LeAnne Howe: 320 (bottom); © James Humphries, Choctaw Nation of Oklahoma: 318; © Richard Hunt: 323, 391; © Shirlee Silvernail Larotonda: 373; © Linda J. Moore: 401; © Leslie M. Newman: 371; © Odyssey Productions: 410; Courtesy of Louis Owens: 322; The Philbrook Museum of Art: 380; © Elaine Querry: 321; © Martha Ann Sheffield, Chickasaw Nation: 298, 299, 300; © Susan Silberberg: 333; © Elliott Smith: 310, 407; © Stephen Trimble: 312, 314, 355, 418, 419; © UPI/Corbis-Bettmann: 301, 341, 392, 393, 396; Courtesy of Craig Womack: 388 (bottom)

Library of Congress Cataloging-in-Publication Data

The encyclopedia of North American Indians.
      p. cm.
     Includes bibliographical references and index.
     Summary: A comprehensive reference work on the culture and history of Native Americans.
     ISBN 0-7614-0230-6 (vol. 3)   ISBN 0-7614-0227-6 (lib. bdg.: set)
     1. Indians of North America--Encyclopedias, Juvenile.
    [1. Indians of North America--Encyclopedias.]
    E76.2.E53   1997
    970.004'97'003--dc20   96-7700
                                                                  CIP
                                                                  AC

Printed and bound in Italy

Title page illustration: The regalia and paint worn by this man, a member of the Mescalero Apache tribe of southeastern New Mexico, clearly represent the plumage and physical characteristics of a bird. The occasion, a powwow at Taos Pueblo, in northern New Mexico, has drawn participants from a great number of Native groups throughout the Southwest.

Editor's note: Many systems of dating have been used by different cultures throughout history. *The Encyclopedia of North American Indians* uses B.C.E. (Before Common Era) and C.E. (Common Era) instead of B.C. (Before Christ) and A.D. (Anno Domini, "In the Year of the Lord") out of respect for the diversity of the world's peoples.

Contents

CHEYENNE

The Cheyennes call themselves the Dzitsiistas, which means "people who are alike" or "our people." The name Cheyenne comes from a Sioux word that means "people who speak a strange language."

The Cheyennes, who are from the Algonquian language family and are considered one of the great tribes of the Plains, were originally farmers and potters. They lived in permanent villages in timber country, now the state of Minnesota, and migrated westward in the 1600s to present-day North Dakota. From their home in North Dakota, the Cheyennes were pushed southwest by other tribes and eventually located in the Black Hills near the headwaters of the Cheyenne River. By the 1800s, they had become buffalo hunters on the Plains.

While moving to their new homeland, the Cheyennes adopted some new customs from allied tribes. Some of their dressing habits, as well as the Sun Dance and buffalo-head medicine ceremonies, were adopted from the Sioux. Other ceremonies and customs have been their own from the beginning of their culture. The Cheyennes were first noted in European historical records around 1680, when a band of the nation from Minnesota visit-ed a French fort on the Illinois River and invited the French to come to their country, which was rich in beaver and other animals.

The Lewis and Clark expedition of 1804 noted the presence of the Cheyennes in the Black Hills of South Dakota. The nation later moved westward to the upper branches of the Platte River, which in turn drove Kiowa inhabitants farther south. In 1825, the first treaty between the Cheyennes and the United States was signed on the Teton River in the Rocky Mountains. The United States promised protection for the Cheyennes, paving the way for the government's building of Bent's Fort on the Arkansas River without opposition from the Cheyennes.

In 1832, the nation split into two groups. A large number decided to relocate along the Arkansas River and became known as the Southern Cheyennes. Other bands of the Cheyennes moved along the headwaters of the Platte and Yellowstone Rivers and became known as the Northern Cheyennes.

In 1840, the Southern Cheyennes made peace with the Kiowas after a battle fought on Wolf Creek in present-day northwestern Oklahoma. Since that time, the Cheyennes, Arapahos, Kiowas,

By 1890, the great buffalo herds were gone, the Plains Indian wars were over, and the Cheyennes had entered a period during which the United States would attempt to assimilate them into U.S. culture. Though these Cheyennes, near Darlington Agency, are pictured in traditional dress, the American-style hats, seen at their feet, are an omen of the changes the Cheyenne people would adjust to over the next several generations.

Intertribal powwows, featuring dance competitions, provide an opportunity for North American Native people of many tribes to gather and celebrate the survival and continuation of their cultures. Here, a Cheyenne young-ster is seen in full regalia at a Shoshone-Bannock powwow.

Kiowa-Apaches, and Comanches—once warring nations—have been allies.

In 1864, Chief Black Kettle and other peace chiefs and their followers were camped at Sand Creek in Colorado. The Cheyennes had made an agreement with government officials that guaranteed their protection from government troops provided that the Cheyennes stayed in the Sand Creek region. But a force of Colorado troops under Colonel John M. Chivington's command attacked the encampment in the early morning hours. The people were stunned and taken completely by surprise. When the soldiers came into the encampment, a woman ran to Chief Black Kettle, who told her everything was all right and raised a white flag outside his home. Despite this offer of submission, the soldiers opened fire on the people. A great number of Cheyennes were killed while a few managed to escape. When the soldiers finally gave up chasing the survivors, they went back and mutilated the bodies by taking scalps, which were displayed to spectators in Colorado. The soldiers were treated as heroes upon their return to Denver. The Sand Creek Massacre changed forever the relationship between the Cheyennes and the United States government.

Under a treaty made at the Medicine Lodge Council in Kansas in 1867, the Cheyennes and the Arapahos were assigned a joint reservation, established by presidential proclamation, north of the Washita River in Indian Territory (present-day Oklahoma). Despite their joint status on the reservation, the Cheyennes and Arapahos steadfastly maintained their separate tribal organizations.

Once in the territory, the Cheyennes found life difficult as they had little interest in farming. Food rations were inferior and were issued at irregular intervals and sometimes withheld. Life on the reservation was more like that in a concentration camp.

In 1868, the Cheyennes took part in the Indian war on the Great Plains. The battles lasted through the summer and into the winter. On November 27, 1868, Chief Black Kettle's band was attacked on the Washita River by troops from the U.S. Seventh Cavalry under the command of Lt. Col. George Armstrong Custer. Black Kettle and many of his band were killed, their horses slaughtered, and their camp destroyed.

From that point, the Cheyennes became enemies of the U.S. government. The Northern Cheyennes became allies of the Sioux (Dakota, Lakota, and Nakota) and were among those who defeated Colonel Custer and his troops in the Battle of the Little Bighorn in Montana in 1876.

After the Battle of the Little Bighorn, the government brought bands of Northern Cheyennes to the Cheyenne-Arapaho Reservation in Indian Territory. The change in climate alone presented a major adjustment for them. Many became sick with malaria, and, as medical supplies ran out, a great number of the Northern Cheyennes died.

In 1878, a group of Northern Cheyennes pleaded with the government to allow them to move back north. After sending word that they were going home and did not want to fight, Little Wolf and Dull Knife led a band of 353 Northern Cheyennes off the reservation in September 1878. Newspapers and various forms of government propaganda sent fear spreading through Kansas and Nebraska, because the Cheyennes had left the reservation.

Even though U.S. Army troops were ordered to capture the Cheyennes, the band managed to move through Kansas unnoticed. U.S. troops eventually caught up with them in Nebraska, and most members of the band were killed. A few were able to reach the North, where they surrendered and remained confined to a reservation in their homeland. In 1883, the last of the Northern Cheyennes in Indian Territory left and settled on the northern reservation, which is located along the Tongue River in south central Montana along the Wyoming state line. Tribal headquarters are in Lame Deer, Montana, which also has a tribal museum. The largest public event is a powwow, held usually in July.

The Southern Cheyennes were assigned individual land allotments under the Dawes Act. Their tribal land holdings were opened up for white settlement on April 19, 1892. Today, the Southern Cheyennes share a tribal office with the Southern Arapahos in Concho, Oklahoma.

— L. Hester

SEE ALSO:

Arapaho; Black Kettle; Custer, Lt. Colonel George Armstrong; Dull Knife; Lewis and Clark Expedition; Little

Bighorn, Battle of the; Sand Creek Massacre; Washita, Battle of the.

SUGGESTED READINGS:

Brown, Dee. *Bury My Heart at Wounded Knee*. New York: Henry Holt and Company, 1970.

Debo, Angie. *A History of the Indians of the United States*. Norman: University of Oklahoma Press, 1970.

Deloria, Vine, Jr. *Custer Died for Your Sins*. New York: Macmillan, 1969.

Lazarus, Edward. *Black Hills, White Justice*. New York: HarperCollins Publishers, 1991.

CHICHÉN ITZÁ

Chichén Itzá is the ruins of an early Mayan settlement in the Yucatán peninsula of Mexico. The name means "mouth of the well of the Itzá" in Mayan. (The Mayans who settled in this region called themselves the Itzá.) Chichén Itzá is believed to have started as a small farming village surrounding a huge sunken well, probably as early as 500 B.C.E., but it did not become a major settlement until the Late Mayan Classic period between 550 and 900 C.E. The city was then abandoned by the Mayans in about the tenth century for unknown reasons and then resettled in about 1100.

Not long after this resettlement, Chichén Itzá was invaded by Toltec armies that had moved down from their highland stronghold in central Mexico. The Toltecs did not replace the existing Mayan culture but, instead, merged with it, introducing Mayans to the cult of Quetzalcóatl, a religious figure who took various forms, including a plumed serpent and a blond king with supernatural powers.

Today, the restored ruins of Chichén Itzá are famous for their remarkable architecture, including the Castillo or great pyramid, the astronomical observatory, and the largest ball court in Mesoamerica. Tourists can see the various temples and platforms and the sacred Cenote, or sunken well.

The buildings, sculpture, and murals that were added to Chichén Itzá after the conquest by Toltec culture have given archaeologists important information about Chichén Itzá's history, especially about the Toltec conquest. But the excavation of the ruins, which began in the early twentieth century, have actually unearthed more questions than answers. There is evidence, for example, of distinctly Toltec designs on some of the Mayan buildings of Chichén Itzá that were built centuries before the conquest by the Toltecs. Some archaeologists have advanced the controversial theory that the Toltecs were originally Mayan settlers who migrated to central Mexico around 600 to 700 C.E. and then, after they had developed their own distinct culture, returned to

Now reclaimed from dense growth that had hidden them for centuries, monuments of Chichén Itzá architecture, such as this one, are yielding valuable clues about an ancient people who made precise astronomical observations and understood the movement of celestial bodies much better than Europeans of their era.

conquer the descendants of their Mayan ancestors.

SEE ALSO:
Culture Areas of North America; Maya; Toltec.

CHICHIMEC

"Chichimec" is from the Nahuatl *Chichimecatl* (plural *Chichimeca*), used in the early 1500s to describe a number of Indian groups inhabiting the northern region of Mesoamerica at the time of the Spanish conquest of Mexico. The term as used by the Aztecs was sometimes derogatory, referring to rural peoples whom the Aztecs considered less civilized than themselves. Yet "Chichimec" was also a term of respect, because of the military skill of these northern tribes, from whom civilized southerners proudly claimed descent. The various northern nations called "Chichimec" remained unconquered by the Aztecs at the time of the Spanish conquest.

The Chichimecs did not represent a single racial or linguistic group but shared similarities in their way of life, their customs, and their social organization. In general, Chichimec groups occupied the high arid plateau situated between the Sierra Madre Oriental and Sierra Madre Occidental mountain ranges in north-central Mexico. The plateau, with vegetation dominated by mesquite, Joshua trees, and cacti, did not have good land for farming.

Living in bands of thirty to fifty people, the Chichimecs harvested the resources of the land by hunting and gathering. These peoples, who carried tribal designations of Guamares, Pames, Zacatecs, Cuachichils, and Conchos, among others, did not survive Spain's colonizing their territory. Spanish intrusions into their region in search of silver and slaves led to a series of bloody conflicts. By the

The Spaniards who conquered Mexico were bewildered by the number of different peoples living in the interior of the country and made little effort to reconstruct the history of the region. This Chichimec artwork might have yielded information about the history of the Chichimecs, if the Spaniards had been interested in them other than for their labor and their lands.

end of the colonial era in the early 1800s, those few Natives of this area who survived were living at Catholic missions or on Spanish haciendas. Some probably joined Apache bands to the north, the last alternative to conquest.

SEE ALSO:
Aztec; Mexico, Indigenous Peoples of.

CHICKASAW

Chickasaws share the same migration story with the Choctaws. In fact, the Muskogean language spoken by the Chickasaws is so similar to Choctaw that both Chickasaw and Choctaw speakers were consulted in the preparation of the newest study of the language, *Chickasaw: An Analytical Dictionary* (1994), by Pamela Munro and Catherine Willmond, published by the University of Oklahoma Press. The Chickasaw and Choctaw language is distantly related to other Muskogean languages, in particular the several dialects of the Creek language.

The Chickasaw migration story is the account of a great journey from the West to the southeastern portion of the North American continent. It was led by two brothers, Chicksa and Chahta. Upon arriving in their new homelands, the followers separated into the Chickasaws and the Choctaws. No one knows when the separation occurred. All that is known is that the two groups were at one time the same people, perhaps until shortly before the arrival of Europeans. This theory is supported by the similarity of their social and political institutions at the time of European contact, by their oral traditions regarding their history, and by their shared language.

The Okla Chahta (Choctaw people) are a confederation of a number of tribal divisions, the Okla Falaya, Okla Hannali, and Okla Tannap. It seems likely that the Okla Chicksa were at one time another major division of the nation. This ancient confederation is known to have lost at least one major division, the Okla Chito, even after the arrival of European colonizers. The Okla Chito disappear from French historical records near the middle of the eighteenth century; it is thought that they were casualties of the disastrous Choctaw civil war that took place at that time. Another Choctaw-Chickasaw-speaking people, the Okla Alabama, apparently separated from the Choctaws at some time in the past. By the time Europeans became acquainted with the Indians of the Southeast, the Alabama had become members of the Muskogee Confederation (Creeks).

Despite whatever shared past the Chickasaws and Choctaws might have had, they had become separate nations by the time Europeans became acquainted with them. The Chickasaw population, however, estimated at five thousand, was only about one-quarter of the estimated populations of their southern neighbors, the Choctaws, Creeks, and Cherokees, who each numbered between twenty and twenty-five thousand. What the Chicka-

The de Soto expedition arrives, on December 9, 1540, at the Chickasaw town called The Place of Two Hundred Fires. The town was located at the headwaters of Suquatonchee Creek in the southern part of what is now Pontotoc County, Mississippi.

In March 1541, the Chickasaws had endured the demands of the de Soto expedition all they could. They attacked the Spanish camp, burning it to the ground, destroying most of de Soto's baggage. The fire was so hot that the Spanish afterward had to build a forge and retemper the steel in their swords.

saws lacked in numbers, however, they compensated for with courage, audacity, and military and diplomatic skills. They exercised an influence in the lower Mississippi River Valley and adjacent areas that had to be reckoned with, both by European colonial powers and indigenous peoples throughout the region.

The ancestral homelands of the Chickasaws are the Tombigbee highlands, which today comprise the northern portion of Mississippi and the northwestern portion of Alabama. They also included in their domain what are today the western portions of Tennessee and Kentucky, which they used as a hunting preserve. To the south, the Natchez and the Choctaws were their close neighbors; to the east were the Creeks and the Cherokees; to the west were various Caddoan and Siouan peoples; and to the north were the Shawnees and other tribes of the Ohio River Valley.

Very early in the colonial era, the Chickasaws cast their lot with the British because the British offered higher-quality trade goods at cheaper prices than the French. This upset the French, who were settling in the colony of Louisiana. In 1698, about the same time that the French were founding their Louisiana colony, two British traders, Thomas Welch and Anthony Dodsworth, arrived in Chickasaw country from the English colonies in the Carolinas. Other English traders soon followed. Many

of them married Chickasaw women and produced mixed-blood families. These families would assume leadership roles in the Chickasaw Nation as interaction first with European governments, and then with the government of the United States, became increasingly more important. One of the English traders, James Adair, retired to England and published a book in 1775 that recounts his experiences with the Chickasaws. Entitled *History of the Indians,* it is a valuable document for students of Chickasaw history and that of other tribes in the region.

During the American Revolution, the Chickasaws sided with the British. After U.S. independence, the Chickasaws engaged in relations with both the Americans and the Spanish, playing each power against the other in the rivalry for the Chickasaw trade. The Chickasaws entered into their first treaty with the U.S. government in 1786 at Hopewell in the Carolinas. In 1801, they granted the United States the right of way for a wagon road through their country. In 1806, 1816, and 1818, they entered into land cession treaties, which left them in possession of only the core of their ancestral homelands, mostly in northern Mississippi.

The Chickasaws resisted removal pressure until Mississippi and Alabama passed laws in 1830 making it a crime for the Chickasaws to govern themselves. The United States was obligated by treaty to prohibit such state interference in Chickasaw

Chickasaw war canoes, made from giant cypress trees, could hold up to sixty men. With these canoes, the Chickasaws ruled the waterways from above present-day Louisville on the Ohio River to below Memphis on the Mississippi River. The French only felt safe on the Mississippi in larger boats equipped with cannons, and even then they traveled in groups that hugged the western shoreline of the river.

affairs and to remove American squatters from the Chickasaw country. However, under the leadership of President Andrew Jackson, the U.S. government refused to intervene on behalf of the Chickasaws. To escape state interference in their affairs, the Chickasaws negotiated a removal treaty with Jackson in 1830. When they could not find land west of the Mississippi River to their liking, they voided the treaty, which a clause in the treaty gave them the power to do. A new treaty was negotiated and later modified. This delayed Chickasaw removal until after the Choctaws had been removed to the West.

The Choctaws offered to share the western portion of their land with the Chickasaws, and in 1837, the Treaty of Doaksville reunited the two people. This treaty allowed the Chickasaws a Chickasaw District plus ten of the forty seats in the legislature of the newly created Choctaw government in the West, at a cost of $530,000. The Chickasaws were then removed to the new land, suffering many hardships and deaths on the journey. They concentrated at first in five temporary camps among the Choctaws in what is today southeastern Oklahoma. These settlements existed until the United States built military posts—Fort Washita and later Fort Arbuckle—at the western edge of Choctaw settlement. At that time, Chickasaws began to settle in

what is today south-central Oklahoma, which had been designated as the Chickasaw District of the Choctaw Nation. As late as 1844, 75 percent of the Chickasaws still remained in their temporary camps, refusing to leave until the U.S. government could offer them protection from Plains Indians. By 1853, about 90 percent of the Chickasaws had finally moved into their district.

Chickasaws were never happy with their minority role in the Choctaw Nation. In 1855, they negotiated the purchase of their district from the Choctaws for $150,000 and re-formed their separate nation, writing a constitution modeled after the U.S. Constitution. By that time, the Chickasaw Manual Arts Academy had become the first of five schools for older students within the nation. A system of elementary schools was also created. Most Chickasaws engaged in agriculture in the rich bottom lands, or in cattle and horse ranching on the lush prairies. Their ancient patterns of settlement in village concentrations were broken by the dispersal of their population across their domain, although a number of towns developed as economic hubs for the local rural populations.

At the outbreak of the U.S. Civil War in 1861, the U.S. government abandoned all of its military posts in the Chickasaw and Choctaw countries. This was in violation of its treaty obligations to provide military protection. Confederate forces moved in, and the Chickasaws and Choctaws negotiated treaties with the Confederacy. A number of prominent, mixed-blood families in the Chickasaw and Choctaw nations owned Black slaves. At the end of the war, the slaves were freed; at the end of the century, they were entitled to receive allotments from the tribal estate.

During the last half of the nineteenth century, the Chickasaws were swamped by an influx of Americans, especially after railroads were built through the nation. Reacting to pressure from Americans who wanted to gain title to Indian lands, Congress forced the Chickasaws to accept individual allotments of their property. In 1907, when their land became part of the new state of Oklahoma, the U.S. government dissolved their nation.

Throughout the twentieth century, Chickasaws have tenaciously refused to disappear as a separate people, and the United States finally abandoned efforts to try to force them to do so. Following passage of the Indian Self-Determination Act of 1975, the Chickasaws were able to write a new constitution, re-form their government, and build a new tribal headquarters facility in Ada, Oklahoma. They were also able to either inaugurate or take over administrative control and expand many health care, housing, and education programs. Profitable tribal enterprises include businesses in the retail sales and tourism industries and high-stakes bingo. Disputes over taxation and other matters regarding tribal sovereignty have brought the Chickasaws into conflict with the state of Oklahoma, which still maintains that it exercises some authority over Chickasaw citizens. These disputes are being worked out in the courts. And Oklahomans, who have largely ignored the Indians among them for most of the twentieth century, are gradually becoming aware that they share the land with people who may eventually be judged to have a stronger legal and moral claim to it.

— D. L. Birchfield

SEE ALSO:
Choctaw; Five Civilized Tribes.

SUGGESTED READINGS:
Debo, Angie. *And Still the Waters Run*. Princeton: Princeton University Press, 1940.

Foreman, Grant. *The Five Civilized Tribes*. Norman: University of Oklahoma Press, 1932.

Gibson, Arrell M. *The Chickasaws*. Norman: University of Oklahoma Press, 1971.

Hale, Duane K., and Gibson, Arrell M. *The Chickasaw*. New York: Chelsea House, 1991.

Munro, Pamela, and Pamela Willmond. *Chickasaw: An Analytical Dictionary*. Norman: University of Oklahoma Press, 1994.

CHIEF EAGLE, DALLAS (1925–1978)

Dallas Chief Eagle, a Teton Sioux (Lakota) born on the Rosebud Reservation in South Dakota, was orphaned as a child and brought up by tribal elders. In 1967, he was chosen by the Teton Sioux as their chief. He was the first chief of the tribe selected since Red Cloud was chosen in 1868 and served as the director of tourism for the Development Corporation of the United Sioux Tribes of South Dakota.

On April 28, 1970, Dallas Chief Eagle said he had interviewed four Sioux warriors who had been at the Battle of the Little Bighorn and that they told him that Lt. Colonel George Custer had not been killed by Indians but had committed suicide during the battle rather than face the consequences of his defeat.

Chief Eagle assisted Thomas E. Mails in the writing of the biography of Frank Fools Crow, the famous spiritual leader of the Teton Sioux. Chief Eagle also wrote the novel *Winter Count* (1968), the story of Turtleheart's search for his stolen wife, Evensigh. Within the novel, Chief Eagle presents a large portion of the history of the Indian wars of the second half of the nineteenth century, including the Battle of the Little Bighorn. Chief Eagle died in 1978.

SEE ALSO:
Fools Crow, Frank; Little Bighorn, Battle of the.

CHIEF JOSEPH (c. 1840–1904)

His name was Heinmot Tooyalaket (pronounced *In mut Too yah lah kat*), which means "Thunder Coming Up Over the Land from the Water." He became known as Chief Joseph, a respected Nez Perce leader.

In 1805, the Lewis and Clark expedition visited the region of the Nez Perces, which included the present-day states of Washington, Oregon, and Idaho. Non-Indian trappers and fur traders followed and established friendly trading relations with the Nez Perces. In 1836, the first Christian missionaries arrived. Among them were Henry Spalding and his wife, Elisa, who instituted a Presbyterian mission at the mouth of Lapwai Creek in the area now known as northern Idaho.

The Nez Perces were impressed by the guns and other weapons introduced to them by the whites and believed the whites possessed a powerful medicine—thus, some Nez Perces became willing converts to Christianity. Among those converted was Chief Joseph's father, a wealthy Nez Perce chief called Tu-eka-kas. Chief Tu-eka-kas was baptized with the name Joseph (The Older) and became a devout follower of the Presbyterian religion.

Chief Joseph (The Younger) was born in the Wallowa River Valley of eastern Oregon, which was the summer home of the Nez Perces. He and his younger brother, Ollokot, were baptized by Presbyterian missionaries and spent many days of their childhood in the mission community at Lapwai,

Chief Joseph, in traditional dress. Like Sitting Bull of the Sioux, Chief Joseph tried to lead his Nez Perce people to Canada in the hope of being able to continue their traditional life.

learning to read, write, and recite biblical passages in their Nez Perce language.

In 1855, a treaty council was held involving Governor Isaac Stevens of Washington Territory, other government officials, and five thousand Indian people, consisting of the Walla Wallas, Umatillas, Yakimas, and Nez Perces. The assembly was the largest peaceful gathering of the tribes in their history. To ensure peace between the whites and the Indians, a treaty was presented by Governor Stevens offering designated lands, or reservations, to the Indians. The treaty was signed by some of the other Nez Perce leaders, but the Older Joseph refused, saying that no man could own a part of the earth.

When gold was discovered on the land promised to the Indians in the 1855 treaty, fifteen thousand white settlers, mostly miners, spread across the region in violation of the Indians' treaty rights. In 1863, negotiations began in which the government asked the Indians to relinquish a huge amount of their land. The Older Joseph again refused this new treaty, which he referred to as "the thief treaty," for it meant losing the Wallowa valley and giving up the Nez Perces' ancestral lands. Other Indian leaders who had never lived in Wallowa valley did sign the treaty. Despite this, the Older Joseph still claimed the Wallowa valley, planting poles to mark the boundaries of the land on which his people lived.

In 1871, the Older Joseph died, and his son became the principal "peace" chief of the band. The Younger Joseph continued the policy set by his father: to peacefully resist pressures from government officials to relocate and give up Wallowa valley. But in 1877, the government was preparing to force the Indians out of the valley and issued them a final ultimatum. Chief Joseph knew he could not fight the United States Army, and being firmly committed to peace, he made preparations to leave. Before that could happen, however, the news reached Chief Joseph that some Nez Perces had attacked and killed white settlers. Chief Joseph realized that war was now inevitable.

Army troops soon arrived in White Bird Canyon and began firing at the Nez Perce camp there. The Nez Perces had been prepared for confrontation and managed to fight off the soldiers. After several more skirmishes, the Indian leaders

reluctantly gave up all hope of living in peace in the Wallowa valley and decided that their only reasonable alternative was to retreat to the buffalo country of what is now Montana.

During the next four months, the Nez Perces, pursued by General Oliver Howard's troops, covered over fifteen hundred miles (twenty-four hundred kilometers) of rugged terrain through the mountains of present-day Idaho, Wyoming, and Montana. The Nez Perces numbered approximately 550, including only about 150 warriors. Nevertheless, led by Chief Joseph and several other leaders, the Nez Perces outwitted, outmaneuvered, and outfought 5,000 U.S. Army soldiers.

The months of fighting, along with the difficulty of traveling the rough mountain terrain, put a terrible strain on the Nez Perces. Many of the people weakened, while many more were wounded or became ill. The travel was becoming increasingly strenuous, and the U.S. Army was still in fast pursuit. Hoping to escape into Canada, the Nez Perces turned north. Toward the end of September, the Nez Perces ran out of strength. Bad weather, exhaustion, and lack of food caused them to stop in northern Montana, just thirty miles (forty-eight kilometers) from the Canadian border. It was there that they were attacked by fresh military forces and endured a siege that lasted for five days.

Finally, on October 5, 1877, Chief Joseph surrendered with the words that would become famous: "My heart is sick and sad. From where the sun now stands, I will fight no more forever."

Chief Joseph died in 1904, having never returned to the Wallowa River Valley. His descendants still live today in parts of Idaho, Oregon, and Washington, and many of them maintain the ancient traditions of their people.

— T. Midge

SEE ALSO:
Howard, Oliver O.; Lewis and Clark Expedition; Nez Perce.

SUGGESTED READINGS:
Beal, Merrill D. "I Will Fight No More Forever": Chief Joseph and the Nez Perce War. New York: Ballantine Books, 1963.

Champagne, Duane. Native America: Portrait of the Peoples. Detroit: Visible Ink Press, 1994.

CHIEF SEATTLE (1788–1866)

Chief Seathl, who has become known as Seattle, was born of a mother from the Duwamish people and a father from the Suquamish. Both of these tribes were allied groups who lived in fishing villages along what is now called the Puget Sound in the state of Washington. The people in these villages were fishers and hunters, and like other tribes of the Northwest Coast, their culture included the skillful making of dugout canoes used for their travel, fishing, and warfare.

While Seathl was still very young, a ship called the *Discovery*, chartered by the English navigator and explorer George Vancouver, arrived in 1792 in the region of the Puget Sound. The Indians called it the "white winged bird ship." Vancouver

Though Chief Seattle has become one of the most famous of American Indians, his Duwamish people are today not recognized by the U.S. government, despite repeated efforts by the Duwamishes to regain their autonomy. In 1962, the Indian Claims Commission awarded the Duwamishes $1.32 per acre (0.4 hectare) for land unjustly taken from them. This land consists of the city of Seattle.

was on an expedition to map and survey the Pacific Northwest Coast, and until his arrival to the area, the Northwest Coast Natives had encountered almost no whites.

As a young man, Seathl adopted many of his father's fine qualities of chieftainship and became the principal chief of a confederation of the Suquamish, Duwamish, and other groups. Much of the respect he earned from his tribe was due to his successfully leading wars against certain other tribes within the area. He held the position of chief for the remainder of his life.

Chief Seathl converted to Christianity during the 1830s, when French Catholic missionaries, among the earliest European immigrants, came to the area. Seathl took the baptismal name Noah, and he made it a practice of his people to have prayer services twice a day.

In 1851, Chief Seathl welcomed the first permanent white settlement, and at his suggestion, a trading post was established on the east side of the sound, which is now the heart of the city of Seattle. A year later, the settlement's name, which was Alki Point, was changed to Seattle, a version of Chief Seathl's name.

As the region grew and prospered, conflict between the Indians and the whites became more frequent, and Chief Seathl, along with members from other tribes, were summoned in January 1855 by Governor Isaac Stevens of Washington Territory. The governor proposed a treaty that would take control of the tribes' lands and move them onto a reservation. To ensure peace, Chief Seathl was one of the first Native leaders to sign the Port Elliott Treaty.

Despite the treaty, conflict still arose between the colonizers and Native groups from eastern Washington and the coast. The trouble lasted for many years, and during this time, Chief Seathl and his followers moved to a reservation on the western side of Puget Sound.

Seathl was known as a strong orator. An interpretation of his 1854 speech to Governor Stevens was published, portraying Chief Seathl as the eloquent and dignified man he was. Seathl died in 1866.

SEE ALSO:
Washington State.

CHILD WELFARE ACT, INDIAN

The Indian Child Welfare Act is a landmark federal law that defines the rights of tribes to assume jurisdiction over children who are members or eligible to be members of a tribe.

Enacted in 1978, the act is intended to protect Indian children from being taken away from their families. Its purpose is also to preserve the cultural heritage of Indian children by immediately identifying these children and connecting them to their tribes through early communication by the various state and federal social, health and family service agencies.

Historically, Indian children have been the focus of certain non-Indian groups. Beginning in the mid-1800s, missionary groups were represented in force on Indian reservations. Although adoptions of Indian children were unknown at that time, the majority of children were removed to institutions such as boarding schools, a required practice when children reached a certain height and age. Abusive practices were rampant and discipline was harsh at the boarding schools. The missionary's misguided justification for interfering with Indian families and taking their children was to supposedly save the children's souls, educate their minds to the ways of the dominant, European-American culture, and break their bonds to their tribes and families.

Indian cultures traditionally have high regard for their children. Children are highly valued, and most tribes, by custom, forbid harsh discipline and other abusive practices like those that were a part of European North American culture. Non-Indians have also historically misunderstood the importance of extended family in Native cultures. Grandparents, aunts, and uncles traditionally assisted in raising Indian children and often took children into their own homes. The non-Indian system considered these children abandoned and took them away from their relatives.

The Indian Child Welfare Act was established because higher-than-average numbers of Indian children were continuing to be taken from their families, tribes, and culture, and serious social problems had developed because of the lack of traditional cultural influence associated with removing them to non-Indian families. The act was designed to prevent their unnecessary removal and to pre-vent their being completely cut off from their culture if removal becomes necessary. If taking a child from his or her immediate family is necessary, procedures under the act include the following: notifying the child's tribe as well as his or her parents or custodians; transferring child custody cases from state courts to tribal courts; allowing the child's tribe the right to intervene in custody proceedings; placement of Indian children in Indian homes; stricter standards than those usually applied to child custody cases; special procedures for court approval to place, voluntarily relinquish, and adopt Indian children; and special rights for Indian adoptees.

The Indian Child Welfare Act requires that preventive measures be offered to Indian families before placing children in out-of-home care; that services be provided for family rehabilitation; and that Indian children be returned to their families whenever possible. The act also requires that preference be given to placing an Indian child with a member of that child's extended family, a foster home selected by the child's tribe, or an Indian foster home or institution for children approved by the tribe or operated by an Indian organization.

SEE ALSO:
Boarding Schools; Children.

CHILDREN

Children are a valuable and beloved resource in American Indian communities, both because of the tradition of giving care and respect to each new generation and also because parents and others today understand that the young represent the future and hope of each tribe. At a time when tribes are reclaiming their cultures, children are being asked to play an important role: They must remember the past and carry it into the future.

A Valued Member of the Family
American Indian children hold another special distinction as the twentieth century turns into the twenty-first century. They represent a larger proportion of their families than do children of other races and ethnic groups. That is because, according to U.S. Census officials, American Indians are

In most traditional Indian cultures, a mother does not face the burden of raising her children alone. She is surrounded by relatives, all of whom help to care for and instruct the children. With so many relatives on the scene, spouse abuse and child abuse were virtually unheard of in traditional Indian communities. Forced assimilation has made inroads into traditional Indian life, and today, as in other communities, some women and children are at risk.

the fastest-growing ethnic group and because Indians tend to die younger on average than do members of other groups.

Officials estimate that there are almost one-half million Indian children of school age, so wherever American Indians are gathered, it is almost certain that there will be large numbers of children present. It is just as certain that those Indian children will be showered with attention and love.

This is not a new attitude. For generations, Indians have believed that children born to any tribal member are a blessing for all. In addition to the sacrifices and special treatment that children receive from their parents, relatives and others pitch in to raise and protect a child as if he or she were their very own.

From the first moments of their lives, American Indian children are extremely close to their parents, and although discipline is different in many Native families from that practiced by the dominant culture, Indian parents have their own way of dealing with good and bad behavior. Traditionally, most tribes believed it was more effective to reward good behavior than to punish bad, and most Indian parents would rather scold than spank a

child. But as Indian tribes intermingled with other ethnic groups, many families' views toward punishment changed. Today, many Indian parents or grandparents, especially those who were physically punished in the off-reservation boarding schools, will spank a child or withhold privileges as consequences for being "bad."

As a result of generations of forced assimilation, American Indian children typically are given names at birth that are similar to those of other children in the dominant American culture. Thus, Indian kids usually have whatever names are popular at the time, such as John, Tiffany, Danny, or Jennifer. But depending on their tribe and how closely their family holds to Native traditions, children also may be given names from their own language.

In some tribes, parents ask a spiritual leader to provide an appropriate name, often in the tribe's language. The elder who names the child will receive a gift. In other cases, a group of older men or women of the tribe may make a group decision, often naming the baby after a perceived characteristic or anticipated talent. In a few tribes, it is a grandparent who must bestow a name of honor on a child.

In some tribes, children do not take on special names until they undergo coming-of-age ceremonies in their early teens. For example, a boy going on a vision quest ceremony in the Lakota tradition may take on a special name according to a vision or a natural occurrence that happens during the period of fasting and meditation. Such ceremonies not only are symbolic but also prove to young men or women that they can endure much as an adult.

Children enjoy the support they receive in close-knit Indian communities. The closeness also helps working parents on reservations with inadequate day care. More than likely, relatives or friends will provide free or inexpensive care for young children.

A Living Culture

Many American Indian children demonstrate the same talent for artistic expression that their forebears displayed. Arts and crafts exhibits often showcase the works of children, and visitors are often surprised by the skilled drawings, paintings, and sculpture that are displayed. The artwork of children is taken so seriously in Native communities that some schools and reservations have elaborate art training programs. The Taos Pueblo in New Mexico even has a children's art gallery.

One of the most popular American Indian activities—the powwow—is a mixed blessing for Native children. While more and more young American Indians are being encouraged to learn about their own tribes as they participate in these social and competitive dances, the powwows tend to mix tribal cultures together, and they often emphasize the cultures of Plains tribes. Children who are not instructed in the lifestyles and dress of their own tribes sometimes adopt a "pan-Indian" culture similar to the blended image of Native cultures portrayed in mainstream media.

For example, it is not unusual to see a young Ottawa child wearing the feathered bustles of a

Today, after generations of repression, Indian children are allowed to experience their cultures. In earlier times, they were forcibly removed from their parents and sent far away to boarding schools, where they were punished for speaking their language. This youngster is displaying traditional dress at an Indian exposition in Idaho.

fancy dancer at a powwow, even though the outfit is far from his own family's tradition. Many young girls may choose brilliantly colored clothing worn by the fancy shawl dancers when such attire is far from what their own tribal ancestors wore. Sometimes, boys from non-Plains tribes may be spotted dancing in moccasins that have beadwork patterns reserved only for young women.

Although powwows have created a kaleidoscope of Indian cultures to some degree, they also have created great interest among the young in keeping the indigenous ways alive. Almost every powwow has special activities and provisions for children. Some give small cash prizes to every child

Navajos have been more successful than most Native peoples in North America in retaining their culture. They have also been able to maintain their nation in their ancestral homelands. These Navajo children are in Canyon de Chelly, in the Navajo Nation, in northeastern Arizona.

under five or six years old who competes in full dance regalia. Other powwows, in addition to selecting and honoring a princess, also choose junior princesses.

Encouraging children to dance in powwow competitions can be a very expensive proposition. It typically costs several hundred dollars to put together an outfit that will catch the eyes of the judges. A teenage girl's beaded buckskin dress may cost a couple of thousand dollars alone; leggings, a beaded fan, and other items may push the cost of her competition outfit to almost twice that price. It takes much love and sacrifice from parents to provide a powwow outfit like this, especially when it will be outgrown in a year or less.

A Matter of Identity

When not competing or dancing in required events, Native children play informal games or find other ways to pass the time with friends. In fact, on most days, the children of American Indian and Alaskan Native communities look and play like kids in the dominant non-Indian culture of North American society. Even on the far reaches of the enormous Navajo Nation, children are influ-

enced by fashions they see on video music channels and on televised athletic events. Like kids elsewhere, they ask for high-priced sneakers, sweat suits, and T-shirts with the names of professional sports teams or athletic apparel lines. Non-Indians are sometimes surprised to drive by a reservation recreation center and see kids who are dressed exactly like children they might spot at a big-city shopping mall.

Some Indian boys, however, let their hair grow down past their shoulders, and it is not unusual for boys in some tribes to wear their hair in braids tied up with colorful elastic or cloth bands. Some schools have tried to ban such hair styles as disruptive. But when the boys and their parents take their cases to court, judges generally uphold their right to wear their hair long as part of a religious observance.

Although Indian children do not wear full tribal dress on a daily basis, many of them express their Indian identity in other ways. It is common for young members of many Indian tribes, primarily in the Southwest, to wear silver and turquoise jewelry. Beaded hair bands or hats also are common adornments for young girls and boys. T-shirts and other clothing that feature geometric patterns, arrow shapes, and other patterns associated with American Indian tribes often find their way into Indian children's closets. Parents try to foster a sense of pride in their children's Indian identity and are usually glad to provide them with clothing that proclaims a tribal association.

Even with these ways of expressing pride in their tribal affiliation, it is not unusual for young members of almost every tribe to fret over their American Indian identity at some time in their lives. Many older community members can recall times when they wished they were not Indian because of constant harassment or taunting from non-Indian classmates at school. That situation persists in many communities today, particularly where there are large concentrations of Indian families.

Today, there seems to be more and more violence and vandalism within Indian communities. Several large reservations have reported the recent formation of youth gangs, some of whose members have been recruited by members of gangs in large cities. Along with gangs has come an increase in graffiti and available drugs. Tribal officials are trying to warn children about the dangers of gang involvement, but young people are being influenced negatively by movies and music that popularize gang lifestyles.

When non-Indian students or teachers find out that children are Indians, they sometimes ask them strange or difficult question. It is common, for example, for boys and girls to be asked if they live in tipis or wear feathers at home. Even Indian children who live in cities sometimes admit that, like their non-Indian friends, they, too, once thought there were tribal people roaming the Great Plains on horseback and living in tipis—*somewhere* in the United States. And even though recent movies such as *Dances With Wolves* and *Pocahontas* attempt to portray Native people in a positive light and convince audiences that being American Indian is socially acceptable, they have also helped keep many nagging stereotypes alive.

Inuit young people, such as this young man at Cape Dorset, are experiencing rapid change in their cultures. Computerized classrooms and stereo earphones make for a greatly different childhood than that of their parents and grandparents.

Sometimes, other students are surprised to learn that a classmate is an American Indian, particularly when he or she does not "look" Indian. Although most American Indian children have black hair, brown almond-shaped eyes, and dark-colored skin, thousands of young tribal members look significantly different than this characteristic image. In fact, it is not unusual to see tribal members at various Indian events who have blond or light brown hair, blue or green eyes, and freckled, light-colored skin. It is important to remember that many enrolled tribal members have only a small percentage of American Indian ancestry. Because each tribe is able to determine its own standards for enrollment, children can qualify as full tribal members with varying standards of blood. In the Cherokee Nation of Oklahoma, for example, one only has to trace ancestry back to tribal allotment rolls established in the late 1800s. In many cases, children qualify as Indian who may only have had a single grandparent or great-grandparent who was a tribal member.

Telling Tales

By the time they reach their teens, many American Indian children have enjoyed hearing a multitude of stories. In most tribes, stories are designed specifically to help children understand important concepts that improve their lives and help them work with others.

Many of the delightful children's tales are morality stories in which people encounter a variety of obstacles. Some stories explain how the world and parts of creation, such as specific animals, came into being. Other stories tell of times when there were no people on the earth and clever animals, such as the rabbit and the coyote, flourished through cleverness or trickery.

Today's American Indian children also hear real-life stories about their close relatives. Because of a long oral tradition in their cultures, conversation has continued to be a favorite source of entertainment in many Native communities. Whenever large families gather, children can often be found sitting around the kitchen table as family histories are recounted. Often, they are included in the conversation until well past their bedtime.

Grandparents, aunts, and uncles sometimes tell stories to children that they themselves heard when they were young. Most of these stories reinforce concepts that tribal societies needed for the group to succeed. For example, children are instructed through such stories not to steal and to speak kindly of others. They learn that gossiping and tattling are wrong. They are taught through stories to respect nature and not to needlessly destroy animals and plant life. Many stories stress the importance of sharing what one has and illustrate the consequences of selfishness.

Sometimes parents or other relatives will draw from real-life situations to drive home a point. What more powerful example could there be than to point at someone the child knows in the community?

The remoteness of some sections of the Navajo Nation has allowed some Navajo children to experience childhood in much the same way as their ancestors. Each year, however, paved roads, automobiles, and telephones reduce the areas of isolation and bring changes to more and more Navajo families.

Children also enjoy hearing spellbinding tales about ancient monsters, cannibals, or other scary subjects. Many tribes tell these stories as part of their history or to bring to life the histories and practices of neighboring communities.

These stories have formed the basis for many of the books kids read in libraries and classrooms throughout North America. A few educators provide opportunities for Indian children to study work written by other Indians. This helps build pride among Indian boys and girls, who often are called on to share their own family histories when the class reads tribal literature. However, most of the material about Indians that is used in public schools continues to be written by non-Indians.

Education

With Indians burdened by the nation's highest unemployment rate and a poverty rate that is surpassed only by African-Americans, getting Indian children to finish high school has become a major goal of parents and teachers alike. Most studies show that American Indians have a higher dropout rate than kids from all other races. If present statistics hold true in the future, of all Indian children starting school in any given year, 40 to 45 percent of them will not obtain a high school diploma. Of the Indians who do graduate and go on to college, only one out of six will finish with a four-year degree.

Educational experts say a variety of factors work against American Indians in a traditional school setting. One main obstacle is the fact that boys and girls from traditional Indian homes have values that often conflict with the values needed to succeed in a non-Indian classroom. For example, if an Indian student has already answered a question in class, she may not raise her hand again, even if she knows the answer. According to Indian educators, that is because a traditional child may have been taught by her elders to let someone else have a turn in the spotlight. A teacher who is unfamiliar with this group value may think instead that the student is not raising her hand because she is unmotivated or simply does not know the answer.

Those familiar with American Indian students also say that most Native children are hampered in the classroom because the curriculum is biased in favor of the dominant society. Indian students also have learning styles that are different than those of children from other cultures. For example, the *Indian Nations at Risk* report on education points out that Indian children are less adept at tasks that involve sequential logic or figuring, but they stand out from other kids when math or science problems require an ability to figure out spatial relationships.

Depending on where they live and the financial resources of their family, American Indian children may attend regular public schools, private schools, or tribally controlled schools. Attempts to meet the special needs of American Indian children vary greatly from school to school, but generally they receive more attention in schools within or near Indian communities. These schools are usually funded all or in part by the federal government, however, and so the money available to them is sometimes in short supply. Educators say that as many as four or five children in some government-controlled schools have had to share a single math textbook.

American Indian children have been taught according to standards set by non-Natives since 1523, when Spanish settlers set up schools in Mexico to teach Indian boys. Various schools were established by the English and other European settlers during the seventeenth and eighteenth centuries. Not only were they taught the language of the newcomers, but they were introduced to religions that were far different from ones that they knew. They also were prepared by their teachers for careers in which they would be subservient and helpful to the European settlers.

Many of the treaties that American Indians struck with non-Indians to open land to European settlers provided for the education of the various tribes' children. Court decisions have consistently held that the U.S. government has a trust obligation to see that Indian children receive an adequate education. Several treaties specifically stated that tribes would have eternal access to teachers and a blacksmith. But it wasn't until 1972, when the U.S. Congress passed the Indian Education Act, that Indians themselves began to be included in determining how their children would be educated by those teachers. This law also provided federal money to tribally controlled and public schools to set up special Indian education programs outside of the schools. The Title V (now Title IX) program

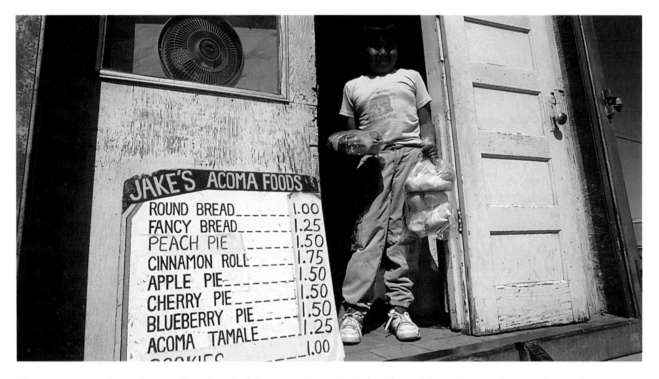

This young boy from Acoma Pueblo is helping to sell freshly baked bread from his family's truck at a flea market in Gallup, New Mexico.

and the Johnson-O'Malley program both gave schools money to teach Indian tribal members or descendants about their culture and to help them improve their grades in regular classes.

Reaching Out to Kids at Risk

In the 1990s, these programs have helped many urban American Indian children find their own cultural identity in mammoth school populations. These programs provide children with mentoring and tutoring, special cultural programs, and a chance to meet and interact with tribal elders.

Many of the entitlement programs focus on substance abuse. By the time Indian children reach their teens, they are three or four times more likely than children of other cultural groups to have had significant problems with drug and alcohol abuse, leading to high rates of substance-related arrests, imprisonment, hospitalization, and even deaths among Native teens. In fact, substance abuse contributes to an abnormally high death rate for Indian children under the age of fourteen, who are more than 25 percent more likely to die than children from other races. The odds get even worse as Indian children reach their later teens and early twenties. At that stage of their lives, according to

the Indian Health Service, they are almost four times more likely to die than are people of the same age from other races and ethnic groups.

In addition to other causes of death, motor vehicle accidents in which alcohol or drugs are considered a factor have become a major killer of children and teens. Young Indians are about 50 percent more likely to be killed in car crashes than others.

Suicide is also a terrible problem for Indian teens, who are about 30 percent more likely than others to kill themselves. Indian children from five to fourteen years old are more than twice as likely to kill themselves than are children from other groups. Indians in their teens and early twenties are twelve times as likely to kill themselves as are Indian children, and they are almost twice as likely to commit suicide than are teens of other races.

Many experts point to high rates of depression among Indian people, including teens, and to the link between depression and suicide. Like other health and social problems in Native America, this often-fatal depression may be related to substance abuse and to the feeling among many Indian youths that they aren't getting a fair shake from society. Health officials and educators are increasing their

This father and son, on Baffin Island in the far north, are of a people who long ago learned to prosper in a harsh climate. They are nearly helpless, however, in dealing with large corporations, such as oil companies, and with environmental pollution, which makes the future of the children uncertain.

efforts to warn Indian children and teens about the link between drug and alcohol abuse and suicide. Recent research shows that the problems exist on the same levels in urban areas as they do within reservation communities.

Indian children are also being warned that substance abuse and other risky ways of living put them at great risk from a variety of health conditions. For example, more young Indian adults become seriously ill or die from diabetes and tuberculosis than do young people from other cultural groups. Today, Indian children are learning in blunt, clear terms why, because of physical hardships and poor health care, so many of their relatives have died at an early age. Authorities and teachers explain to them that the same thing doesn't have to happen

to them if they take care of themselves and that their chances of getting sick may be greatly reduced if they exercise regularly, eat a nutritious diet, and maintain sanitary living conditions. This emphasis on staying healthy is even extended to preschool programs, which also prepare Indian children to succeed in school.

Facing the Future

Despite many economic, health, and social disadvantages, many Indian children flourish alongside their non-Indian classmates in public schools. Motivated Indian children across the country are succeeding in many ways. They win art contests, excel in sports events, and place high in math and science competitions. Some are graduating at the top of their high school classes and qualifying for scholarships at prestigious colleges and universities.

Some of these star performers get special assistance and career guidance from summer camps and seminars in mathematics, engineering, and other subjects. When they reach their teens, many of these kids qualify for minority internship programs at jobs in government and private business. Tribal officials and school administrators are also working hard to ensure that all children learn basic computer skills. In addition to being sure children take classes that teach them how to type and use different types of computers and software in schools or recreational programs, some tribes have developed computer programs that teach children about their own cultures.

Like young people from other groups, American Indian children begin thinking of possible careers early in life. Some of them also begin developing marketable job skills through the help of parents or other relatives. While some tribal members teach their children how to make money by producing beautiful works of art, others explain how to make money through farming or driving trucks. In rural areas, Indian children may help parents and grandparents raise cattle or sheep. Not only are they learning how to work, but they are also playing a valuable role in their family's economy.

Children in Indian households are frequently required to do chores, particularly as they reach middle school years. If their families can afford it, they may receive an allowance for doing odd jobs

This fifth-grade girl in Peach Springs, Arizona, eagerly awaits the beginning of a traditional dance practice session. Traditional dances are an important part of the celebrations of most Southwest tribes.

around the house, just as in many non-Indian homes. Some older children may even make their own money by doing tasks for others, such as mowing lawns, babysitting, or house painting.

The fact that children are asked to work in and around their own homes is not much different than it was in Indian communities long ago. Families often assigned Indian boys and girls important tasks. Often, boys would fish or hunt for small game with their friends. The food they brought in was an important means of sustenance for the tribe. Girls also would be involved in gathering food, picking berries, vegetables, or nuts either alone or with older women.

Many Indian boys and girls have particularly close relationships with their grandparents, even more so than children of other races and cultures. In almost every North American tribe, grandparents take time to give children special instructions for life while parents are tied up with other duties and activities.

Prospects for education, health, and the preservation of their heritage should continue to improve for Indian children as we move into the twenty-first century. Children have always been the center of attention in most Indian communities. But now more than ever, parents and other adults are trying to find ways to guide them successfully into the future.

— D. Pego

SEE ALSO:
Alcoholism; Boarding Schools; Enrolled Indians; Fancy Dance and Fancy Shawl Dance; Infant Death Rate; Johnson-O'Malley Act; Powwows; Storytelling; Tribal Membership.

CHINOOK

The traditional homeland of the Chinook people stretches over 100 miles (160 kilometers) inland from the Pacific Ocean along the Columbia River. Recent studies estimate the Chinook population at nineteen to twenty thousand before white contact.

Chinookan bands known as the Clatsop and Multnomah lived on the south side of the river. Their territory extended south through the Willamette River Valley to present-day Oregon City. Also on the south side of the Columbia, to the east, lived the Wasco band.

On the north side of the Columbia River were the people known as the Chinook proper. Their territory extended north along the Pacific coast to Willapa Bay. The Cathlamet were another Chinookan band who lived east of the Chinook proper.

The Chinookan bands were fishing people, whose food—mainly salmon, sturgeon, and eel—came mostly from the river. Their diet also included smelt and herring; jerked (sun-dried) venison; camas, fern, and flag roots; salal berries and huckleberries; and wappatos, a potatolike bulb. The coastal Chinooks relied on whale and seal oil as well.

Chinook longhouses were built of cedar planks, and each housed several families during the winter months. Archaeological evidence indicates some cedar longhouses were as long as 150 to 200 feet (45.5 to 60.6 meters) and 20 to 30 feet (6 to 9.1 meters) wide. Bunk beds were built along the inside walls, with mat partitions woven from cattail or tule rushes. A fire pit for cooking and other activities was located in the center of the longhouse. A hole in the middle of the roof let the smoke out, and fish were often cured on overhead poles inside the longhouse.

The Chinooks' earliest contact with non-Natives may date back to the explorers Francis Drake and Juan de Fuca. It is recorded that James Cook, George Vancouver, and other early explorers were in contact with the Chinooks as well.

The Chinooks were influential and skillful traders. By necessity, they developed a trade language, which came to be called Chinook Jargon and which Native tribes of the Pacific Northwest used to communicate with one another for untold centuries. The first recorded words of this language are found in the journals of the Lewis and Clark expedition, which encountered the Chinook Chief Concomly on the north banks of the Columbia River in 1805. Early white explorers and maritime traders adopted Chinook Jargon to use in their relations with the Chinooks. By 1875, English and French words had been added to the language and fully one hundred thousand people were using it.

The numerous Chinook bands made thirteen treaties in the early 1850s with Governor Anson Dart of Oregon, but not one of those treaties was ratified by the U.S. Congress. Today, the Chinook Indian Tribe is recognized by the state of Washington but not by the U.S. government. The Chinooks are currently petitioning for federal recognition status. The tribe has fourteen hundred members. Tribal headquarters are in Chinook, Washington, near the mouth of the Columbia River. Individual Chinook descendants are on the tribal rolls of the Confederated Tribes of the Siletz and the Confederated Tribes of Grand Ronde in Oregon and the Shoalwater Bay Indian Tribe and the Quinault Indian Nation in Washington.

SEE ALSO:
Chinook Jargon; Lewis and Clark Expedition; Slaves, Indian as; Washington State.

CHINOOK JARGON

In many parts of the world, mixed languages have developed as a result of contacts between different peoples. One such language is Pidgin English, a simplified form of English developed among traders speaking different languages and today used mostly in parts of Asia and Africa.

The Chinook intertribal language developed in the Pacific Northwest to meet the needs of Native Americans speaking various languages from different language families. Chinook Jargon is comprised mostly of words from old Chinook but includes many other words from Salish, Nootka, and other languages. Chinook Jargon words include *tillicum* (people, nation), *nesaika* (our), *alki* (the future), *wawa* (speech, to speak), *mackamuck* (goods, possessions, big shot), *kokshut* (no good, bad, broken), *skookum* (power), *naika* (I, my), and *maika* (you, your).

The jargon began as a trade language, but eventually it came to be used for other purposes. After Native contact with British, French, and Métis traders, the jargon was enlarged to include words of English, French, Algonquian, and other languages. In turn, the English language has borrowed many words and phrases from Chinook Jargon, including *hike* (from *hyak*, hurry up!), *chuckhole*

(from *chuck* or *cha-ak*, water), and *living in the sticks* (from *stick*, forest or wood). Until the 1880s or 1890s, Chinook Jargon was widely spoken by both non-Natives and Natives from southern Alaska southward to northern California.

The Chinook Jargon is still spoken in the Pacific Northwest, and attempts have been made to revive it. It is a very easy language to learn since verbs do not change with different tenses. It has been proposed that the jargon be enlarged by adding to its vocabulary the eight hundred to one thousand Native American words currently in English, such as *hammock*, *caucus*, *tomato*, *potato*, *okay*, *wow*, *puma*, *skunk*, *raccoon*, and others.

SEE ALSO:
Chinook; Métis.

CHIPPEWA

SEE Ojibwe.

CHIVINGTON MASSACRE

SEE Sand Creek Massacre.

CHOCTAW

Choctaws tell a variety of stories to account for their origin. Some stories tell of a great migration from some distant land to the northwest. Most Choctaw creation stories describe the people emerging from the earth near the Choctaw sacred mound, Nanih Waiya. Nanih Waiya, now a state park, is located near the headwaters of the Pearl River in the east-central portion of the present-day state of Mississippi. *Mississippi* itself is derived from a Choctaw word, Misha sipokni. It means "older than time"— the Choctaw designation for the great river of the North American continent.

The Choctaw language belongs to the Muskogean language family, which is one of the families of the large Algonquian language group. Choctaw is closely related to the language of the Seminoles and Creeks and is virtually the same as Chickasaw. Until recent times, these two tribes were one people; their separation took place probably not long before European contact. Of the languages of the so-called Five Civilized Tribes (Choctaws, Chickasaws, Creeks, Seminoles, and Cherokees), only the Cherokee language is not a Muskogean language. A simplified, pidgin version of the Choctaw language became the universal trade jargon for the Native peoples of the southeastern portion of the North American continent. In much the same way, Chinook Jargon was used for commerce by the Native peoples of the Pacific Northwest.

Watersheds were important boundaries in the ancient homeland of the Choctaws. In fact, with only a few exceptions, the villages of each tribal division were located within their respective watersheds. The villages of the Okla Falaya (Long People) were found mostly within the watershed of the Pearl River, along the western edge of the confederacy. Those of the Okla Tannap (People of the Opposite Side) were to be found within the watershed of the Tombigbee River on the eastern side. Those of the Okla Hannali (Six Towns People) were located within the watershed of the Chickasawahay River to the south. The Okla Falaya, being close neighbors of the Okla Chickasaw to the north, maintained close relations with the Chickasaws. Similarly, the Okla Tannap, being close neighbors to the Creeks on the east, maintained close relations with the Creeks, and the Okla Hannali maintained close relations with neighboring tribes to the south around Mobile Bay.

For sport and adventure, Choctaws ventured far to the west to the great buffalo herds of the southern Great Plains. These expeditions, consisting largely of young men eager to prove themselves, ordinarily began at the conclusion of the winter bear hunts in the Louisiana bottom lands. The most famous Choctaw, Pushmataha, who lived from 1764 to 1824, rose to the position of Okla Hannali war chief because of his exploits in the West. Demonstrating leadership on exploits in the West was a time-honored path for upward mobility among the ancient Choctaws.

In their Mississippi homeland, the Choctaws were skilled agriculturists, raising large crops of corn. The ancient Choctaw confederacy was dis-

tinguished for its love of free speech and public exhibitions of oratory. Gideon Lincecum, an early nineteenth-century observer, in describing the Choctaw public meetings, was particularly struck by the architecture of the large brush arbors under which they gathered for such events in the summer. A hole was left in the center of the roof, and anyone desiring to address the assembly was required to stand directly beneath the hole, in the full heat of the Mississippi sun. When he asked about the reason for this arrangement, Lincecum was told that it was to encourage the speaker not to talk too long. The rest of the Choctaws could remain comfortably seated in the shade for as long as the speaker desired to stand in the sun and speak.

Choctaws first entered European historical records when the expedition of Hernando de Soto passed through Choctaw Country in the 1540s. The Choctaws maintained a close and troubled relationship with the French in particular. This relationship began at the time the French founded the cities of Mobile (in present-day Alabama) and New Orleans (in present-day Louisiana) early in the eighteenth century; it ended when the French were expelled from North America at the end of the French and Indian War in 1763. The Choctaws never engaged in hostilities against the French, but they were drawn into French hostilities against other Indians, primarily the Natchez and the Chickasaws.

By the 1730s, some Choctaws desired the less expensive and higher quality trade goods of the English colonial merchants in the Carolinas, who had established trade relations with the Chickasaws. The French, hoping to maintain their trade monopoly with the Choctaws, resisted Choctaw trade with the English. Soon a rivalry for the Choctaw trade developed between the French and English colonial empires. This divided the Choctaw confederacy and eventually led to the catastrophic Choctaw Civil War of 1747 to 1750. Red Shoe, an Okla Falaya chief, was the most prominent leader in this struggle.

During the American Revolution, Choctaws sided with the rebelling English colonists and provided scouts for generals Morgan, Wayne, Sullivan, and Washington. The Choctaws entered into their first treaty with the new United States government in 1786. In 1801, they granted the government

Tushka Homma, the capitol building of the Choctaw Nation of Oklahoma, was built in 1884. The U.S. government has changed the spelling of Tushka Homma (Choctaw for *Red Warrior*) to Tuskahoma, but the Choctaw Tribal Council has kept the original name. Inside the building are a museum, a gift shop, and the Tribal Court.

the right of way for a wagon road through Choctaw country, and from that time onward, Americans poured into and through their lands. By 1817, enough non-Indians had surrounded the Choctaws to form the state of Mississippi and covet the rich Choctaw agricultural lands.

Under the leadership of Pushmataha, who was said to be the greatest orator in the nation, the Choctaws sided with the United States government in the War of 1812. Pushmataha met the Shawnee leader Tecumseh in open debate in November 1811 when Tecumseh came south to try to recruit the southern nations for his pan-Indian alliance. Persuaded by Pushmataha to remain loyal to the United States, the Choctaws expelled Tecumseh from their country. They then worked hard to keep all but the Red Stick faction of the Creeks from joining Tecumseh.

To accomplish this, Pushmataha visited the Creek councils and made speeches to them urging their loyalty. In the ensuing war, Pushmataha, as a lieutenant colonel in General Andrew Jackson's U.S. Army, led hundreds of Choctaws first against the Red Stick Creeks, then against the British at the Battle of New Orleans, and later against the Seminoles in General Jackson's Peninsular Campaign. Despite their loyalty, the Choctaws were pressured into negotiating another treaty with the United States government, in 1816. In it, the government demanded a large parcel of their land.

In 1805, at the negotiations for the Treaty of Mount Dexter, the U.S. government began pressuring the Choctaws to remove themselves as a nation to land west of the Mississippi River. Finally, in the Treaty of 1820, the Choctaws accepted an exchange of some of their Mississippi land for a huge tract west of the Mississippi. It extended from present-day central Arkansas to present-day northeastern New Mexico. In 1830, the United States government forced the Choctaws to give up the remaining portion of their Mississippi homeland and remove to their land in the West.

The removal, poorly planned and allowing only starvation rations and little protection from the elements, killed twenty-five hundred Choctaws. It was executed in successive, brutal installments during the winters from 1831 to 1834. Most of the old people and many of the young died. The Choctaws were the first people to suffer removal as an entire nation, and their "trail of tears," as the removal journey is often called, would soon be experienced by many others, notably the Cherokees, later in the decade.

Some Choctaws refused to be removed and took to the swamps instead. There they lived on the margins of southern society until their existence was finally recognized by the U.S. government early in the twentieth century. Today, they are the Mississippi Band of Choctaw Indians, a federally recognized tribe with several blocks of non-contiguous reservation land near Philadelphia, Mississippi.

In the West, the Choctaws wrote a constitution modeled after that of the United States government, established schools, and, within a generation, had recovered from the trauma of removal. Their republic enjoyed a vigorous, independent political life until the tide of U.S. westward expansion once again overwhelmed it. Although their nation in the West had been guaranteed to them "forever" by the explicit provisions of Article Four of the Removal Treaty of 1830, the nation was dissolved by the United States government in 1907 when the state of Oklahoma was formed.

Finally, in the 1970s, the Choctaws managed to reassert their existence as a nation, write a new constitution, and gain recognition by the U.S. government as the Choctaw Nation of Oklahoma. Today, the federal courts are grappling with the problems that have arisen because three entities—the state of Oklahoma, the United States government, and the Choctaws—are seeking to exercise sovereignty over the same land and people. This process will likely require at least another generation before a solution agreeable to all parties can be worked out.

— D. L. Birchfield

SEE ALSO:

Chickasaw; Choctaw Literature, Contemporary; Five Civilized Tribes; Mississippi Band of Choctaw Indians; Pushmataha; Red Shoe; Removal Act, Indian; Trail of Tears.

SUGGESTED READINGS:

Debo, Angie. *The Rise and Fall of the Choctaw Republic.* Norman: University of Oklahoma Press, 1934.

Foreman, Grant. *The Five Civilized Tribes.* Norman: University of Oklahoma Press, 1934.

Lewis, Anna. *Pushmataha: American Patriot.* New York: Exposition Press, 1959.

Wright, Muriel. *A Guide to the Indian Tribes of Oklahoma.* Norman: University of Oklahoma Press, 1951.

CHOCTAW LITERATURE, CONTEMPORARY

Choctaws have distinguished themselves in many fields of literature, but nowhere more so than in the field of history. In 1930, Anna Lewis, a Choctaw woman and a historian, became the first woman to receive the Ph.D. degree from the University of Oklahoma. Shortly afterward, her doctoral dissertation was published as *Along the Arkansas, a Study of French-Indian Relations on the Lower Arkansas River Frontier in the 18th Century.* She then pursued a distinguished teaching career at the Oklahoma College for Women, now the University of Science and Arts, in Chickasaha, Oklahoma.

In addition to teaching, Lewis devoted her life to researching a biography of Pushmataha. This war chief of the Okla Hannali Choctaw tribal division was the most influential Choctaw leader of the early nineteenth century. The book was published in 1959 under the title *Chief Pushmataha, American Patriot.*

Another Choctaw woman who distinguished herself in the field of history was Muriel Wright, granddaughter of Allen Wright, who was principal chief of the Choctaw Nation in the nineteenth century. For two decades, she served as editor of *The Chronicles of Oklahoma,* the quarterly historical scholarly journal of the Oklahoma Historical Society. In 1959, she produced her greatest work, *A Guide to the Indian Tribes of Oklahoma.* It provides a summary of the history, culture, and contemporary status of each of the sixty-five Indian nations that either were original residents of or were removed to the area before statehood.

Scott Kayla Morrison, an Oklahoma Choctaw and an environmental attorney, was named to *Who's Who in Indian Country* in 1993 by *Oklahoma Today* magazine. She writes model environmental codes for tribal governments.

Playwright Leanne Howe, an Oklahoma Choctaw, also does investigative journalism and writes poetry, essays, and fiction. She reads French, is a student of Choctaw-French relations during the first half of the eighteenth century, and is skilled at portraying Choctaw culture during that era in works of fiction.

Though both Anna Lewis and Muriel Wright are now deceased, other Choctaw women continue the tradition of leadership in scholarly pursuits regarding Choctaw history. One such scholar is Choctaw-Chippewa author Clara Sue Kidwell, formerly an associate professor at the University of California at Berkeley, later with the Museum of American History at the Smithsonian Institution, and now director of Native American Studies at the University of Oklahoma. In 1980, Kidwell co-authored the invaluable study *The Choctaws: A Critical Bibliography*. Her detailed history of early missionary activity among the Choctaws, *Choctaws and Missionaries in Mississippi from 1818 to 1918*, was published in 1995.

Choctaw author Beatrice Harrell has contributed memoirs of her mother's experiences in the Choctaw boarding schools in such publications as *The Four Directions: American Indian Literary Quarterly* and books recounting Choctaw traditional stories. One of these is *The Choctaw Story of How Thunder and Lightning Came to Be*.

In investigative journalism, two Choctaw women, Scott Kayla Morrison and Leanne Howe, have demonstrated both courage and resourcefulness. Their jointly written article, "Sewage of Foreigners" (*Federal Bar Journal & Notes*, July 1992), for example, is a long, detailed exposé on contract negotiations by the Mississippi Band of Choctaw Indians to allow for the dumping of toxic waste on Choctaw lands in Mississippi. In publishing this article, Morrison, an attorney, and Howe, a journalist and playwright, forced a difficult, controversial topic into the national spotlight. In the winter of 1994, the newspaper *News from Indian Country* reported that Morrison and Howe had signed a contract with the University of Oklahoma Press to expand the journal article into a book.

Morrison, who has worked as a legal services attorney among the Choctaws in Mississippi, is now director of the Native American Office of Jobs in the Environment (formerly the National Toxics Campaign Fund). She travels around the country doing environmental work and writes model environmental codes for tribal governments. She is also accustomed to asking tribal leaders questions that many of them would prefer not to be asked, such as, "Why doesn't your government have a Freedom of Information Act?"

For her environmental work, the magazine *Oklahoma Today*, in the summer of 1993, named Morrison to its *Who's Who in Indian Country*. Her short stories and essays have also appeared in many publications, among them *The Four Directions: American Indian Literary Quarterly* and *Turtle Quarterly*, and in such anthologies as *The Colour of Resistance*, which was published in Canada in 1994. She is currently editing an anthology of Native American environmental writing, tentatively titled *This Handful of Dirt*.

Howe's poetry, essays, short stories, and plays have been widely published and performed. Her poetry has appeared in such anthologies as *Gatherings IV: The En'owkin Journal of First North American People* (published in British Columbia, Canada) and in *Studies in American Indian Literatures* (summer issue, 1990); her short stories can be found in *A Stand Up Reader* and *Coyote Papers* and in such anthologies as *Earth Song, Sky Spirit: Short Stories of the Contemporary Native American Experience* (published by Doubleday in 1993).

Howe is perhaps best known for her saucy essay "An American in New York" in *Spiderwoman's Granddaughters*, edited by Paula Gunn Allen. The recent radio broadcast of one of her plays, *Indian Radio Days* (co-authored with Roxy Gordon), was broadcast by satellite to stations as far away as Alaska and became the occasion for a long interview, published in the November 1993 issue of *Native Playwrights Newsletter* (Madison, Wisconsin).

Choctaw men have made their mark in both scholarship and the arts. In 1992, for his play *Fire on Bending Mountain*, Choctaw playwright Wallace Hampton Tucker became the first three-time winner of the Best Play Prize of the Five Civilized Tribes Museum in Muscogee, Oklahoma. The competition has been held biennially since 1974. Tucker also won the first two competitions in 1974 and in 1976. His plays have been widely performed.

Choctaw playwright Roxy Gordon has published more than two hundred poems, articles, and stories in such publications as *Rolling Stone*, *Village Voice*, *Texas Observer*, *Greenfield Review*, *Dallas Times Herald*, and *Dallas Morning News*. His fiction has appeared in such anthologies as *Earth Power Coming*, edited by Simon J. Ortiz, in 1983. His volumes of poetry include *Unfinished Business*, *West Texas Midcentury*, and *Small Circle*.

Ron Querry, an Oklahoma Choctaw, left college teaching to become a cowboy in New Mexico. His first novel, *The Death of Bernadette Lefthand*, sold out of its first printing in thirty days, becoming an instant classic in the literature of the Southwest.

Choctaw writer Gary McLain has contributed such nonfiction works as *Keepers of the Fire*, *Indian America: A Traveler's Companion*, and *The Indian Way*.

A descendant of Okla Hannali Choctaws, Ronald Burns Querry has, at various times in his life, been a professor of English at the University of Oklahoma, an editor of horse industry magazines, and a professional farrier (horseshoer). He is the author of *The Death of Bernadette Lefthand*, which received both the Border Regional Library Association Regional Book Award and the Mountains and Plains Booksellers Association Award for one of the best novels published in 1993. Querry is also the editor of *Growing Old at Willie Nelson's Picnic and Other Sketches of Life in the Southwest* and is the author of his "unauthorized" biography, *I See By My Get-UP*. In 1995, Bantam reissued *The Death of Bernadette Lefthand* worldwide in a trade paperback edition in many languages, including French and German.

Louis Owens, a Choctaw-Cherokee, made Choctaw cosmology a major part of his murder mystery, *The Sharpest Sight*, which alternates between settings in California and Mississippi.

Choctaw poet Jim Barnes has long been the editor of *Chariton Review* at Northwest Missouri State University, Kirksville, Missouri. He won the Oklahoma Book Award for his volume of poetry, *The Sawdust War*, and in 1993-1994 he was awarded a Fulbright Fellowship to the University of Lausanne in Switzerland. His books of poetry include *American Book of the Dead*, *A Season of Loss*, *La Plata Cantata*, *The Fish on Poteau Mountain*, and *This Crazy Land*.

Choctaw novelist Louis Owens, an English professor at the University of New Mexico, formerly at the University of California at Santa Cruz, is co-editor of the *American Indian Literature and Critical Studies Series* of the University of Oklahoma Press. Owens's novels include *Wolfsong*, *The Sharpest Sight*, and *Bone Game*. His critical studies include *Other Destinies: Understanding the American Indian Novel*.

— D. L. Birchfield

SEE ALSO:
Mississippi Band of Choctaw Indians; Pushmataha; Returning the Gift.

CHOLOS

In essence, a *cholo* is a Native-looking person who has lost his or her sense of indigenous identity and is, therefore, somewhat marginalized—or on the outer edges of both Native and white or European society. The term first appears in writing in the Peruvian region of South America. Native American writer Garcilasco de la Vega el Inca tells us that cholo was a word from the language of the island of Barlovento (off the coast of Venezuela). He states that it was being used in the early 1600s to refer to persons of mixed Native American and African ancestry. For centuries, the term had also been used throughout the Andean region (Ecuador, Peru, Bolivia, northern Chile, and northern Argentina) to refer to people of mixed Native American and European ancestry or to persons of Native descent but of mixed culture. In other words, cholo has been used in a manner very similar to the word *mestizo*, especially for people with mixed blood, darker skin, and indigenous features.

In the Spanish Empire, the term mestizo was used primarily for people of half-Native American and half-European ancestry. But the term has also come to refer to people of mixed culture and Native American appearance, to people of any known degree of Native American and European mixture, or to people with African ancestry (even if not very noticeable) along with a mix of Native American and European ancestry.

The word *cholo* has also evolved in a similar manner, except that its meaning has changed somewhat as its use spread northward to Mexico and California. In the latter areas, cholo has come to refer to a detribalized person of Mexican indigenous ancestry, who belongs to the lowest economic strata. It has also come to be a self-selected term for some youth who feel like outcasts from the dominant society and who refer to themselves as cholos, perhaps without being aware of the history of the word. Nonetheless, it may indicate some pride in indigenous ancestry. In the Andean region, the

Like these children playing in Belize, in Central America, many people in the Americas are of mixed ancestry. Whether they lose their Native identity depends upon their upbringing. Some people who have very little Indian blood are Indians in every cultural sense of the word, being raised within the tribal environment and sharing its worldview. Many people of mixed ancestry become separated from their culture, however, and no longer identify themselves as Indians.

word *cholo* is a rather derogatory term, although in the diminutive form *cholita* it is sometimes used affectionately for a mistress or girlfriend of indigenous race who is Spanish-speaking (as opposed to speaking Quechua, Aymara, or other indigenous languages).

CHRISTIAN COLONISTS' VIEWS OF NATIVES

Most European missionaries sent to the North American continent came with the idea that civilized society among Native cultures was impossible without knowledge of the Bible. Ironically, some of the most glowing reports of American Indians' societal harmony came from these same missionaries. These missionaries returned from their exposure to Indian cultures carrying accounts of government without force, religion without churches, and charity without knowledge of Christ.

As Britain and France became military rivals in North America, both bid for alliance with its Native peoples. In an effort to win Indians over to their side, these European powers often used religious belief and symbolism as instruments of propaganda. For example, French Catholic missionaries sometimes told Christianized Indians that Christ, the savior, was born in France and crucified in Protestant England.

Many of these missionaries also reported on the resistance of Native Americans to efforts at converting them to Christianity. One such French missionary, a Jesuit priest named Le Jeune, opened a school for Indian boys in Quebec. But he soon complained that introducing Indians to the "yoke of Christianity" was easier said than done. "All these barbarians have the law of wild asses," he wrote to his superiors. "They are born, live and die in a liberty without restraint. They do not know what a bridle is." Another Jesuit, named Father Charlevoix, agreed with this assessment of Native resistance to efforts at conversion: "These Americans are perfectly convinced that man was born free, that no power on earth has a right to infringe his liberty, and that nothing can repay him for the loss of it."

While some of the colonists complained about Indian attitudes toward Christianity, others used the Native point of view to criticize the shortcomings of people who called themselves Christian.

Throughout North America, non-Natives showed no respect for Native beliefs. Converting Indians to Christianity was an objective of virtually every European colonial power. This goal often created friction within a tribe, where harmony and a unified worldview gave way to competing religious factions. Europeans, however, had a romantic view of the religious conversion of Indians, as in this picture of a baptism at Port Royal, in Nova Scotia, Canada.

One such seventeenth-century colonist was Thomas Morton, an English-born American who so displeased Puritan authorities with his playful, high-spirited ways that he was twice deported from the colonies back to England. Morton left no doubt whose company he preferred: "The one Christian, the other Infidels, these [Indians] I found most full of humanity and more friendly than the other."

Roger Williams was a religious leader who rebelled against the structures of Puritan Boston in the mid-seventeenth century and went on to found Rhode Island, a colony based on principles of religious tolerance. He, too, used the example of Indians to criticize European religious customs. Although Williams presented his ideas on freedom as they applied to religion, these ideas also spoke to notions of political liberty that would fire the revolution of the English colonies more than a century later.

Like many of the United States' founders, Williams also often used his perceptions of American Indians and their societies to illustrate his displeasure with European-based colonial life. As the founder of Providence Plantations (later called Rhode Island), Williams tried to put into practice his ideas of "soul liberty," political freedom, and economic equality. His experiment was a forerunner of the later revolution that swept all thirteen original colonies.

Williams argued for a more personal religion, a religion that was closer to Native conceptions of faith than the Puritanism under which he was raised. Other colonial religious leaders had also looked to Indian spirituality as an alternative to the structures of European Christian religion. As early as 1624, one religious leader, Joseph Le Caron, reminded his brethren that no "savage" had ever killed a Christian colonist for religious reasons. Like Le Caron, other Euro-American Christians recognized differences between Native Americans and Europeans such as the English, with their secret and often harsh courts called Star Chambers, or the Spanish, whose brutal Inquisition trampled over Muslims and Jews who refused to accept the authority of the Catholic Church. Unlike these Europeans, Native Americans had no institutions that compelled obedience to any particular ruler's version of the Great Spirit's wisdom. Indians fought with each other for many reasons, but none of them were religious.

In some ways, Roger Williams found what Europeans called Christian values better embodied in Native American societies: "There are no beggars amongst them, nor fatherless children unprovided for." Williams's sermons were directed at the most pompous and chauvinistic of the English. "They [Indians] were hospitable to everybody, whomsoever cometh in when they are eating, they offer them to eat of what they have, though but little enough [is] prepared for themselves," Williams wrote. He continued, "It is a strange truth that a man can generally find more free entertainment and refreshing amongst these Barbarians than amongst the thousands that call themselves Christians."

Williams also wrote poetry that expressed his feeling that Indians had more worthwhile customs and life ways than most English colonists could imagine:

> I've known them to leave their house and mat
> To lodge a friend or stranger
> When Jews and Christians oft have sent
> Jesus Christ to the Manger.
>
> Oft have I heard these Indians say
> These English will deliver us
> Of all that's ours, our lands and lives
> In the end, they'll bereave us.

By the time of the revolution of the English colonists against British rule, these images of Indian ways as an alternative to English customs, including religions, had spread throughout the colonies.

— B. E. Johansen

SEE ALSO:
Catholic Church in the Spanish Empire; Franklin, Benjamin; Jefferson, Thomas.

CHURCHILL, WARD (1947–)

Ward Churchill, an associate member of the United Keetoowah Band of Cherokees, was born on October 2, 1947. He is an author and scholar on topics concerning Native American political issues.

Churchill is the associate director of the Center for the Study of Ethnicity and Race in America, an associate professor, and coordinator for the American Indian Studies program, all at the University of Colorado. He is also the codirector of the Denver/Boulder, Colorado, chapter of the American Indian Movement (AIM), and he has been a highly visible participant in AIM for more than a decade. The Denver/Boulder chapter of AIM has been instrumental in preventing the celebration of Columbus Day activities in Colorado for several years.

Churchill received both a bachelor's degree in technological communications and a master's degree in communications from Sangamon State University, in Springfield, Illinois. In 1992, he was awarded an honorary doctorate by Alfred University in Alfred, New York.

He is the author, coauthor, or editor of ten books, including *Critical Issues in Native America* (1989) and *Agents of Repression: The FBI's Secret Wars Against the Black Panther Party and the American Indian Movement* (1988), and he has been a contributor of articles to many journals and anthologies, such as "The Earth Is Our Mother: Struggles for American Indian Land and Liberation in the Contemporary United States," in *The State of Native America: Genocide, Colonization, and Resistance*, edited by M. Annette Jaimes (1992). Two of his books, *Agents of Repression* and *Fantasies of the Master Race*, received the Gustauvus Myers Award for Outstanding Books on the Subject of Intolerance in the United States, from the Center for Human Rights in the United States, at Fayetteville, Arkansas.

SEE ALSO:
American Indian Movement.

CIGAR-STORE INDIAN

Cigar-store sculptures of Indians appeared from the late sixteenth century through the early twentieth century and had both commercial and decorative functions. These figures were the best-known visual representations of Indians and were so popular they inspired jokes, elements of popular speech, plays, cartoons, and anecdotes. While many kinds of store figures existed, for the most part, statues representing Indians were the most widely used.

A "cigar-store Indian" outside a shop in New York City. Perhaps it was inevitable that European-Americans would associate Indians with tobacco, since the cultivation of tobacco was learned from Indians. But this logic did not carry over to potatoes and all the many other crops that Indians taught Europeans to cultivate.

A large industry produced the figures for display in the storefronts or on the counters of tobacco shops. Carvers gave different types of names based on the statue's stance, dress, or gender. "Chiefs," as male figures were called, were divided into warriors, hunters, scouts, trappers, bucks, braves, and Captain Jacks. Many were given specific names of real or fictional figures like Keokuk, Sitting Bull, Black Hawk, or Hiawatha, while others had comic names like Big-Chief-Me-Smoke-Em. Many exhibited stereotypical features, stance, and clothing, and most were indistinguishable from one another as differences were often subtle. Unrealistic portrayals often made Indians appear grotesque and comic.

The female types were called "Pocahontas," "maiden," or "squaw." The Pocahontases and maid-

ens embodied the Indian princess stereotype, were smaller than the squaws, and wore classical or romantic dress. Squaws were more likely to have exposed or prominent bosoms with an Indian baby on their backs. Many of these types of statues still appear as displays in tobacco shops today.

The images portrayed in these sculptures are dehumanizing, portraying Native people as stoic and without feelings. They are an example of the exploitation of Native people and cultures for commercial uses.

SEE ALSO:
Captain Jack (Kintpuash); Pocahontas; Tomahawk Chop; Westerns, Portrayal of Indians in.

CIVIL RIGHTS ACT OF 1968

SEE American Indian Civil Rights Act of 1968.

CIVIL WAR, U.S., INDIANS IN THE

Like other groups in the United States, American Indians were divided by the Civil War, which was fought between the Confederacy (the South) and the Union (the North) from 1861 to 1865. Some members of the tribes that had settled in Indian Territory (now Oklahoma) during the forced removal of the 1830s supported the Confederacy, some supported the Union, and some preferred to remain neutral. However, various factors, including the location of Indian Territory, made neutrality difficult if not impossible. All five nations in Indian Territory—Cherokee, Creek, Chickasaw, Choctaw, and Seminole—would become involved in skirmishes and in full-scale battles during the war.

On March 15, 1861, about a month before the war actually began, the Confederate Congress established a Bureau of Indian Affairs within its War

Department and provided appropriations for a commissioner and a clerk. Albert Pike of Arkansas was chosen to negotiate with the tribes in Indian Territory. At a large council meeting held at North Fork Town in Creek Nation territory, members of the various nations established a league called the United Nations of the Indian Territory and adopted a constitution. The purpose was to support the Confederate cause and government, which agreed to recognize the sovereign powers of the tribes and provide for tribal representation in the Confederate Congress.

Not all tribal members in Indian Territory were in agreement with the allegiance to the Confederacy. Within the Creek Nation, for example, people's loyalties were divided along mixed-blood and full-blood lines, with full-bloods tending to support the Union or to seek neutrality. On August 5, 1861, a full-blood faction from the Canadian District met in council and elected Oktarharsars Harjo, also known as Sands Harjo, as their chief. On August 15, Sands Harjo and another full-blood leader, Opothle Yahola, pleaded for protection in a letter to President Abraham Lincoln. Unfortunately, the federal (Union) government was too burdened by the war to provide such protection.

Opothle Yahola and a group of his followers soon packed up their belongings and food, intending to journey to the territory of the Cherokees, many of whom—like Opothle Yahola—preferred neutrality. Opothle Yahola's plan was to wait out the war with the Cherokees and those members of other tribes who also wanted no involvement in the war.

On November 19, 1861, during their journey to Cherokee territory, Opothle Yahola's followers were attacked on the south side of the Arkansas River. In this battle, known as the Battle of Round Mountain, he and his small force managed to hold off the Confederate troops that included Chickasaw, Choctaw, and white soldiers. The Confederates lost one hundred men, and two hundred were wounded.

Opothle Yahola's followers continued their journey. Troops led by Confederate Colonel Douglas H. Cooper, a Choctaw agent, caught up with them near Bird Creek on December 8. Here, it is reported, a large number of Confederate soldiers deserted their posts and joined the Union supporters.

Albert Pike (1809–1891), a Confederate general, was forced to resign after being severely criticized for inept leadership of a brigade of Indian soldiers from Indian Territory (present-day Oklahoma) in March 1862 at the Battle of Pea Ridge.

Opothle Yahola, a Creek leader, tried to get President Abraham Lincoln to honor Indian treaties guaranteeing that federal troops would provide protection for Indians in Indian Territory. The United States was unable or unwilling to do so, leaving Indian Territory at the mercy of Confederate forces at the beginning of the Civil War.

John Ross, Chief of the Cherokee Nation, tried to maintain neutrality in the Civil War, but when the United States withdrew its troops from Indian Territory, the Cherokees had no choice but to enter into diplomatic relations with the Confederacy.

The day after Christmas, the Indians were again attacked near Hominy Creek by a white force from Arkansas. Opothle Yahola and his followers escaped to Kansas, which was loyal to the Union, in hopes of protection and survival. Many of the people froze to death during their journey, and everyone lost possessions. Opothle Yahola, who only wanted peace, later died in Kansas.

John Ross, chief of the Cherokee Nation, tried to stay neutral, but when Stand Watie sided with the South, Cherokee neutrality ended. Stand Watie became one of the strongest Confederate leaders in Indian Territory. He commanded his own regiment of Cherokee, Creek, and Seminole soldiers and was eventually promoted to brigadier general. His regiment, as well as the Choctaw-Chickasaw regiment, fought in the Battle of Pea Ridge in March 1862. One of the more important Union victories in Indian Territory occurred at Honey Springs on July 17, 1863.

As the end of the war approached, it seemed imperative for tribes to unite for their own protection and to save their land from settlers and the railroads. On May 26, 1865, about a month after the Confederate surrender, fourteen tribes agreed on a declaration that no Indian should spill another Indian's blood. The tribes also agreed to maintain the integrity of Indian Territory as their home.

The United States government later sent Commissioner of Indian Affairs Dennis N. Cooley to meet with tribal leaders at Fort Smith, Arkansas. There, tribal leaders were severely reprimanded for the alliance with the Confederate government. The commissioner told the leaders that they had forfeited all their treaty rights and annuities and had to make new treaties with the federal government—despite the fact that many tribal members of the various nations had supported and even fought on the side of the Union.

When the council at Fort Smith ended, the tribes agreed to meet again in Washington, D.C., to make final treaty provisions. In the end, they agreed to the construction of one north-south and one east-west railroad through Indian Territory. All five nations were required to make provisions for their freed slaves. The Creeks, Seminoles, and Cherokees immediately provided citizenship and property rights for the former slaves, as did the Choctaws and Chickasaws some years later.

The war provided nothing for the Indians except a loss of lives and resources. All were penalized for the role that some had played on the side of the Confederacy. However, once the peace treaties were signed, the people began to return to Indian Territory and once again rebuild their nations.

— S. Arkeketa

SEE ALSO:

Lincoln, Abraham; Pea Ridge, Battle of; Removal Policy; Trail of Tears; Watie, Stand.

SUGGESTED READING:

Debo, Angie. *A History of the Indians of the United States.* Norman: University of Oklahoma Press, 1970.

CIVILIZATION POLICY

The so-called Civilization Policy was a partnership established in the early 1800s between the U.S. government and various religious missionaries in an attempt to use education to force Indians to assimilate into the dominant U.S. society. In 1819, Congress passed the Civilization Fund Act, which set aside ten thousand dollars per year for various religious groups to teach Indians the "habits and arts of civilization." Actually, the government's real purpose with the Civilization Policy was neither education nor assimilation of the Indians but to force the Indians, in an underhanded way, to give up more and more of their land.

The first official U.S. policy toward Indian education was a treaty clause in the 1794 agreement with the Oneidas, Tuscaroras, and Stockbridges that stipulated that Indians would exchange their land for a number of things, including education. Ninety-five of the 371 treaties the United States negotiated with Indian tribes over the years carried such a provision. Through these treaties, Indians were forced to give up over one billion acres (four hundred thousand hectares) of land.

By giving money to missionaries for Indian education, the U.S. government made their Civilization Policy appear humane and moral. The U.S. government rationalized that these treaties enabled church groups to "put into the hands of Indian children the primer and the hoe" so they would "grow up with the habits of morality and industry."

Both United States government-run schools and missionary-run schools worked to destroy Indian culture and to force Indians to adopt white culture. By 1838, more than three thousand Indian children had been separated from their families and shipped to missionary schools in the eastern United States. Missionaries at the time held to the theory that the farther away children were from their parents, the easier it would be to get them to give up their Indian traditions.

In virtually all of the missionary schools, students were forced to give up their tribal languages and customs, to wear military uniforms, to march to class, and to learn practical skills such as agriculture, printing, and mechanics. Discipline in these schools was harsh—especially for those children who tried to escape or who were slow to give up their tribal cultures. Students were often kept away from their families for years at a time.

Many schools were underfunded and had to be supported by the manual labor of the children. This meant the boys had to do heavy construction and farming work. They also had to make shoes, boots, and wagons. The girls were forced to do sewing,

Indian training schools were used in an attempt to force Native children to adopt non-Native habits. This school, as it looked in 1882, was located in Forest Grove, Oregon.

washing, and ironing, as well the cooking and cleaning for the whole school. These chores were in addition to their schoolwork, and it was not unusual for students to spend more time working every day than studying in the classroom.

Many Indian parents rebelled against the government policy, refusing to allow their children to be taken to Indian boarding schools. Students were often forcibly taken away from their parents anyway and then held as virtual hostages in the schools to make sure their parents did not become more disruptive. In the 1890s, when most of the Plains tribes were confined to reservations, forbidden to hunt, and dependent on the government for food rations, the government often threatened to withhold food from families who kept their children out of the boarding schools.

It was not until 1928, when the Institute for Government Research released the Meriam Report—a study of the Indian educational system based on the government's Civilization Policy— that anyone admitted officially that the policy had been a failure. Reforms were finally begun during John Collier's term as Commissioner of Indian Affairs (1933–1945). The Civilization Policy is widely viewed today as an organized practice of cultural extermination against Native people.

SEE ALSO:
Acculturation; Boarding Schools; Collier, John; Meriam, Lewis.

CLARK, CARTER BLUE (1946–)

Carter Blue Clark (Creek) is an ethnohistorian and university administrator. He is a member of the Muscogee Nation of Oklahoma and received B.A., M.A., and Ph.D. degrees in history from the University of Oklahoma.

Clark has served as coordinator of the History of the Indians of the Americas Graduate Program at the University of Utah, director of Indian Studies at Morningside College, associate professor in the Department of Indian Studies at San Diego State University, and visiting professor in American Indian Studies at UCLA. For fifteen years, he taught in the American Indian Studies Program at California State University at Long Beach. He currently serves as executive vice president of Oklahoma City University.

Clark has received many awards, including an academic fellowship at the Newberry Library in Chicago and the Muriel Wright Heritage Endowment Award for writing the best article in 1977 in *Chronicles of Oklahoma*, the quarterly scholarly journal of the state historical society. He is a member of many professional and educational associations concerned with Indian education and has served on the National Advisory Caucus and as regional coordinator for Wordcraft Circle of Native American Mentor & Apprentice Writers.

Clark is the author of more than fifty scholarly, academic, literary, biographical, or historical articles in professional journals and anthologies, and he serves on the editorial board of the *American Indian Culture and Research Journal*, published by UCLA, and the *Native Press Research Journal*,

Carter Blue Clark, a member of the Creek Nation of Oklahoma, is an authority on the allotment of Indian lands in Indian Territory in the late nineteenth century and its effect on tribal sovereignty.

published by the University of Arkansas at Little Rock.

Clark's most recent academic project is a revision of his doctoral dissertation, *A History of the Ku Klux Klan in Oklahoma,* for publication by Texas Tech University Press. In 1994, he published *Lone Wolf v. Hitchcock: Treaty Rights and Indian Law at the End of the Nineteenth Century,* University of Nebraska Press, an important case study of the United States Supreme Court decision of January 5, 1903. The decision proved to be a rationale to abrogate, or annul, the 371 treaties between the Indian nations and the United States by placing Native people at the mercy of unilateral decisions of the United States Congress. The work is distinguished not only for its thoroughness and scholarship, but also for the dignity and restraint with which Clark surveys the devastating impact of the decision on Native tribal sovereignty.

SEE ALSO:
Lone Wolf v. Hitchcock.

CLIFF DWELLINGS

Throughout the arid Southwest, beneath overhanging cliffs in remote canyons, in the entrances to large natural caverns, or perched atop steep, virtually inaccessible canyon walls, stone masonry apartments stand silent and abandoned. Many of them are multistory structures, some of them are remarkably well preserved, and most of them are at least six to eight hundred years old. The abandonment of these structures is a testimony to the fragile nature of the climate in this arid region and to the capacity of prolonged drought to disrupt agricultural communities. For some of the ruins, especially those with dependable sources of water, the reason for their abandonment is a profound mystery.

Most of the cliff dwellings were constructed by people of the Anasazi, Mogollon, Sinagua, and Salado cultures. There are hundreds of sites throughout the Southwest, concentrated in New Mexico, Arizona, southern Utah, and southwestern Colorado. The ones open to the public, which are also

The arid environment of the Southwest has helped preserve remarkable structures of earlier civilizations, such as these Puye cliff dwellings in New Mexico.

331

The entrance to an individual apartment in a cliff dwelling is often through a hole in the roof, which is reached by means of a ladder.

the ones most easily reached, are found in national monuments and national parks. The largest and most spectacular cliff dwellings are found in Mesa Verde National Park in southwestern Colorado, which includes Cliff Palace, the largest cliff dwelling in the Southwest, with more than two hundred rooms and twenty-three *kivas,* or underground chambers used for ceremonies.

Montezuma Castle National Monument in central Arizona contains the best-preserved cliff dwellings in the Southwest. They are found at several locations along Beaver Creek in the Verde Valley, within the more than 800-acre (320-hectare) expanse of the monument. In the nineteenth century, Americans mistakenly believed that the ruins had been built by Aztecs fleeing from Hernando Cortés and other Spaniards in central Mexico during the sixteenth century; thus they were misnamed for the Aztec ruler, Montezuma. The ruins are now known to date from about three centuries before the time of Montezuma, and they had been abandoned for about half a century by the time he was born.

The misconception about the origin of these ruins is instructive about U.S. attitudes in the 1800s regarding the Indians within the region that now encompasses the United States. At that time, for example, even distinguished U.S. scientists refused to believe that the ancestors of the resident Native people could have constructed the elaborate earthen mounds found throughout the Ohio River Valley in the Midwest. Discover-

ing these mathematically precise, geometric arrangements, the scientists attributed their impressive construction to some vanished race.

The multistory stone masonry structures in the Verde Valley are found in limestone cliffs. Montezuma Castle is the most impressive of these structures, perched high on a cliff, towering above the valley floor. A few miles away, Montezuma Well, a natural spring with a flow of more than one million gallons (3.8 million liters) of water per day, was diverted to croplands in the valley floor through stone irrigation ditches.

Many cliff dwellings were built under the protection of an overhanging outcrop of rock, such as this structure at Walnut Canyon, Arizona.

Grand Canyon National Park in northwestern Arizona contains hundreds of cliff dwelling ruins throughout its vast expanse. No one knows how many cliff dwellings may be within the park. More than six hundred sites have been located thus far, and many of them are virtually inaccessible. Many of the ruins cannot be seen from either the rim of the canyon or from the bottom of it, and many of them require technical climbing equipment to reach a vantage point from which the ruins can be seen. Artifacts from some of the ruins are on display at Tusayan Museum within the park, near Tusayan Ruin, one of the few sites that can be easily reached and that is open to the public.

At Bandelier National Monument, 50 miles (80.5 kilometers) west of Santa Fe, New Mexico, are cliff dwellings constructed between the twelfth and sixteenth centuries. These ruins are known as *talus* villages because they were built at the base of the cliff. They extend for 2 miles (3.2 kilometers) along the Rito de los Frijoles, Bean Creek, the only dependable source of water in the area. Constructed of stone masonry, some of the structures were as much as three stories high and have additional rooms carved into the walls of the cliff.

At Gila Cliff Dwellings National Monument, a remote site 50 miles (80.5 kilometers) north of Silver City, New Mexico, a total of thirty-five rooms were constructed in about 1100 C.E. in six natural caverns. They were abandoned in about 1350. Pottery found at the site was crafted with great skill, but many precious artifacts were removed from this site between the 1870s and 1907, when the dwellings received protection as a national monument.

At Tonto National Monument, about 50 miles (80.5 kilometers) east of Phoenix, Arizona, are some of the most intriguing ruins in the Southwest. They were built and occupied for less than one hundred years during the fourteenth century by a people who are credited with being the first people in the world to cultivate the grain amaranth as a crop. They also were the only ancient people of the Southwest who are known to have developed dark green and blue-black dyes, which were used for dying cotton. Skilled farmers, they built irrigation ditches to divert water from the Salt River for their crops. Their multi-story masonry dwellings, constructed of unshaped native quartzite with adobe mortar, completely fill three large caverns in the cliffs. The sites are known

as Lower Ruin, Lower Ruin Annex, and Upper Ruin. Their irrigated fields were located from 2 to 4 miles (3.2 to 6.4 kilometers) from these structures. With a dependable water supply and a flourishing civilization of skilled potters, weavers, and farmers, no one knows why they suddenly abandoned the site at the end of the fourteenth century.

Nineteenth-century Euro-Americans are usually given credit for the discovery of most of the cliff dwellings in the Southwest. These discoveries were almost always followed by a period of looting of artifacts from the structures until the sites could be given some sort of protection. Contemporary Native peoples of the area have been aware of the sites for centuries. The state of their preservation at the time Euro-Americans found them is testimony to the respect accorded to the ancient ones by Native people. Had the sites not been found by European-Americans, chances are that most of them would today be largely as they were at the time they were abandoned by the people who constructed them.

— D. L. Birchfield

SEE ALSO:
Anasazi; Mesa Verde; Mogollon Culture.

SUGGESTED READINGS:
Ferguson, William, and Arthur Robin. *Anasazi Ruins of the Southwest in Color.* Albuquerque: University of New Mexico Press, 1987.
Noble, David Grant. *Ancient Ruins of the Southwest.* Flagstaff, AZ: Northland Press, 1981.
Warren, Scott. *Cities in the Sand.* San Francisco: Chronicle Books, 1992.

CLOTHING

SEE Regalia.

CLOVIS CULTURE

Clovis culture is a name archaeologists have given to a distinctive culture of Ice Age hunters that flourished in North America about thirteen thousand years ago. It is the oldest culture in North

America that can be dated with a high degree of reliability.

No skeletal remains of Clovis people have been found, but much is known about them, nonetheless. They left behind a unique kind of spear point made from stone, which is now called a Clovis point. These projectile points are about two to five inches (five to thirteen centimeters) long and are fairly heavy, being rather thick through the middle. Their distinctive feature is a groove in one of the flat sides of the spear point, sometimes on both flat sides, usually extending about half the length of the point, but sometimes only for a short distance near the base. This groove, called a flute, required a lot of extra work and was not necessary for attaching the spear point to the spear shaft, though it did make it a little easier. Fluted points have not been found anywhere except in North America. Why Clovis people spent so much time making fluted points, when they were really not necessary, is a mystery. Another culture that came a little later than Clovis culture, called Folsom culture, made even more finely crafted fluted points. But later inhabitants of North America did not make fluted points at all and got along fine without them.

A spear shaft was made by cutting a split into the end of a pole and then fitting the blunt end of the spear point into the split. The shaft of the spear was then bound to the spear point with strings of plant fiber or small strips of animal hide.

Clovis points were usually made from flint or chert, but sometimes they were made from beautiful pieces of transparent stone that are much more difficult to work with. For many years, archaeologists could not explain how they were made, until a technique called flaking was rediscovered by trial and error. The spear points were crafted by removing tiny flakes of stone. Either another piece of stone was used to strike them off (called percussion flaking), or a hard piece of bone was used, such as the tip of an antler, to remove the flakes by pressing down hard on the stone (called pressure flaking).

Flaking required great skill as the craftsperson removed tiny flakes one at a time all along the edge of the spear point until it had been fashioned into a thin, sharp blade. Flaking was also the method used to cut the groove into the flat side of the spear point.

The discovery of Clovis points in the 1930s was an important event in the history of archaeology in North America. Before that time, archaeologists had argued that humans had only inhabited North America for three or four thousand years. But in 1933, near Clovis, New Mexico, campsites were discovered around the edges of a series of ancient lake beds.

The bones of extinct Ice Age animals, such as mammoths and camels, were found in close association with the campsites. It was obvious that these sites were much older than three or four thousand years. Excavation of the sites was begun under the direction of Dr. Edgar B. Howard of the University of Pennsylvania Museum. In 1936, John L. Cotter found the first two Clovis points at one of the sites.

Archaeologists were finally able to date Clovis culture when Dr. E. H. Sellards led investigations by the Texas Memorial Museum in 1949, 1950, and 1951. Arriving at the site near Clovis, New Mexico, they chose an area called Blackwater Draw for their excavations.

Digging down into eighteen feet (five meters) of deposits, they discovered Clovis sites in the very bottom three-foot (one-meter) layer of earth, a layer that rested on bedrock. Here, they found Clovis points in close association with the bones of extinct Ice Age mammals in a layer of earth that geologists were able to date to about thirteen thousand years ago. Clovis points were soon discovered in other layers of thirteen thousand-year-old strata at other sites in New Mexico, Arizona, and Texas.

Once archaeologists learned to look in thirteen thousand-year-old layers of earth, Clovis points were soon discovered in California, Nevada, Oregon, Washington, Mexico, and Alberta, Canada. The discovery of Clovis points, and the reliability of their dating, changed the way archaeologists think about the antiquity of humans in North America. There is much debate about how long humans have been in North America, but now the debate is focused on the distant past, on how long people might have been on the continent before they began making Clovis fluted points.

SEE ALSO:

Folsom Culture.

COCHISE (c. 1815–1874)

Cochise was known to his people by the name Cheis, meaning "oak," a name that refers to the strength and quality of oak, rather than to the tree itself. European-Americans added a prefix to his name, and he is now most widely known by that name, Cochise. He was a member of the Chokonen band of Apaches, which has become known as the Chiricahuas.

Cochise was a leader of the Chiricahua Apaches during the time the Chiricahuas were forced to make the transition to life on a reservation as a result of the Euro-American colonization of Arizona. The United States claimed ownership of the Chiricahua Apache homeland in present-day southeastern Arizona and southwestern New Mexico as a result of conquest in the war with Mexico, which ended in 1848. Soon after the war, citizens of the United States began moving into the region in ever-increasing numbers. Conflicts with the resident Apaches soon developed.

After the Mexican War, the U.S. Congress moved quickly to incorporate the Apache homelands into territories of the United States. In 1850, Congress created the Territory of New Mexico, which encompassed most of the land in the present states of New Mexico and Arizona. In 1854, the United States acquired an additional tract of land from Mexico, known as the Gadsden Purchase, that is now the southern portion of the state of Arizona, south of the Gila River. This land was added to the Territory of New Mexico. In 1863 Congress divided the Territory of New Mexico in half, creating the Territory of Arizona from the western half.

Apaches soon became victims of aggression within their homeland. U.S. officials were aware at the time that the Apaches were not to blame for the violence that would trouble the region for an entire generation. Upon becoming governor of the Territory of New Mexico in 1853, David Meriweather said, "I had heard on my arrival in the territory that the Indians were not the aggressors, but I well knew that when the Indians and the whites once commenced fighting, the Indians would never make peace until whipped, and, therefore necessity compelled me to whip them." This unsympathetic attitude would characterize U.S. colonization in the Southwest. The Apaches would find no justice for wrongs committed against them and would have no recourse but to attempt to defend the invasion of their homeland as best they could. Rather than attempt to redress Apache griev-

Cochise, a leader of the Chiricahua Apaches, was on friendly terms with the United States, until an army officer summarily hanged his younger brother and two of his nephews.

ances, the United States would respond by attempting to subdue the Apaches militarily.

Though the Chiricahuas and other Western Apaches had for many years been engaged in warfare with Mexicans, who occupied Apache lands in northern Mexico and against whom Apaches had many bitter and long standing grievances, Cochise was an Apache leader who tried to coexist with the newly arrived Euro-Americans, even in the face of provocation. Not only was he an influential Chiricahua, but he was married to Dos-teh-seh, the daughter of Mangas Coloradas, a leader of the Mimbrenos Apaches. Cochise remained on good terms with Euro-Americans even after his father-in-law, Mangas Coloradas, was attacked by a group of miners in 1851, tied to a post, and whipped until nearly dead. Mangas Coloradas then waged war against the miners, but Cochise would not join him.

Cochise regularly sold firewood to a remote station on the Butterfield stagecoach line in Siphon Canyon, near the entrance to the rugged Apache Pass, within the Chiricahua homeland. He enjoyed good relations with the Butterfield employees and visited them frequently. In 1861, however, Cochise's friendly relations with Americans were shattered by an incident that he had nothing to do with.

In that year, members of some Western Apache bands were thought to have captured a twelve-year-old boy named Felix Ward and to have stolen some cattle from the boy's stepfather. The boy may have been half Apache and he might also have been running away from an abusive stepfather and not have been kidnapped at all. In any event, he ended up being raised by the Apaches and later became known as Mickey Free when he served as a scout and interpreter for the U.S. Army. The boy's stepfather, without any evidence—and, as it turned out, erroneously—accused Cochise and the Chiricahua Apaches of stealing the boy and the cattle. The stepfather demanded that the U.S. Army take action, and an inexperienced lieutenant named George N. Bascom was sent with a detachment of soldiers to confront Cochise.

Cochise, upon learning that the lieutenant wanted to talk to him, and unaware that anything was wrong, came to the stagecoach station in Siphon Canyon to meet with the lieutenant, bringing with him his wife and children and his brother and nephews. Lieutenant Bascom, after luring Cochise and his relatives into his tent on the pretext of serving them dinner, suddenly seized all of them as hostages for the return of Felix Ward. Bascom's brash and foolish plan was immediately upset when Cochise slashed a hole in the tent and bolted away as fifty startled soldiers fired their rifles at him.

Events became more confused when Cochise and his Chiricahuas managed to capture a Butterfield employee as a hostage of their own, as well as some nearby teamsters, and demanded an exchange of hostages. When Lieutenant Bascom refused to enter into any discussions with the Chiricahuas, the situation quickly deteriorated. Fighting waged back and forth until another force of soldiers arrived and the Chiricahuas had fled to the mountains. The incident ended in tragedy for all parties, with Cochise killing his hostages and the U.S. Army hanging six of their Chiricahua hostages before leaving the canyon, including Cochise's two nephews and his younger brother, Coyuntara. Cochise became bitterly distrustful of non-Native Americans and joined Mangas Coloradas against them, engaging in warfare that would rage for twelve years.

In the end, it was friendship between Cochise and an American named Thomas Jeffords that would lead to peace. Jeffords was an employee of the Butterfield stage line, which had lost more than a dozen employees to the Chiricahuas during the war. Somehow, Jeffords and Cochise met. Some accounts say Jeffords sought out Cochise in the mountains. Others say that Jeffords had been captured by the Chiricahuas. In any event, the two men came to know and trust one another. Jeffords became an important emissary in negotiations in 1872 between the Chiricahuas and General Oliver Howard, talks that eventually resulted in a reservation for the Chiricahuas within their homeland and relative peace during the last few years of Cochise's life. After his death, however, Cochise's people were forced to move to another reservation, outside their homeland, in violation of the agreement between Cochise and General Howard.

— D.L. Birchfield

SEE ALSO:
Apache; Arizona; Geronimo; Howard, Oliver O.

SUGGESTED READINGS:

Roberts, David. *Once They Moved Like the Wind: Cochise, Geronimo, and the Apache Wars.* New York: Simon and Schuster, 1993.

Sweeney, Edwin R. *Cochise: Chiricahua Apache Chief.* Norman: University of Oklahoma Press, 1991.

Worchester, Donald E. *Apaches: Eagles of the Southwest.* Norman: University of Oklahoma Press, 1979.

COCHISE CULTURE

Cochise culture is a term used by archaeologists for the Archaic period ancestors of the Mogollon tradition. The Cochises and their Mogollon descendants inhabited a mountainous territory in present-day southeastern Arizona and southwestern New Mexico extending into the Mexican state of Chihuahua.

The introduction of pottery sometime around 300 B.C.E. is generally regarded as marking the end of the Cochise culture and the beginning of the Mogollon tradition. Prior to that change, Cochise culture had been developing for thousands of years.

Originally a group of nomadic gatherers, the Cochise people entered the region as early as 7300 B.C.E. In contrast to the extremely dry country of the Anasazi people to the north and the Hohokam to the west, the Cochise country is mountainous. It is well timbered, with grassy meadows and dependable sources of water.

The nature of the land made food gathering, rather than hunting, the base of their early economy, though they are credited with being the first people in the Southwest to make bows and arrows. Food gathering included such items as seeds, berries, nuts, acorns, cactus fruit, and agave roots. Cochise artifacts dating before 6000 B.C.E. are primarily grindstones (metates and manos); they are the oldest such implements thus far found in the Southwest.

Between 3500 B.C.E. and 1500 B.C.E., the design of the metate, formerly flat, was improved by hollowing it out. During this period, the Cochise people also developed split-twig figurines. These deerlike animal figures, made of split willow twigs, are considered among the most delicate and artistic of Archaic period artwork.

Between 1500 B.C.E. and 500 B.C.E., the climate of this region became wetter. As a result, agriculture, which depends on adequate rainfall, became more attractive. The Cochise people became partially sedentary, cultivating corn, beans, pumpkins, and sunflowers. These crops had originally been domesticated in Mexico and had spread north along the trade routes. Simple clay pots also originated during this period.

The Cochises gradually began to construct permanent dwellings, called pit houses, and became more dependent upon agriculture. They also developed pottery—the first true pottery in the Southwest—an activity at which their descendants would excel. The Cochises then entered into a long and distinguished period of cultural development called the Mogollon tradition, which would last until the fourteenth century C.E. The Mogollon culture is especially known for its outstanding arts, particularly pottery. The Cochise people are also known for their skill in constructing items from plant fibers. These include not only baskets but also sandals.

The Cochise people offer an example of the long and gradual development of sedentary culture in the Southwest. They also offer an example of the influence and spread of cultural developments from Mexico, particularly regarding domesticated plants.

SEE ALSO:
Archaic Period; Mogollon Culture.

CODE TALKERS, CHOCTAW

The use of Native American soldiers speaking their Native languages for battlefield radio communications in World War II, especially the military service of Navajos, Choctaws, and Comanches, is becoming increasingly well known in popular culture. The Navajo Code Talkers, especially, have been the subject of several books. The use of Native Americans as "code talkers," however, began in World War I with Choctaws serving in the U.S. Army in Europe, and that service is much less well known in popular culture than that of the code talkers of World War II.

Choctaws were the first soldiers to use their Native language for the purpose of transmitting military radio field communications that could not be understood by the enemy. In World War I, the Choctaw language was the only "code" used by the Allies that was never "broken" by the German Army code breakers.

Fifteen Choctaw men, serving in the 36th Division of the American Expeditionary Force, became the Choctaw Code Talkers of World War I. They were Robert Taylor, Jeff Nelson, Calvin Wilson, Mitchell Bobb, Peter Maytubby, Solomon Louis, Charles Jones, James Edwards, Ben Carterby, Walter Vech, Albert Billy, Ben Hampton, Joseph Oklahombi, Victor Brown, and Tobias Frazier. The Choctaw Code Talkers are credited with playing an important role in key battles in the Meuse-Argonne campaign in the decisive final days of World War I.

At least one Choctaw Code Talker was placed in each field company headquarters, where he transmitted military communications by field telephone and by radio. Code talkers also wrote field orders in the Choctaw language that were dispatched between units by couriers. The Germans were able to intercept and capture about 25 percent of the messages sent by courier, but German intelligence officers were at a complete loss in attempting to "decode" the messages.

In at least one instance, a trick attempted by the Germans backfired badly, thanks in large part to Choctaw Code Talkers. At Ferme Forest on the Aisne River, the Germans, upon retreating, intentionally left much of their communication network intact, hoping that the American Expeditionary Force would use the captured lines and then the Germans would be able to listen to the transmissions. The Americans did use the captured telephone lines for their own military transmissions, but Choctaw Code Talkers from Company E of the 142nd Infantry made it possible for the Americans to make good use of the extensive German communications network and for the Germans to gain no benefit from the sacrifice.

The Choctaw Code Talkers received no recognition for their work in World War I until the Choctaw Nation of Oklahoma honored them in ceremonies at the annual Choctaw Nation Labor Day Festival in 1986. The event took place at Tuskahoma, Oklahoma, site of the historic nineteenth-century Choctaw Nation Capitol Building, which is

now a Choctaw Nation museum. Some of the surviving World War I Choctaw Code Talkers were able to attend the ceremonies. They were awarded the Choctaw Nation Medal of Valor for their service. Medals were posthumously awarded to families of deceased code talkers.

In November of 1989, on the steps of the Oklahoma State Capitol building in Oklahoma City, Oklahoma, representatives of the government of France recognized the World War I Choctaw Code Talkers with the highest honor that France can bestow upon a citizen of another nation, the Chevalier de L'Ordre National du Merité.

SEE ALSO:

Choctaw; Code Talkers, Navajo.

CODE TALKERS, NAVAJO

Navajos have served with distinction in the armed forces of the United States in every war in the twentieth century, including World War I, even though they, like other reservation Indians, did not become citizens of the United States until citizenship was extended to them by an act of Congress in 1924. Their most heralded service, however, came during World War II in the United States Marine Corps. Their contribution was to employ the Navajo language for military communication in the field as the Marines stormed Japanese-held islands in the Pacific. They became known as the Navajo Code Talkers.

Philip Johnson, a son of missionaries to the Navajos who was raised on the Navajo Reservation, is credited with a leading role in the formation of the Navajo Code Talkers. As a child, he learned fluent Navajo, as well as Navajo culture and traditions. At the age of nine, he served as an interpreter for a Navajo delegation that had traveled to Washington, D.C., to present Navajo grievances to President Theodore Roosevelt. After serving in World War I, Johnson was a civil engineer in California when World War II broke out with Japan.

Upon learning that the military hoped to develop a code using American Indians as signalmen, Johnson met with Marine Corps and Army Signal Corps officers and arranged a demonstration of

Judge William Wilson, shown here in traditional Navajo dress, was a Navajo Code Talker in the U.S. Marine Corps in World War II.

Training Center at Camp Pendleton in Oceanside, California. There they received 176 hours of instruction in basic communications procedures and equipment.

They were then deployed to Guadalcanal, a Pacific island, where their use of the Navajo language for radio communication in the field proved to be so effective that recruitment for the program was expanded. Eventually, some four hundred Navajo Code Talkers saw duty in the Pacific in the Marine Corps. By the end of the war, they had been assigned to all six Marine Corps divisions in the Pacific and had taken part in every assault, from Guadalcanal in 1943 to Okinawa in 1945. Today, the surviving Navajo Code Talkers maintain an active veterans organization. In 1969, at the 4th Marine Division Association reunion in Chicago, they were presented with a specially minted medallion in commemoration of their services.

SEE ALSO:
Code Talkers, Choctaw; Navajo.

SUGGESTED READING:
Wright, David K. *A Multicultural Portrait of World War II.* New York: Benchmark Books/Marshall Cavendish, 1994.

Navajo as a code language. This took place on February 28, 1942, at Camp Elliott, California, with the cooperation of four Navajos from Los Angeles and one who was in the navy in San Diego.

Within a year, the Marine Corps authorized the program, which at first was classified as top secret. Philip Johnson, although over the age for military service, was allowed to enlist in the Marine Corps and was assigned to help supervise the establishment of the program at Camp Pendleton, California. In May 1942, the Marine Corps, with the approval of the Navajo Tribal Council, began recruiting Navajo men at Window Rock, Arizona, for the program. The first group to receive training consisted of twenty-nine Navajos. They underwent basic boot camp training at the San Diego Marine Corps Recruit Depot, and then they were sent for four weeks to the Field Signal Battalion

CODY, BUFFALO BILL

SEE Buffalo Bill Cody; Buffalo Bill's Wild West Show.

COLLIER, JOHN (1884–1968)

John Collier was an author, editor, reformer, and for twelve years commissioner of Indian Affairs (1933–1945). Educated at Columbia University and the College de France, he was editor of *American Indian Life Magazine* from 1926 to 1933.

On March 7, 1934, Commissioner of Indian Affairs John Collier met with leaders of the Blackfeet Nation in Rapid City, South Dakota, to hear their views on legislation pending in Congress known as the Wheeler-Howard Act.

Before he developed an interest in Indian affairs, Collier had established a reputation as a social worker and reformer. On a visit to the Taos Pueblo in December 1920, the ceremonies he observed and the people he met influenced his future work on behalf of Indian rights and laws. After his experience at Taos Pueblo, Collier, who was not a Native American, wrote, ". . . what I observed and experienced was a power of art—of the life-making art—greater in kind than anything I had known in my own world before."

The next year, Senator Holm Bursum of New Mexico introduced legislation that threatened the Pueblos' ownership of their land. Collier helped the Pueblos to fight against the Bursum Bill, which was eventually defeated. Afterward, he helped organize the American Indian Defense Association in May 1923, and he remained its most important executive until it suspended operations in the 1930s. In *The Nations Within*, Lakota educator and historian Vine Deloria, Jr., says of Collier, "He was not the first non-Indian to appreciate the Indian tradition. He certainly became the first to understand, appreciate, articulate, and fight zealously for it."

In 1928, Collier organized a tour of Indian Country by the senators from North Dakota, Wisconsin, Oklahoma, and Montana. Although these senators represented states with significant Indian populations, they knew nothing about the living conditions or concerns of Native people in their states. They learned about those conditions and the abuses caused by the Bureau of Indian Affairs. The senators became concerned about the lack of an organized way for the various tribes to deal with the U.S. government. It was this concern—that Native Americans needed to represent themselves to the federal government—not a concern for Indian self-government, that led the senators to look at reorganization of the tribal governments. The Klamaths had already sought congressional help in working with the federal government directly and bypassing the Bureau of Indian Affairs—an approach Collier supported the rest of his life.

Lawrence Kelly in his article "The Indian Reorganization Act: Dream or Reality?" published in 1976 in *Pacific Historical Review*, wrote that "the genius of John Collier . . . was that he saw the bankruptcy of federal Indian policy more clearly than anyone else in his generation." Deloria points out that everyone knew Indian policy was "bankrupt"; they just didn't know what to do about it. Except for Collier, all reformers before and since have accepted the federal institutions as a constant in the equation. Collier attempted to change the institutions themselves.

President Franklin Delano Roosevelt appointed Collier to head the BIA in 1933 on the basis of Collier's work with the American Indian Defense Association. Even before his appointment, Collier had begun efforts to get major changes in tribal government policy put into law. He wanted a corporate structure for the reservations to give Indians decision-making powers for management of Indian lands and eliminate the BIA from this function. He also fought for the "restoration of Indian societies and culture." He got a bill creating tribal councils introduced, but the Senate, distracted with other matters, never took action. In 1994, many tribes continued to call for the elimination of the BIA or at least the elimination of its area offices.

On February 12, 1934, Congress passed the Indian Reorganization Act, which had been introduced by Representative Edgar Howard of Nebraska and Senator Burton K. Wheeler of Montana. Opponents of the Indian Reorganization Act (Wheeler-Howard Act) have sometimes attacked Collier as the source of that legislation, but in fact the 1934 law modified and changed the legislation that Collier had sought. While the discussions about, receptions of, and controversy over his proposals were as complicated as most Indian law, generally the defeat of his legislation came from senators and representatives who were concerned about Indians gaining self-government and too much control over their lands.

The legislation Collier had sought included sections dealing with Indian self-government, special education programs for the training and development of young Indians, Indian lands, and a Court of Indian Affairs. Only the education section was not controversial. Seeking support for the legislation he desired, Collier then looked to the tribes for help.

In addition to the congressional hearings in Washington, Collier held hearings throughout Indian Country on his proposed legislation. However, small and large reservations could not agree about

supporting the legislation, and most people were confused about the bill's terms. These differences prevented all-out support from Indian Country, although a majority of Indians appear to have supported the Collier bill. He also got strong support from President Roosevelt.

By the time the Wheeler-Howard Act reached Congress, the Indian Court of Law and the detailed elements of tribal government creating home rule were gone. The Indian Reorganization Act (IRA) held only a hint of what Collier had originally proposed.

Collier remained BIA commissioner until 1944 and never quit opposing the IRA. Abe Fortas compiled a report to Congress as assistant secretary of the interior in the Roosevelt administration, supporting the IRA and resisting Collier's opposition. Fortas was later a cabinet member and Supreme Court Justice in the administration of President Lyndon Johnson, during which some of Collier's concepts were implemented.

Collier did have some success in encouraging economic development on reservations by insisting that Indians as citizens (whether they acknowledged citizenship or not) were entitled to benefit from any public program, not just those specifically meant for Indians. He used his abundant administrative skills to overcome his unpopularity with appropriations committees.

Collier's approach foreshadowed the policies of the Johnson War on Poverty. His major concern, however, was over the loss of the Indian land base, and the land restoration policy was highly successful while he was commissioner. As a result, several million acres/hectares of grazing land and 400,000 acres (160,000 hectares) of croplands were restored to Indian reservations.

Collier does not appear to have become bitter over his defeats and continued to write about Indian causes, issues, and reforms until his death. His books include *The Indians of the Americas* (1947) and *Patterns and Ceremonies of the Indians of the Southwest* (1949), which was reprinted in 1962 under the title *On the Gleaming Way*.

— C. Hamilton

SEE ALSO:
Bureau of Indian Affairs; Indian New Deal (Indian Reorganization Act).

COLONIALISM

Colonization is a process that begins with the settlement of foreign territories by countries that retain absolute power. At first, social and political rights are not usually extended to the Native peoples, creating an exploitative relationship between the mother country and the people living in the colony. Some common features of colonization include political and legal control by an alien minority, economic exploitation, and racial and cultural inequality. *Colonialism*—the policies and practices leading to colonization—has become synonymous with conquest and exploitation. Historically, colonialism in the Americas is most often associated with the European countries of Britain, France, Portugal, Spain, and the Netherlands. In addition to these nations, Russia also had a colonial presence in regions of Alaska and the Pacific Northwest.

Colonization is a major force in shaping the economic and political character of the Americas. It is an ongoing process that imposes foreign ideas upon Native populations. The forced participation of indigenous peoples in the economy of the dominant society is one of the characteristics of colonization. This process does not end when the colony achieves the status of an independent nation. The colonization of the Native population continues. In the United States, since it became a separate nation, the ongoing colonization process has been one of attempting to extinguish Native languages, religions, and cultures and of forcing the Native peoples to assimilate into the dominant culture. If Native peoples were allowed to maintain their cultures, then issues of Native freedom and sovereignty would have to be acknowledged and dealt with. In this regard, the cultural oppression waged against Native peoples is a way of gaining and maintaining control of their lands and resources.

Historically, colonies were seen as both sources of raw materials and markets for manufactured goods. Many of the original American colonies were set up with the intention of generating a profit for the founders; a number were chartered by commercial companies.

European colonizers considered North America uninhabited land. They regarded the indigenous peoples who occupied the continent as being racially inferior; they granted them no rights, and

indeed, they felt that they were doing Native peoples a favor by "civilizing" them.

In colonizing the Americas, Europeans acquired land. The transfer of land from the Indians to the colonists occurred in many ways. The three main methods were conquest, trade, and treaty. The following paragraphs summarize the pattern of conquest for each the major European countries that claimed colonies in North America.

Spanish Colonial Empire

The Spanish colonial presence in the Americas was spearheaded by the expeditions of Christopher Columbus to the Caribbean starting in 1492. In the 1500s, the Spanish established large colonies in Mexico and South America, where the Aztec and Incan empires were conquered by the conquistadors. Spanish explorers also entered the American Southwest, where they made some attempts at colonization. Juan de Oñate established a colony in New Mexico in 1598. The Spanish colonies in North America were primarily missionary outposts, especially in California and New Mexico. The Spanish were known by the indigenous peoples for their brutality and violence. Yet the Spanish made an important impact on Native culture in the Southwest and vice versa. Like the French, the Spanish intermixed with the Native Americans.

In the eastern section of North America, Pedro Menendez de Aviles established a Spanish colony in San Augustine, Florida, in 1565. As with other Spanish colonial efforts, a string of missions was established throughout the area.

English Colonial Empire

The first successful English colony was founded in 1607 at Jamestown. Captain John Smith led the colonists who founded this settlement. The colony was financed by the Virginia Company, a large English commercial enterprise.

New England was founded primarily as a result of the Puritan religious movement in England. The Puritans received a land grant from the second Virginia Company (the two Virginia Companies divided the English claim to North America). Shortly before the arrival of the Puritans, an epidemic of European diseases, spread by fishers and traders who visited the shores of North America, wiped out nearly 90 percent of the Native inhabitants of the coastal villages of the region. This made it fairly easy for the Puritans to claim and settle the land.

The New England colonies were unique in that the Puritans transplanted their culture intact. In contrast to the Virginia settlement, whole families migrated to New England. Compared to other colonists, they encountered relatively little hardship and opposition in North America.

Nonetheless, the New England communities did not establish friendly relationships with the Native peoples. As early as the seventeenth century, reservations were created for the Indians. For the most part, New Englanders demonstrated intolerance and racial hatred toward the Indians.

French Colonial Empire

Samuel de Champlain established the first French colony at Quebec in 1608. His fellow countryman Jacques Cartier explored the North American continent from 1534 to 1542. He helped extend the profitable fur trade already established by the French with the Indians of North America. The French fur trade extended from Quebec along major rivers,

deep into the north woods around the Great Lakes and throughout the watershed of the Mississippi River. Of all the European groups, the French entered most deeply into the Native American world, often marrying and living among the Indians. The French commercial goals with the fur trade were generally complementary to the goals of the Native Americans: Both were interested in preserving the natural resources of the continent for their needs.

Dutch Colonial Empire

On the East Coast of North America between the two English colonies, the Dutch East Indies Company established the colony of New Netherlands, which would later be renamed New York. New Netherlands began as a trading post colony in 1624, and the Dutch port of New Amsterdam quickly became the fur trading center of North America. The Dutch had little interest in obtaining land in North America. With their focus on commerce and communication, the Dutch developed a friendlier relationship with their Native American trad-

Most U.S. historians teach that colonialism is something that ended when colonies became independent states. Indians, however, know that the colonization of their cultures is an ongoing process that did not end when the United States gained independence. Here, in a Sunday School scene in Indian Territory about 1900, Indian religions were still under assault by foreign religious ideas.

After forcing many Indian nations to move to land set aside for them in the West, the United States eventually colonized even these few remaining parcels of Indian land. Once whites were allowed to move in, their sheer numbers overwhelmed the Indian population. Here, a busy street scene is shown in Oklahoma Territory in 1894.

ing partners than the English did. Nevertheless, the good relations enjoyed by the Dutch and the Native Americans resulted in the same thing as had contact with the English for Native peoples: destruction and removal of Indian villages, death by introduced disease, and the disintegration of the Indian traditional lifestyles.

Russian Colonial Presence

Russia's interest in North America was based mostly on the possibilities of fur trade, and so its presence was usually in the form of trading communities and outposts. Russian sailors first happened upon the Aleutian Island chain off the coast of Alaska in 1741, and in 1784, the first permanent Russian colony in North America was established by a fur trader on Kodiak Island, the easternmost Aleutian island. This settlement was followed by an influx of Russian farmers and Russian Orthodox missionaries to the Alaskan mainland.

Relations between Alaska's native population and the Russian settlers were mixed. The first gov-

ernor of Russian Alaska, Alexander Baranov, learned the language of the Aleuts and married an Aleut woman. His treatment of other Alaskan Natives, particularly the Tlingit, was not always so friendly, however. For example, in setting up the capital of Russian America, Sitka, in the heart of Tlingit country, Baranov set the stage for bloody conflicts between Russians and Tlingits for years to come.

Russia sold Alaska—and with it, a virtual gold mine of opportunity for further exploitation of its natural and human resources—to the United States in 1867. To this day, onion-shaped spires of Russian Orthodox churches may be spotted in small Alaskan villages as evidence of Russia's former— and limited—colonial presence.

Summary

The colonial experience has had a devastating effect on the Native peoples of the Americas. Contact often resulted in hostilities between the indigenous people and the colonists. The carving up of the North American continent led to conflicts among the European colonists, into which Native populations were inevitably drawn. The combination of warfare, introduced diseases, and dislocation that resulted from contact with the European colonizers caused a very serious decline in population and cultural integrity for all Native American groups.

Once the colonies became independent nations, the colonization process gradually shifted to attempting to absorb Native populations by assimilating them into the dominant culture, a process that might lead to extinguishing their claims to political sovereignty. This process continues today, and Native peoples continue to resist it.

— M. A. Stout

SEE ALSO:
California Missions; Columbian Exchange; Columbus, Christopher; Demography, Native; Dutch Colonists; England; France; Missions for Indians, Christian; Oñate Expedition; Spain.

COLORADO

Colorado, sometimes called "the Centennial State," became a U.S. state on August 1, 1876. *Colorado* is Spanish for "reddish" and probably refers to the red stone formations that early Spanish explorers saw in the state.

Colorado has a long history of Indian habitation. As long as fourteen thousand years ago, Paleo-Indians established hunting camps in Colorado as they pursued big game. Many stone Folsom projectile points, dating back ten thousand years, have been found throughout Colorado.

The spectacular Cliff Palace in southwestern Colorado, an Anasazi ruin, is but one of many well-preserved Anasazi sites now under the care of the National Park Service at Mesa Verde National Park.

Members of the Basket Maker culture lived in the southwestern part of Colorado as early as the first century C.E. The Basket Maker culture merged with the Anasazi culture by 800 C.E. The Anasazis, "the ancient ones," encountered pressure from other tribes and built defensive communities on cliffs. Some of these famous sites, such as Mesa Verde and Hovenweep, still remain. Cliff Palace at Mesa Verde contains over two hundred rooms. Hovenweep, "deserted valley" in Ute, has six separate groups of defensive towers. After 1300 C.E., the Anasazi culture vanished; no one knows why, but a thirty-year drought is known to have occurred at about the time the Anasazis left the region. Their descendants may have become the Pueblo people of the upper Rio Grande river valley in New Mexico.

In any event, at the time of the first European contact in 1541, when Francisco Coronado entered Colorado in search of the "Seven Cities of Gold," the Anasazis were gone and tribes such as the Utes, Cheyennes, Arapahos, and Comanches inhabited the state. Following Coronado, the next European to enter Colorado was Silvestre Velez de Escalante, who traveled from Santa Fe to the present-day site of Provo, Utah, and back. Spanish settlers entered southern Colorado as early as the 1700s, well before the United States gained control of that part of Colorado in the early 1800s. Zebulon Montgomery Pike explored Colorado in 1806, and many American "mountain men" lived in Colorado in the early 1800s.

During the 1800s, the United States waged many wars against the Indians of Colorado. The Sand Creek Massacre, which was not so much a battle as a slaughter, was one of the most notorious of the actions taken against Colorado Native Americans. In 1880, the Ute chief Ouray signed a treaty that officially ended the Colorado Indian wars.

Two reservations remain in Colorado. The Southern Ute Reservation has 310,002 acres (124,001 hectares), and the Ute Mountain Reservation has 477,850 acres (191,140 hectares). A small tip of the Navajo Reservation also extends into southwestern Colorado. The 1990 Census lists 27,776 Indians as Colorado residents, making the state the sixteenth in terms of Native population.

SEE ALSO:
Anasazi; Basket Maker Culture; Coronado Expedition; Folsom Culture; Mesa Verde; Sand Creek Massacre.

COLUMBIA RIVER AND ITS NATIVE PEOPLES

The Columbia River is called Nch'i-Wana (Big River) by the Sahaptin Nations who live midway along the watercourse. People have inhabited this river basin since the retreat of the cordilleran glaciers over ten thousand years ago. The Columbia begins in central British Columbia, Canada, and its watershed is ultimately joined by the extensive networks of the Snake, Warm Springs, John Day, Yakima, Spokane, Palouse, Kootenai, and other drainages. Many cultures have been nurtured by this flow.

In addition to the Canadian Shuswap and Okanagan areas, there are at least twelve other language groups living along the main tributaries of the Columbia River in the states of Washington, Oregon, Idaho, and Montana. They include Cayuse, Nez Perce, Coeur d'Alene, Kalispel, Columbia, Chinookan, Coast Salish, and Northern Paiute—all of which are bound by the waters of this great watershed.

In the 260,000 square miles (676,000 square kilometers) of the Columbia drainage basin, the river runs through many different ecosystems. There are environmental differences between the Kalapuyan area in the low, green Willamette Valley, for example, and the Kutenai in the drier heights of the Rocky Mountains. But all Native American Columbia River drainage inhabitants are bound together by being salmon people. They all have some form of the First Salmon Ceremony, and they all have an economy and spirituality based on the gifts of the six major salmon runs. They are distinguished by where and how different nations fished. Before the arrival of Europeans, it was the salmon by which the river maintained its nations. Salmon provided slightly more than 30 percent of the nutrition for people living along the river, who supplemented their diets by hunting, root and herb gathering, and seed farming. Salmon was and is viewed as a sacred gift of the Creator.

Each nation had special spiritual centers and trading sites. Some of the vision quest sites, such as in the high rocks of Saddle Mountain or along the Columbia Gorge, were located near great trading centers. Among the best known of these was the Dalles, known as Wanapum, near Priest Rapids.

Celilo Falls, an ancient fishing site on the Columbia River, is now buried beneath a reservoir. The site has deep significance to indigenous peoples of the region, and its loss is keenly felt. Native poet Elizabeth Woody conveys the depth of feeling over the loss of the falls in *Hand into Stone,* winner of the 1988 American Book Award.

Good fishing sites were owned by specific communities. Goods were either shared or traded with people from the hills, who brought bitterroots, camas, huckleberries, and a variety of roots, fruits, and game animals. The trade was lively for such items as finely woven rush mats, beaded leather clothing, cedar ceremonial clothing and rainwear, moccasins (nearly thirty varieties), and various breeds of horses. Travelers compared these trading sites to the great marketplaces of Mexico. At Celilo Falls, with its famous salmon catchment, traders brought dentalium (tooth) shells, blankets, beads, bone and shell work, baskets, obsidian (a type of volcanic glass), buffalo products, and pipestone. Thousands of celebrants came for great festivals that lasted for months.

The Nch'i-wana peoples are known for their highly democratic villages, which had a variety of methods of sharing and maintaining intercultural harmony. People demonstrated their generosity by exchanging wealth through feasts and sharing their hunting, fishing, and gathering sites. They also shared information through complex ceremonies. These included extended storytelling and ritualistic presentations by spiritual teachers.

Today, thirteen treaty nations live along the Nch'i-wana and its branches. These include the Yakama and Colville Confederated Tribes; the Nez Perce, Fort Hall, and Flathead nations; and the Warm Springs, Spokane, Kalispel, and Umatilla Agencies. These treaty nations encompass a number of cultures, including Sahaptin, Wishram, Wasco, Northern Paiute, Walla Walla, Kootenai, and Coeur D'Alene. In all, a total of nearly thirty thousand people live on tribally managed lands. Some major victories in the courts have recently returned river areas controlled by the Nuclear Reservation to the Yakama Nation. The struggle to restore the fishing rights and sustain the spirit of Nch'i-wana continues for those peoples who honor the great waters.

— T. Heidlebaugh

COLUMBIAN EXCHANGE

The phrase *Columbian exchange* is used by ethnobiologists to describe the transfer of biological materials between the Americas and the "Old World" (Europe, Africa, and Asia) during and after the voyages of Columbus. The Columbian exchange included human beings, domesticated plants and animals, and disease germs. Most of the people traveled from Europe and Africa to the Americas, but a few Native Americans were taken to Europe (some against their will). Many American crops, which had first been tilled by Native Americans, were brought to Europe. Some of the best known of these were corn, potatoes, peanuts, tomatoes, and tobacco. European and African plants, including wheat, sugar cane, and citrus fruits, were brought to the Americas.

While some items in the Columbian exchange were beneficial, others were very damaging to Native Americans. The exchange brought to the Americas a number of deadly diseases. The most devastating of these was smallpox. With contact, many Europeans had developed a degree of immunity to smallpox and other serious diseases. Native Americans, however, lacked immunity to these diseases. A large percentage of the Native American population was wiped out by European diseases within one hundred years of the Columbian voyages.

Looked at as a whole, the Columbian exchange was more beneficial to immigrating Europeans than to Native Americans. In his books *Indian Givers* and *Native Roots*, anthropologist Jack Weatherford describes how the infusion of American gold and silver helped to build the empire of Spain, and how American food products, such as potatoes and corn, helped to nourish Europeans. According to Weatherford, 60 percent of the food harvested in the world today was first grown by Native Americans.

SEE ALSO:
Columbus, Christopher; Demography, Native; Epidemic Diseases; Smallpox.

COLUMBUS, CHRISTOPHER
(1451–1506)

When Christopher Columbus went ashore in the Antilles in 1492, he took European and North American Indian history down a path that we continue, in some ways, to travel today. Other Europeans had been to the Western Hemisphere before Columbus: The Vikings had established a short-lived colony five hundred years before Columbus's voyage, and evidence suggests that Basque, English, and Portuguese sailors crossed the Atlantic in the 1300s and landed in Newfoundland and Labrador in present-day Canada.

None of these earlier landings had any lasting effect on the indigenous cultures of North America. Columbus's "discovery" of America was different because his voyages initiated a catastrophic

In 1992, for the five hundredth anniversary of the landfall of Columbus in the Western Hemisphere, American Indians staged Columbus "de-celebration" protests throughout North America, angry that someone who ignited a holocaust for indigenous American peoples should be regarded as a hero. The mainstream media largely ignored the protests.

This oil painting, in the National Naval Museum in Madrid, Spain, is a romanticized, Eurocentric conception of the arrival of Columbus in the Americas. It says more about the European frame of mind that led to the nature of the painting than it does about the arrival of Columbus.

invasion of the Americas and resulted in the deaths of millions of Native Americans and the demise of many Native cultures.

Even the name *Indian* came from Columbus. Whether one believes that Columbus called the Caribbean Taino people Indians because he thought he was in India or because he used the term *in Dios*, meaning "a people of God," to describe them, he certainly used the term to refer to the Native people of the Americas. To this day, *American Indian* remains the most widely recognized name under which most Native Americans are grouped, despite the debates over how appropriate it is to group a vast and varied array of indigenous cultures under one name—and to use the name that may have been bestowed upon them by an oppressive European invader.

Who was this person who left such an imprint on North American history and whose name, in one form or another, is so much a part of the landscape and language of the Americas?

Early Life and Struggle to Gain Support for His First Voyage

Cristoforo Columbo was born in Genoa, Italy, in 1451. He had very little formal education, but his true schoolroom was the sea. As a young boy, Columbus traveled on the Mediterranean Sea. He first traveled through Portugal after he was shipwrecked on that country's shore. He also traveled to England and Ireland and claimed to have been as far north as Iceland. Whether these claims are true is not clear, but what is clear is that Columbus was gaining a greater and greater interest in traveling the world. He became fascinated in learning about what might lie to the west of Europe. He read stories about the legendary land of Atlantis and listened to other sailors as they told stories about lands to the west of the Azores. Columbus studied the maps of his day and came to believe that Japan was 3,000 miles (4,830 kilometers) east of Portugal.

In 1484, Columbus sought support for a voyage of exploration from King John II of Portugal, but the king refused his request. Columbus's wife, Dona Felipa, had died shortly after the birth of a son in 1480. The boy was named Diego. In 1485, Columbus and Diego went to Spain. For the next seven years, Columbus tried to get Queen Isabella I to support a voyage. By 1492, Columbus had given up hope of gaining support from the Spanish crown for his project, and he was preparing to go to France to seek help there. But one last appeal to Isabella finally resulted in support for his voyage.

The First Voyage

Columbus was allowed to outfit three ships—the *Niña*, the *Pinta*, and the *Santa Maria*—at the port of Palos. Columbus was in command of the *Santa Maria*, and two brothers commanded the other two ships. Martín Alonso Pinzón commanded the *Pinta*, and Vicente Yáñez Pinzón commanded the *Niña*.

The ships first sailed to the Canary Islands (off the northwest coast of Africa) and then headed west. On the morning of October 12, 1492, the party landed on an island in the Bahamas. There is some debate about which island the men first landed on. The two most likely islands are San Salvador and Samana Cay.

At this landing, Columbus first met people from the Western Hemisphere, and he called them "Indians." Considering that Columbus probably thought he was near China, as well as the fact that in his day what we call *India* was called *Hindustan*, the old story of Columbus mistaking Native Americans for natives of India seems unlikely.

In any event, Columbus's first meetings with the Arawak people were very friendly. After spending several days on the island, Columbus and his party sailed on to Cuba, still seeking the Chinese mainland. Columbus continued to sail around the Caribbean, and on Christmas Day, 1492, the *Santa Maria* ran aground and was badly damaged near Cap Haitien, a city in present-day Haiti on the island of Hispaniola. The Native population was friendly, so Columbus left thirty-nine men at the site to start the colony of Navidad. Columbus returned to Spain on the *Niña*.

Martín Alonso Pinzón was exploring on his own at this time, but he rejoined Columbus, and they sailed together until being separated again at sea. Columbus made a good crossing and arrived in Portugal in March 1493. He reported about his journey to John II of Portugal and then went on and reported to Isabella and Ferdinand II of Aragon. Columbus brought back a small amount of gold, and he also displayed Indians that he had brought with him. He told the royal courts that there was an easy sea route to China, and he continued to believe that he had been just off the Chinese coast.

The Line of Demarcation

At the time of Columbus's discovery, Portugal and Spain were the two most powerful countries in Europe. Since they were both Catholic nations, the pope at that time, Alexander VI, sought to avoid a war between the two countries by dividing the Americas into two separate areas for Spanish and Portuguese colonization. The pope established this "line of demarcation" in 1493. The two nations revised the line in 1494 at the Treaty of Tordesillas and agreed to abide by the boundary.

The effects of the line of demarcation are evident today: Most of Latin America is Spanish speaking, with the most notable—and largest—exception of Brazil, where the major language and prevailing European cultural influences are Portuguese.

The Second Voyage

Columbus received support for a second voyage from Isabella and Ferdinand. When he set sail on September 25, 1493, Columbus took with him a much bigger fleet of seventeen ships and nearly fifteen hundred men. Again, Columbus had a good crossing to the Caribbean, and on November 3, 1493, he landed near Dominica, a small island in the eastern West Indies. In late November, Columbus returned to the site of the colony at Navidad and discovered that all of the men had been killed. Controversy over Indian and European relations revolves around the destruction of Navidad. Some accounts suggest that the Indians attacked without provocation, while other accounts hold that relations between the Europeans and the Indians turned bad after the Europeans seized women and property.

Columbus set up another colony, which he called Isabella, at another site on the island. He spent the next months exploring Jamaica and the southern coast of Cuba. He also returned to Isabella, where his inability to get along with others led to his first failures as a colonial administrator. In 1496, Columbus returned to Spain, but before he departed, he left his brother, Bartolomé, in charge and told him to move the colony to Hispaniola. This new settlement, Santa Domingo, became the first permanent European settlement in the Americas.

Columbus returned to Spain in June of 1496. By this time, the Spanish court had become dismayed that Columbus had still not found the Chinese mainland, and he brought back little gold to the king and queen.

The Third Voyage

Columbus had a great deal of difficulty gaining support from the Spanish Crown for a third voyage. It was not until word reached the court that Portugal had sent Vasco da Gama to find a sea route to India that a third voyage was authorized for Columbus. In May of 1498, Columbus set sail with six ships. He made another successful crossing and landed in Trinidad on July 31, 1498. On August 1, 1498, Columbus landed on the coast of South America. Columbus next sailed to Santa Domingo, where he faced a revolt from the colonists, who resented Columbus and his brother. In 1500, a commissioner arrived from Spain with full authority over the colony. This man, Francisco de Bobadilla, placed Columbus and his brother in chains and sent them back to Spain.

The Fourth Voyage

Although he was allowed the choice of removing his chains, Columbus insisted on appearing in chains before the king and queen. The court reinstated Columbus and provided him with ships for another voyage. Columbus left Spain in May of 1502. During this voyage, he reached Honduras and other sites in Central America. Columbus was marooned in Jamaica for over a year after his ships had to be abandoned because a shipworm problem had made them unnavigable. Columbus returned to Spain in November of 1504; he would never return to the Americas.

Columbus's Last Days

After Columbus returned to Spain, he continued to seek support from the crown for another voyage. The king and queen refused any more support and sent other explorers to the so-called New World. Columbus died on May 20, 1506, still believing that he had explored the coast of Asia. He never realized that he had happened upon two other continents—North and South America.

From a purely technical point of view, Columbus's voyages were remarkable in their accomplished goals of crossing and recrossing the Atlantic with very simple ships and navigation. From a European point of view, his voyages were noteworthy in their linking of the Old World with the New World that was the Western Hemisphere. From the point of view of the Native cultures that Columbus and the ensuing waves of Europeans would invade, Columbus's voyages brought great and unimaginable change—and destruction.

— T. Colonnese

SEE ALSO:

Arawak; Bahamas; Columbian Exchange; Cuba; Ferdinand and Isabella; Hispaniola; Las Casas, Bartolomé de; Taino.

COLVILLE CONFEDERATED TRIBES

The Colville Reservation in northeast Washington State was established by executive order on April 9, 1872. The Colville Confederation is made up of twelve individual bands that had traditional lands around the Kettle Falls area of the Columbia River.

The Indians who lived at the Kettle Falls were known as the Shwayip, the Chaudieres, the Kettle Falls Indians, or the Colvilles. To the north of Kettle Falls lived the Sinaikst or Lake people. Both of these groups spoke an almost identical dialect. To the east lived tribes who spoke dialects of the Salish or Flathead language, including the Spokane, the Kalispel, and the Chewelah. To the south and the southwest lived the Sanpoil, who spoke a separate dialect of the Colville language. The Okanagan people lived to the west and spoke another language, Okanagan.

What brought all of these people together were the falls and their great runs of salmon. Every summer, all of the tribes came to fish. The fish were a very valuable resource, however, and complex rules dictated who could fish in which areas; other rules limited the catch amounts of different types of fish.

The Kettle Falls area was also a great social hub. There is evidence suggesting that humans have been at the falls for nearly ten thousand years, and one can imagine that the falls served as a kind of magnet that drew people together. Since the Colville people have been at the falls, their villages were the largest concentration of dwellings within a 10,000 square-mile (26,000-kilometer) area. One would have had to travel 100 miles (161 kilometers) in any direction of the falls to come upon a larger village. Indians traveled to the falls to join with other people and to trade, take part in marathon gambling games, and participate in great dances.

Although the Colville Reservation consists of only a small portion of the traditional lands of the confederated bands, it is still the eleventh-largest Indian reservation. It contains 1,063,043 acres (425,217 hectares) and a Native population of 3,788.

SEE ALSO:
Columbia River and Its Native Peoples.

Quanna Parker, pictured above, has been the subject of many books and articles about his life in the nineteenth century. Many of these works are subtitled "the last Comanche chief." Indians in the United States complain bitterly about being referred to in the past tense, and with good reason. As of 1996, for example, Wallace Coffey was tribal chairman of the Comanche Nation, with tribal headquarters in Lawton, Oklahoma.

COMANCHE

The Comanches call themselves *Neum* in their own language, which means "people of people." They are of the Shoshonean linguistic family, which also includes the Shoshonis, Bannocks, Paiutes, and Utes. The Comanches and other Shoshonean peoples originally came from the Shoshoni and Snake River regions of Wyoming and Idaho, and also from other areas within the upper Great Basin region. The Comanches are the only nation of the Shoshonean family who left their homes in the Rocky Mountains and established themselves on the Plains. They became divided into about twelve different bands in their later history.

The Comanches were considered to be among the most skillful horsemen of all Indian nations and were the most powerful nomadic tribe on the Plains of the Southwest. They were noted for their hospitable and generous nature and their courage.

Before the 1500s, the Comanches roamed the Rocky Mountain region, hunting, fishing, and supplementing their diet of meat with wild berries, fruits, and roots. They also took expeditions to the Plains to hunt buffalo. After the Spanish colonization of Mexico, the Comanches acquired horses, which were brought to the Americas by the

Spanish. With horses, the Comanches left their Rocky Mountain homes and adapted to life on the Plains.

They moved out toward the east, establishing home bases on the North Platte River until about 1700. Over the next few decades, they were driven from this area by the Sioux, who came down from the north. The Comanches began moving southward. Early in the eighteenth century the Comanches began appearing on the northeastern frontiers of Spanish New Mexico. They remained in contact with their Shoshoni relations and visited them occasionally in the Rocky Mountain regions. They also would travel as far as 1,000 miles (1,610 kilometers) to replenish their herds of horses, sometimes raiding settlements far into Mexico to acquire more animals.

On their southward migrations, the Comanches sometimes displaced other Indian nations such as the Plains Apaches, especially the Jicarilla Apaches. In 1787, the Comanches entered into an historic peace treaty with the Spanish in New Mexico, after which the Comanches became allied with the Spanish in campaigns against the Apaches. They also fought the Kiowas, but by about 1790 the Comanches and Kiowas made a peace agreement that has never been broken.

In 1815, the Comanche bands met English-speaking traders for the first time. General Thomas James established a profitable trade agreement with Comanches in 1822, although he mistakenly referred to them as "Pawnee."

In 1834, the Comanches met with the Dragoon Expedition. This was the first meeting between the Comanches and official representatives of the United States government. They held council along with other Indian delegations. Through this meeting, the Comanches signed their first treaty with the United States, and with eight other Indian nations, at Camp Holmes on the Canadian River, in present-day Oklahoma, in August 1835.

The southern branch of the Comanches was assigned a reservation located west of Clear Fork, in north-central Texas, in 1854. Most of the Comanches settled peacefully on this reservation.

With an increase in white travelers heading across the Plains in the mid-1800s, the Northern Comanches faced difficulty living as hunters on the Plains. Conflicts with settlers and traders, espe-

cially along the Santa Fe Trail, ensued. In July 1853, a peace agreement with the United States was signed, but only one of the Comanche bands was represented, and conflicts continued between Comanches and non-Natives in the region.

In the spring of 1858, a Comanche village near the mouth of Little Robe Creek, in the Antelope Hills of present-day Oklahoma, was attacked by white militia from Texas. Seventy-six Comanches were killed, including the Comanche chief, Pohebits Quasho, or Iron Jacket. Later that year, a Comanche encampment on Rush Creek, at the present-day site of Rush Springs, Oklahoma, was attacked by the U.S. Army. The band of Comanches were returning from a friendly meeting with U.S. Army officers, where they had just concluded a treaty of peace and friendship with the United States. On the way back to their own territory, they had then stopped to visit with the Wichitas at Rush Springs. The loss of life in the Rush Springs attack was great for the Indians and added greatly to their mistrust of the United States.

In 1859, the Southern Comanches were forced to abandon their reservation in Texas and to relocate to a leased area in Indian Territory (present-day Oklahoma). They settled along the Washita River under the supervision of U.S. government agents.

In 1865, the Comanches attended two peace councils. One in May was held at Camp Napoleon, and more than five thousand Indians from Indian Territory were there. Terms for peace were set, with the agreement that "an Indian shall not spill an Indian's blood." The second peace council was held at the Little Arkansas River in October; there a peace treaty was signed by U.S. commissioners and the Comanches.

Another council was conducted on Medicine Lodge Creek in Kansas in 1867. Thousands of Indians attended, all from nations of the southern Plains. The chiefs signed agreements that provided that their tribes would settle on reservations in Indian Territory, now Oklahoma.

The Comanches began settling on reservation lands in Indian Territory in 1868. Raids and fights broke out between Indians and non-Indians with the encroachment of settlers on Comanche land and the disappearance of the buffalo, which the Comanches depended on for food. The last of the

Al Wahnee, a Comanche, displays traditional dress at a powwow. Throughout Indian Country, Comanches are known as some of the finest powwow dancers and singers.

Comanches to come to the reservation were led by Quanah Parker. They had remained in Texas and had not signed the treaty agreements. They surrendered on June 24, 1875, at Fort Sill, in Indian Territory.

Confinement on reservations changed the lives of the Comanches. They had their last big buffalo hunt in 1878 and soon afterward started raising cattle and leasing their lands to ranchers. Quanah Parker was the first recognized chief on the reservation in Indian Territory. He encouraged Indians to adopt the customs of white settlers.

With more and more Indian land taken over by white colonizers and the passage of the Severalty Act, sometimes called the Dawes Act, the Comanches were forced to accept individual plots of land. The tribal lands that were not allotted were opened for settlement by non-Indians on August 6, 1901. Breaking up the tribal land estate was a blow to tribal sovereignty for the Comanches and to all the other tribes in Indian Territory, which soon became Oklahoma, in 1907. All of the Indians in the new state of Oklahoma were forced to become U.S. citizens, in violation of treaties that had guaranteed their sovereignty as individual nations. Comanche children were sent away to boarding schools, as were the children of other Indian nations, where attempts were made to force them to assimilate into the dominant U.S. culture.

In the face of these difficulties, the Comanches have managed to preserve their culture and traditions through the years of change. Today, they are widely known for their dances and ceremonies. They are a federally recognized tribe and share jurisdictional territory with the Kiowas and Plains Apaches. They have reorganized their tribal government, which today is managed by a business committee elected by Comanche voters. The tribal headquarters of the Comanche Nation is now located in Lawton, Oklahoma.

— S. S. Davis

SEE ALSO:
Boarding Schools; Dawes Commission; General Allotment Act; Kiowa; Oklahoma; Texas.

SUGGESTED READINGS:
Brown, Dee. *Bury My Heart at Wounded Knee*. New York: Henry Holt and Company, 1970.

Debo, Angie. *A History of the Indians of the United States*. Norman: University of Oklahoma Press, 1970.
Deloria, Vine, Jr. *Custer Died for Your Sins: An Indian Manifesto*. Norman: University of Oklahoma Press, 1988.
Wright, Muriel H. *A Guide to the Indian Tribes of Oklahoma*. Norman: University of Oklahoma Press, 1951.

COMMISSIONER OF INDIAN AFFAIRS

SEE Bureau of Indian Affairs.

CONLEY, ROBERT J. (1940–)

Robert J. Conley (United Keetoowah Cherokee), born December 29, 1940, in Cushing, Oklahoma, is a poet and an author of popular western novels, many of which have Indians as their main characters. He earned undergraduate and graduate degrees at Midwestern University in Wichita Falls, Texas. For many years, he was known primarily as a poet and editor of poetry anthologies, a professor at a number of colleges, and the director of Indian Studies at Morningside College and Eastern Montana College. He also has served as assistant programs director for the Cherokee Nation of Oklahoma.

Conley began publishing westerns in the mid-1980s. In 1988, he won the coveted Spur Award from the Western Writers of America for his short story "Yellowbird: An Imaginary Autobiography" in *The Witch of Goingsnake and Other Stories*. He won the Spur Award again in 1992 for his novel *Nickajack*, which was nominated for the American Library Association's Best Book for Young Adults award. Conley has served on the board of directors for Western Writers of America.

In recent years, Conley has been writing a series of novels about the Cherokees. He calls the series, which he intends to carry to the present day, the *Real People* series because that is what the Cherokees call themselves.

Although Conley's works are fictional, the historical references are well researched and accurate.

He describes Native culture as it was and is today; he also retells ancient stories and prophecies, especially in the *Real People* series, which begins before the coming of Europeans.

In 1992, one of Conley's novels, *Mountain Windsong: A Novel of the Trail of Tears,* was published by the University of Oklahoma Press. In 1995, Conley and New York songwriter Lendar Clarson adapted the novel for the stage. It was performed at the Cherokee Nation Amphitheater featuring international Cherokee opera star Barbara Macalister and a large cast of both Native and non-Native performers.

Conley is a member of the National Advisory Caucus for Wordcraft Circle of Native Writers and Storytellers. He has been very active in helping to organize and teach workshops for emerging Native writers at Oklahoma City University, the University of Oklahoma, Northeastern State University, and the University of Memphis.

Conley is an enrolled member of the United Keetoowah Band of Cherokees. He lives in Tahlequah, Oklahoma, and devotes his full attention to his writing.

CONNECTICUT

The Indians of Connecticut are linguistically Algonquian. There are two Pequot reservations, as well as Mohegan communities, in southeastern Connecticut; a tiny Paugusett reservation near Bridgeport; and a Schaghticoke reservation in the hills of western Connecticut. Members of other tribes reside throughout the state.

Traditionally, Connecticut's Indians lived in palisaded wigwam villages as hunter-gatherers and farmers. They reckoned descent matrilineally, and women were respected decision makers. After additional European explorers followed Giovanni da Verrazano (1524) and Samuel de Champlain (1605), diseases devastated the Indian population. The Pequots continued exerting might and influence, however.

In 1614, an English captain abducted twenty warriors and sold them into slavery in Spain. This event triggered periodic conflicts culminating in the Pequot War. In May 1637, a combined English and Narragansett force staged a predawn attack on the Pequots' village at Mystic, killing several hundred.

Small bands of Indians survived this period, some on acreages that were dwindling in size. In the 1760s, the Reverend Samson Occam (Mohegan, 1723–1792) helped raise funds for what became Dartmouth College in New Hampshire; in 1772, he became the first Indian to publish in English. William Apees (1798–1838) emerged as a militant preacher and author. One of the earliest Native poets writing in English was Ann Plato, who published her work in New Haven, Connecticut, in the 1840s. Gladys Tantaquidgeon is a respected Mohegan elder and scholar; and Trudie Lamb Richmond (Schaghticoke) is a noted educator.

Today's Connecticut Indians promote cultural understanding while seeking to have treaties and deeds honored. *The Eagle,* an award-winning newspaper, was established in 1981. The Mashantucket Pequots' casino gambling enterprise makes them a recognized force in the state's affairs.

SEE ALSO:
Algonquian ; Pequot; Pequot War.

CONQUISTADORES, SPANISH

SEE Spain.

CONSENSUS IN NATIVE AMERICAN GOVERNANCE

Because they had lived in societies based on hierarchy, early European explorers and colonizers came to America seeking kings, queens, and princes. What they sought, they believed they had found, at least for a time.

Quickly, however, some Europeans began to sense a difference. In most Native societies, the people they were calling "kings" and "queens" had few trappings that distinguished them from the people being "ruled." This "royalty" only rarely behaved with the pomp of European rulers. More important, Indian "kings" usually did not rule. Rather, they led, using such mechanisms as consensus and public opinion instead of coercing belief and action. Many Europeans found this admirable. The English had no other generally accepted way to describe such a leader, so they often used the Indians' own words, such as *sachem* and *sagamore*.

The Europeans observed that all along the Atlantic seaboard, Indian governments showed a remarkable similarity. Everywhere they looked, the immigrants found confederacies of Native nations. These nations were loosely governed by the kind of respect for individual liberty that European philosophers had envisioned only in theory. The Indians' languages, customs, and material possessions varied widely, but their democratic form of government seemed to be nearly everywhere.

An Extract from the Journals of Reverend Mr. Bolzius, published in London in 1734 by the Society for Promoting Christian Knowledge, contained this description of Indians' governance: "Their Kings do not reign with absolute power, but give Counsel. The King proposes to the Old Men, and the Old Men to the Young men; after which it is put in Execution. . . . When a King is not fit for his office, they choose another. The wisest is their King; who doth not distinguish himself from others by Clothes. . . . If a present is made to the King, he doth not keep it, but he distributes it among all, and keeps nothing for himself."

Bolzius also penned another description of the Native peoples he knew: "They love equality. . . . They account laboring and working for hire to be slavery; therefore, they will not work for Gain."

Native leaders had to become very good at persuasion. In his *History of the Five Nations* (1747), Cadwallader Colden attributed the Iroquois' skill at public speaking to "a perfect republican government." Colden described the intense study that the Iroquois applied to the arts of oral persuasion, to the acquisition of "grace and manner" before councils of their peers. According to Colden, Iroquois speakers became "very nice in the turn of their expressions. . . . They have, it seems, a certain *urbanitas*, or Atticism, in their language to which the common ears are ever sensible, though only their great speakers ever attain it."

The system of the Hurons was remarkably similar to that of their neighbors, the Iroquois. According to Bruce J. Trigger's *Children of the Aataentsic: A History of the Huron People*, the Hurons' system,

like that of the Iroquois, was rooted in family structure. Leaders of the various clans used public opinion and consensus to shape decisions. Issues "were usually decided upon by majority vote . . . [and] discussed until a general consensus was reached." No one was expected to be bound by a decision to which he or she had not given conscious consent.

Robert Rogers, a frontier soldier who studied the Indians' war tactics and later turned to writing for the press and stage, said that Native children were introduced very early into "public councils." This practice, he wrote, produces young adults "with a composed and manly air, inspires them to emulation, and makes them bold and enterprising."

European observers often compared Indians' councils to public meetings in Europe and often found the Indians' in better order. As early as 1635, an Indian was recorded in the *Relation of Maryland*, asserting that the members of the Virginia Assembly all talked at once. Comparing European-style assemblies to those he knew, the Native informant stated, "Wee doe not so in our Match-comaco [councils]."

Tench Tilghman, George Washington's secretary during the Revolutionary War, served on diplomatic assignments among the Iroquois. He was adopted by the Onondagas on the eve of the war and given the Iroquois name *Teahokalonde*. Upon observing the Iroquois Grand Council at Onondaga, Tilghman remarked that the debates of the Iroquois "ought to put us civilized people to the Blush." Benjamin Franklin had a similar impression: "To interrupt another, even in Common conversation, is reckon'd highly indecent. How different this is to the conduct of a polite British House of Commons, where scarcely a day passes without some Confusion, that makes the Speaker hoarse in calling *to Order*."

Franklin contrasted the way Indians listened quietly to speakers with "the mode of Conversation of many polite Companies of Europe, where, if you do not deliver your sentence with great Rapidity, you are cut off in the middle of it by the impatient Loquacity of those you converse with, and never suffer'd to finish it!"

— B. E. Johansen

SEE ALSO:

Franklin, Benjamin; Iroquois Confederacy.

CONSTITUTION, UNITED STATES

The United States Constitution mentions American Indians as people "not taxed" and not counted for representation in Congress. When the Constitution was written, many Native neighbors of the former colonies were distinct nations. Thus, the Constitution gives Congress the power to regulate trade with them, as with other nations outside the United States. The Constitution also gives the federal government the authority to make treaties with Indian nations, as with other nations.

Models of Native American government were discussed at the Constitutional Convention of 1787. Political leaders of the 1700s were aware of Native American governments. Benjamin Franklin, who served as a delegate to the Constitutional Convention, believed that there should be a unicameral, or one-house, legislature, as in the Iroquois Confederacy's Grand Council. The Grand Council had served as a model for the Albany Plan of

Union that Franklin had proposed for the colonies in 1754 and for the Articles of Confederation, the national government plan that had been in effect since 1781 and that the delegates to the Constitutional Convention wanted to replace.

Another important leader, John Adams, held a view different from Franklin's. Adams had been selected as a Massachusetts delegate to the Constitutional Convention but was serving as a United States ambassador in Europe and was unable to attend the convention. On the eve of the convention, Adams published an essay titled "Defence of the Constitutions of Government in the United States of America." The essay was a critical survey of world governments, including a description of the Iroquois and other Native American political systems as Adams believed them to exist. Adams's grandson later pointed out that the essay "was much circulated in the convention, and undoubtedly contributed somewhat to give a favorable direction to the opinion of the members." On June 6, 1787,

The form of this Plains Indian council, a circle, is indicative of the great contrast between Native and non-Native worldviews. No one sits at the head of this council; indeed, it does not even include such a position of authority. Native people arrive at decisions by consensus of the group, and everyone is likely to be allowed to express an opinion.

James Madison reported the opening of the convention to Thomas Jefferson (who, like Adams, was serving as a U.S. ambassador in Europe), writing that "Mr. Adams' Book . . . has excited a good deal of attention." Madison believed that Adams's essay would be read and "praised, and become a powerful engine in forming the public opinion."

In his essay, Adams stated his opinion that Franklin and certain other politicians and philosophers were ". . . attempting to . . . set up governments of . . . modern Indians." An ardent believer in the fundamentals of the British constitution, Adams opposed Franklin's belief that the new United States government should resemble Native confederacies. However, he did believe it would be productive to have ". . . a more accurate investigation of the form of governments of the . . . Indians." In addition, Adams wrote that it would be ". . . well worth the pains [effort] . . . to collect . . . the legislation of the Indians . . ." for study while creating a new constitution. Adams thought that in studying American Indian governments such as the Iroquois Confederacy, Americans could observe the best examples of separation of powers among the legislative, executive, and judicial branches of government. In fact, Adams stated that "the three powers [of government] are strong in every tribe" and that separation of powers in American Indian governments ". . . is marked with a precision that excludes all controversy."

Adams also noted that Native governments were so democratic that the "real sovereignty resided in the body of the people." He stated that the Mohawks could be characterized as having "complete individual independence," providing an example of the importance of personal liberty to the Indians.

Adams, however, believed that the new United States government must incorporate certain checks on freedom and power: for example, a bicameral, or two-house, legislature. Otherwise, he thought, the system would succumb to special interests and dissolve into anarchy or tyranny. Fearing unrestrained freedom, he cited the Iroquois Grand Council as a negative example of government, apparently ignoring the fact, as Franklin wrote, that it "has subsisted [lasted] ages." Franklin was more of a utopian than Adams; that is, he sought a government based on the best in human nature, calling its citizens to rise to it. However, Adams's ideas had the greater influence on the delegates to the Constitutional Convention.

— B. E. Johansen

SEE ALSO:
Albany Plan of Union; Declaration of Independence, U.S.; Franklin, Benjamin; Iroquois Confederacy; Jefferson, Thomas.

CONTRIBUTIONS, NATIVE AMERICAN

SEE Native American Contributions.

COOK, JAMES (1728–1779)

James Cook, British naval officer and explorer, was born on October 27, 1728, in Marton-in-Cleveland, Yorkshire, England, and he died on February 14, 1779, at Kealakekua Bay, Hawaii. Cook is known for his leadership of three exploring expeditions to the Pacific Ocean. The first expedition spanned the years 1768 to 1770. Cook transported members of the Royal Geographical Society to the Tahitian Islands to observe the transit of Venus across the Sun, and afterward, he charted the islands of New Zealand and the eastern coast of Australia. On the second expedition, from 1772 to 1775, Cook searched for the Antarctic land mass.

It was during Cook's third expedition, from 1776 to 1779, that he encountered indigenous peoples of the Western Hemisphere. The purpose of this expedition was to chart the northwest coast of North America in search of a "Northwest Passage," via the Arctic around the North American land mass. On the last leg of the voyage, outbound from Tahiti, Cook's expedition encountered a group of islands inhabited by Polynesian Natives. Cook named the islands the Sandwich Islands (later Hawaii) in honor of the Earl of Sandwich. Cook found poor anchorage at the Island of Atooi (Kauai) and so only stayed long enough to provision his ships with food and water before setting sail for North America.

Cook's ships, the *Resolution* and the *Discovery*, made landfall in North America on March 7, 1768. Cook began charting the coast as his ships sailed northward fighting heavy seas, rain, and gale-force winds. Cook's first anchorage on the North American coast was at Nootka Sound on present-day Vancouver Island, British Columbia. The sound was named after the people inhabiting the area, the Nootka. Cook's ships remained in the sound for four weeks while repairs were made. The interaction between the British seamen and the Native inhabitants was marked by brisk economic activity and a lack of violence.

In April of 1778, with ships repaired, Cook continued his voyage north. The route carried his ships around the western extremity of Alaska and into the Bering Sea, with no Northwest Passage to be found. In late fall, the *Resolution* and the *Discovery* turned around when faced by a solid sea of ice, resupplied, and set sail for the Sandwich Islands

This undated watercolor portrays Captain James Cook sailing in New Zealand waters in 1769.

to spend the winter months. The ships reached the island of Hawaii in early December and cruised the coastline slowly, trading with the Natives as they went, until finding anchorage at Kealakekua Bay on January 17, 1779.

The first two weeks at Kealakekua were uneventful. The Englishmen and Natives treated each other with respect. By mid-February, the ships were repaired and ready for sail, and it was clear that the Natives were not displeased at the imminent departure of their uninvited guests. The ships set sail on February 4, but as fate would have it, they encountered a violent gale two days later that damaged the ships sufficiently to cause Cook to order their return to Kealakekua Bay for repairs. Confronted once again with the unwelcome Englishmen, the Hawaiians made their displeasure

known, and tensions mounted. A plot to ensure the return of an English boat taken by the Hawaiians involved the attempted kidnapping of a local leader by Captain Cook. Cook and four marines died in the ensuing confrontation with the Hawaiians as they defended against the kidnapping attempt.

The consequences of Cook's third expedition would prove to be severe for the Native populations of both Hawaii and the Pacific Northwest region of North America. As a result of his "discoveries," the English laid claim to an area already inhabited by its Native populations but also claimed by Spain, almost leading to armed conflict with the latter. In addition, with the publication of Cook's journals (completed by James King, one of his lieutenants) in 1784, Europeans became aware of a region that, until then, had been relatively unknown. At least partially because of Cook's and King's account, the first trading vessel appeared off the northwest coast in 1785, and by 1792, that number had increased to twenty. The traders would winter in the Sandwich Islands, and so the Native populations of both the Northwest and the Sandwich Islands experienced increased contact with Europeans. In this meeting of cultures, the Natives were not in a position to dominate. Increased contact meant not only the diminution of Native cul-

ture but possibly death from European diseases as well.

— P. Press

SEE ALSO:
Alaska; British Columbia; Hawaii.

COOKING

SEE Foods and Cooking, Native American.

COOK-LYNN, ELIZABETH
(1930–)

Elizabeth Cook-Lynn (Sioux) is a poet, editor, and professor who for many years has edited one of the leading scholarly journals for Native American studies professionals, *Wicazo Sa Review*. She was born on the Crow Creek Reservation at Fort Thompson, South Dakota, in 1930. Her grandfather was a Sioux linguist who participated in the development of early dictionaries for the Dakota dialect of the Sioux language. Both her father and her grandfather served on the Crow Creek tribal council.

Cook-Lynn received a B.A. in English and journalism from South Dakota State College and an M.A. in education, psychology, and counseling from the University of South Dakota. She has undertaken additional postgraduate studies in literary criticism at the University of Nebraska and at Stanford University. Her first volume of poetry, *Then Badger Said This* (1978), was published by Vantage Press and was later reissued (1983) by Galleon Press. Her second volume of poetry, *Seek the House of Rel-*

For many years, Elizabeth Cook-Lynn, through the pages of *Wicazo Sa Review*, prodded Native intellectuals to think more deeply into issues. In the fall of 1995, she retired from her editorial duties and turned over the management of the review to the American Indian Studies Program of the University of Minnesota.

atives (1983), was published by Blue Cloud Quarterly Press. Her volume of short fiction is entitled *The Power of Horses & Other Stories* (1990), and her novel is entitled *From the River's Edge* (1991), both published by Arcade/Little Brown. Her work has appeared in a number of publications and anthologies, including *Pembroke, Great Plains Observer, Sun Tracks, The Greenfield Review, Prairie Schooner, South Dakota Review, The Remembered Earth, A Gathering of Spirit,* and *Returning the Gift: Poetry and Prose from the First North American Native Writers Festival.* Her poetry and prose are known for focusing on the geography of the northern Plains and the culture of the Dakota Sioux.

From 1970 until her retirement as professor emeritus in 1993, she taught English and American Indian studies at Eastern Washington State University in Cheney, Washington. Since her retirement from this university, she continues to teach, most recently as Visiting Professor at the University of California at Davis. A substantial interview with her can be found in *Survival This Way: Interviews with American Indian Poets* (1987). She also shared the story of her life in *I Tell You Now: Autobiographical Essays by Native American Writers* (1987).

COOPER, JAMES FENIMORE
(1789–1851)

Few people have had a greater hand in shaping the popular image of Native Americans than European-American novelist James Fenimore Cooper. Author of more than a dozen works about the sea and American life, Cooper is best known for a series of five novels, collectively called the *Leatherstocking Tales,* about life in the forest. These books, *The Pioneers* (1823), *The Last of the Mohicans* (1826), *The Prairie* (1827), *The Pathfinder* (1840), and *The Deerslayer* (1841), were the first to feature Indian characters and make Indian life central to their plot and themes. Not only were they enormously popular and widely imitated, both in the United States and in Europe, but the best known of the lot, *The Last of the Mohicans,* continues to be widely read today and has served as the basis for no fewer than five Hollywood movies and a television series.

This illustration appeared in James Fenimore Cooper's novel *The Prairie*.

An illustration of a scene from Cooper's most famous novel, *The Last of the Mohicans*.

Although much of his knowledge of Indians and the woods was gathered firsthand during his childhood in New York State, Cooper has been criticized for oversimplifying his Indian characters. His plots are action packed, but his writing was breezy and careless, and critics often have taken him to task for inaccuracies about Indians and woodsmanship. In his serious but very funny essay, "Fenimore Cooper's Literary Offences," Mark Twain rips Cooper apart for showing a group of Indians to be so inept that they actually fall out of a tree and into a river while trying to jump onto a passing barge. More recently, Cooper has been criticized for his shallow treatment of women characters, Indian and white.

In fairness, however, Cooper's responsibility for American Indian stereotypes is more indirect than direct. It was Cooper's imitators who substituted a whoop and a dash of war paint for characterization and whose stereotypes linger today. Cooper's favorite theme is the conflict between European and Native American cultures played out in the vanishing American forest. His hero is the woodsman, Hawkeye (also known as Natty Bumppo), whose life is a doomed struggle to combine the best of the Indian's and the colonist's ways of life. Hawkeye rejects the colonist's greed and hypocrisy and the violence of the Indian wars. His code combines the Indians' laws of the forest, represented by his lifelong companion, Chingachook the Mohican, with an ideal of reason and civility.

Unlike later imitators, Cooper populated his forests with a diverse group of many different Native peoples. In *The Last of the Mohicans*, for example, which is based on an historical incident of the French and Indian War of 1757, there are Indian characters from almost a dozen tribes, including the Huron, Mohican, Lenape, Oneida, and other tribes of the Iroquois Confederacy. Bands from each tribe fight for either the British, the French, or in some cases both sides in a complex picture of intertribal alliances.

But for all his sympathies and the variety of Indian tribes in his novels, most of the Indian characters emerge as one of two types: the vicious savage and the noble man of the forest. In *The Last of the Mohicans*, Uncas, son of Chingachook, is the consummate hunter and tracker. Completely guid-

ed by the laws of the forest, he knows when to be violent and when to be compassionate. Magua, his rival, is equally skilled, but he is treacherous, corrupted by deals with Europeans and disregardful of human life. At the end of the novel, Uncas dies at the hand of Magua as he tries to save Cora, the British woman he loves. With the deaths of Uncas and Cora, so too dies Cooper's romantic vision for an America born from a union of Indian and white settler.

SEE ALSO:

French and Indian War; Iroquois Confederacy; Lenape.

COPWAY, GEORGE (1818–c. 1863)

Scholar Charles Hamilton suggests that George Copway, an Ojibwe (Chippewa) who was also known as Kahgegwagebow ("Stands Fast"), may have been the model for Henry Wadsworth Longfellow's Hiawatha. Copway was a close friend of Longfellow's, and he was noted among the Ojibwes for his physical strength and skill at hunting. Copway also was one of the first Native Americans to write books that were widely read by non-Indians.

Copway was born near the mouth of the Trent River in what is now Ontario, Canada. He was raised as a traditional Ojibwe. His father was a noted leader and medicine man, but the family often went hungry during Copway's youth. His traditional training included stress on physical strength; Copway once carried two hundred pounds (ninety kilograms) of flour and other supplies on his back for 0.25 mile (0.4 kilometer) without rest. In the spring of 1841, he is said to have run 240 miles (386 kilometers) in four days, across much of present-day Wisconsin, to warn the Ojibwes of a Sioux raiding party.

Copway was converted to Methodism in 1830 and attended Ebenezer Academy in Jacksonville, Illinois, for two years. He became a Methodist minister in 1834, after which he translated several religious texts from English into Algonquian and worked with several religious publishers. In New York City, Copway started a newspaper about American Indian affairs, called *Copway's Ameri-*

can Indian. Only one issue is known to have been published, on July 10, 1851.

Copway wrote *The Life, History, and Travels of Kay-ge-ga-gah-bowh* (1847), which was revised in 1850 as *The Traditional History and Characteristic Sketches of the Ojibway Nation.* The same book was reissued in 1858 as *Indian Life and Indian History.* Copway also wrote *The Ojibway Conquest* (1850), *The Organization of a New Indian Territory East of the Missouri River* (1850), and *Running Sketches of Men and Places in England, Germany, Belgium, and Scotland* (1851). Copway toured Europe; in England, he denounced European and American deals for Ojibwe ancestral lands as frauds and robberies. Copway died near Pontiac, Michigan, at the age of forty-five.

SEE ALSO:
Hiawatha; Ojibwe.

CORNPLANTER (1735–1836)

Cornplanter (Seneca) was a major Iroquois leader of the late eighteenth century. Also known as John O'Bail, he figured prominently in the shifting alliances that accompanied the American Revolution, and he became a personal friend of George Washington. Cornplanter's father was a white trader, John O'Bail (sometimes "Abeel"). Some sources contend O'Bail was Irish; others say he was Dutch. All agree, however, that he was one of the biggest sellers of liquor to the Senecas. Cornplanter was raised by his Seneca mother.

As an ally of the French in the French and Indian War (1754 to 1763), Cornplanter and his fighting men attacked several British settlements. He may have been part of the French force that defeated British General Edward Braddock and his aide George Washington at Fort Duquesne (now Pittsburgh).

As the Revolutionary War got underway, the Iroquois Grand Council could not reach consensus on which side to join. The majority of the Six Nations took up the British cause. Cornplanter, however, generally favored neutrality.

After the war, Cornplanter secured from George Washington a tract of land for his people on both

Cornplanter, an influential Seneca leader in the League of the Iroquois during and after the American Revolution, was a supporter of the young American nation.

sides of the Allegheny River. He brought in Quaker teachers and helped sustain a prosperous agricultural community that included large herds of cattle. Cornplanter signed several treaties on behalf of the Senecas. These included treaties concluded at Fort Stanwix in 1784 and others at various locations in 1789, 1797, and 1802. Through his many associations with Euro-Americans, including a trip to England, Cornplanter picked up English clothes and mannerisms, which upset some of his people. On one occasion, some angry Senecas tore off his English clothes and dressed him in traditional attire, greasing his body.

In April 1786, the Tammany Society welcomed Cornplanter and five other Senecas to Philadelphia. The Tammany Society was a voluntary organization of Native Americans and Euro-Americans formed before the American Revolution. The group, which included some of the most influential people in both cultures, had rituals that blended Native American and European ideas and traditions. In a remarkable ceremony, the Tammany sachems (leaders) escorted the Senecas from their lodgings at the Indian Queen tavern to Tammany's wigwam on the banks of the Schuylkill River for a conference. Within a few days, Cornplanter and the Senecas proceeded to New York City to address Congress.

Later in his life, Cornplanter lost some of his prestige among the Senecas because of his ready agreement to land cessions. He retained enough influence to bring the Senecas to the U.S. side in the War of 1812, however. Shortly before he died in 1836, Cornplanter had a dream that indicated his friendship with all Euro-Americans had been mistaken. After the dream, he destroyed all the presents that had been given him by non-Indians.

Cornplanter's people occupied the 1,300-acre (520-hectare) piece of land along the Allegheny River until the mid-twentieth century, when the Army Corps of Engineers decided that the land better suited the public convenience and necessity under water. The scope of the army's engineering projects had grown grandiosely since George Washington himself helped survey the mountains that now comprise West Virginia, long before the pursuit of electricity became an excuse for the state to seize Indian land. In 1964, the bones of Cornplanter's people were moved from their land to make way for rising waters behind the Kinzua Dam.

SEE ALSO:

American Revolution; French and Indian War; Iroquois Confederacy; Tammany Society; War of 1812.

CORONADO EXPEDITION

On January 6, 1540, Antonio de Mendoza, viceroy of New Spain, received word that his proposed *entrada de conquista* (expedition of conquest) into regions north of Mexico had been approved by the king of Spain. Don Francisco Vasquez de Coronado, governor of the province of Galicia, had been chosen to lead the expedition. They expected great wealth, based on rumors heard about the region by Alvar Nuñez Cabeza de Vaca and Fray Marcos de Niza. The viceroy himself had poured much of his personal fortune into the venture.

An advance party left Compostela, Mexico, in February 1540. By later that month, the main body, led by Coronado, was on the move. It consisted of 230 cavalry, 62 infantry, and 800 Indian auxiliaries. Also in the group were three women, who were wives of the men, and Spanish priests, including Fray Marcos de Niza, who had gone to the Zunis during an earlier exploration. Other men, not yet at Compostela, were to leave later.

Coronado, moving ahead with about one-third of the force, reached the Zuni pueblo of Hawikuh on July 7, 1540, in present-day western New Mexico. The Spaniards had to fight their way into the pueblo, where they were bitterly disappointed at not finding the riches they sought. While the main body of the army was being brought up to Zuni, Coronado sent Don Pedro de Tovar with Fray Juan de Padilla and a dozen soldiers to explore the land of the Hopis in present-day northeastern Arizona. There, the Hopis told the Spaniards about a great river to the west. Upon hearing this, Coronado sent a group of soldiers under Garcia Lopez de Cardeñas to investigate. They returned with incredible descriptions of the Grand Canyon but no wealth.

Meanwhile, a delegation of Pueblo people had arrived at Hawikuh from the Pecos pueblo, east of the Rio Grande in present-day eastern New Mexico. Hernando de Alvarado, with twenty soldiers, was dispatched to investigate the Pecos country. They went even farther than Pecos, out onto the southern Great Plains, where they got their first look at the great buffalo herds. At Pecos, they met a Pueblo, whom they called "the Turk," who had some amazing stories to tell.

The Turk, acting on behalf of his kinsmen who were determined to rid themselves of the Spaniards, told fantastic stories of great wealthy cities far to the north and the east, out on the plains. When Alvarado reported these tempting stories to Coronado, he decided to move the entire expedition to the Rio Grande Valley for the winter so that they would be near the plains when spring arrived.

The winter of 1540–1541 was unusually severe. The Spaniards suffered miserably, and they disrupted Pueblo life all along the Rio Grande with their demands for food, warm clothing, and many other things. Fighting raged off and on all winter between the Spanish and groups of Pueblos. Final-

Coronado, leading his troops onto the Great Plains, was pursuing stories of fabulous wealth in gold and silver at Quivira. He found only the grass huts of the Wichitas.

ly, in April 1541, the expedition moved eastward, where it encountered Plains Indians and buffaloes but no gold or silver. Leaving the main force behind, Coronado and a small group of soldiers ventured as far as present-day Wichita, Kansas, which the Spanish called Qtiuivira. Finding nothing but Indians living in thatched huts and tipis, the Spanish strangled the Turk.

Coronado remained in the area for about a month, exploring as far east as the Smoky Hill Valley, before finally giving up and returning to the main force of the expedition, which had returned to the Rio Grande Valley. The winter of 1541–1542 was not as severe as the previous one, but the presence of the Spanish was no less disruptive to the lives of the Pueblos.

The Spanish, most of them disillusioned at finding nothing that they valued, could not agree about whether to explore further in the spring or return to Mexico. An injury to Coronado, suffered in a riding accident, helped them make up their mind to leave. They left behind two priests, Fray Juan de Padilla, who traveled back across the plains to Quivira, and Fray Luis de Ubeda, who remained at Pecos pueblo. Natives promptly killed both after the Spanish left.

Coronado reached Mexico by early summer, and in July 1542, he reported to the viceroy in Mexico City. The Spanish were so disappointed by what had been found that it would not be until the end of the century that they would attempt to colonize the region. However, a number of unauthorized expeditions would venture there for brief, but disruptive, visits in the last half of the sixteenth century.

— D. L. Birchfield

SEE ALSO:
Cabeza de Vaca, Alvar Núñez; de Niza, Marcos; Pueblo; Spain; Zuni.

CORTÉS, HERNÁN (1845–1547)

Hernán (or Hernando) Cortés was born in Medellín, Spain. At the age of thirteen, he was sent to Salamanca to study law but dropped out of school shortly after he learned that Christopher Columbus, another Spaniard, had made his first voyages to the New World in search of adventure and riches. Cortés sailed for Hispaniola in 1504; he eventually became Spain's best-known conquistador.

In Hispaniola, Cortés took part in battles against Native peoples. Then, in 1511, he traveled to Cuba to take part in its conquest under Diego Valazquez. Valazquez later heard of a rich Native empire to the west of Cuba and designated Cortés to lead an expedition there. Realizing that he was appointing an overly ambitious man who might someday replace him, Valazquez withdrew the commission. Cortés ignored him, and set sail with six hundred men in February of 1519.

This was to be the first Spanish expedition into the heart of the Aztec Empire. Ultimately, with just a few hundred men, Cortés was able to subdue the strongest empire in the Americas. He did this by making alliances with the Aztecs' enemies and using intrigue and deception. He was also helped by the fact that his men carried European diseases against which the Aztecs had no resistance.

In 1519, Cortés looked out over Tenochtitlán, the Aztecs' capital city (which occupied the site of present-day Mexico City). It struck him as a world-class metropolis, and he called it the most beautiful city in the world. It has been estimated that Tenochtitlán contained about 250,000 people at a time when Rome, Seville, and Paris contained only about 150,000 people each. The Aztec ruler Moctezuma welcomed Cortés and his men, presenting them with gifts of flowers and gold.

But within a decade, Tenochtitlán lay in ruins. Cortés first imprisoned Moctezuma, then killed

An undated painting by Diego Rivera depicts the arrival of Cortés at Vera Cruz, on his way to the conquest of the Aztec Empire of central Mexico.

him. The Spanish conquistadors tore down the Native temples, pyramids, and public buildings and used the stones to build Spanish-style government buildings and churches. They filled in rivers and canals and burned the Aztec gardens. In the process, Cortés survived a major rebellion, thus solidifying the Spanish hold on the land that was becoming known as Mexico.

Worst of all, epidemics of smallpox and other diseases carried by the conquistadors had killed at least half the Aztecs. One of the Aztec chroniclers who survived wrote, "Almost the whole population suffered from racking coughs and painful, burning sores." Within thirty years of Cortés's arrival in Mexico, the Native population had fallen from about 25 million to roughly 6 million.

SEE ALSO:
Aztec; Columbus, Christopher; Las Casas, Bartolomé de; Moctezuma; Spain.

COSTO, RUPERT (1906–1989)

Early in his life, as a football player in the 1920s at Haskell Institute and Whittier College (where he played with future President Richard M. Nixon), Rupert Costo (Cahuilla) demonstrated his athletic and intellectual aptitudes to the Indian and non-Indian world alike. From the 1930s to the 1950s, he was active in national and tribal politics, serving both as a vocal critic of the Indian New Deal in the 1930s and as tribal chairman of the Cahuillas in the 1950s.

For most of his working life, Costo was employed by the state of California in the highway department as an engineer. In 1964, upon his retirement, Costo and his wife, Jeannette Henry Costo (Eastern Cherokee), founded the San Francisco–based American Indian Historical Society. The society was often in the forefront of such American Indian issues as the protection of Native American human remains and cemeteries. Members of the society also developed publications that accurately reflected the historical role of American Indians in U.S. society.

Initially, the American Indian Historical Society published three such journals, all of them edit-

ed by Costo and his wife: *Wassaja*, a national Indian newspaper (1973–1979); *The Indian Historian*, a respected academic journal (1964–1979); and the *Weewish Tree*, a national magazine for Indian young people. Through his editorial columns in *Wassaja*, Costo argued for increased sovereignty for Native American nations in order to enhance their land and water rights. He also worked tirelessly for the protection of American Indian civil, social, and religious rights.

In 1970, the society founded another publishing arm—the Indian Historian Press, an American Indian–controlled publishing house that boasted no fewer than fifty-two publications. Some of the better-known titles included *Textbooks and the American Indian* (1970), which was edited by Costo, and *The Iroquois and the Founding of the American Nation* (1977), by Donald A. Grinde, Jr. (Yamasee).

Toward the end of his life, Costo set up and endowed the Rupert Costo Chair in American Indian History at the University of California, Riverside. He and his wife also established the Costo Library of the American Indian at Riverside, and today it is one of the most comprehensive collections of American Indian books in the United States. In 1994, the University of California, Riverside renamed its Student Services Building Costo Hall in honor of the outstanding contributions of Rupert and Jeannette Henry Costo to the university.

COUNCIL OF ENERGY RESOURCE TRIBES

The Council of Energy Resource Tribes (CERT) is an intertribal organization formed to help tribes meet a variety of economic, social, and environmental needs.

A tribal government spends money to meet the needs of its members. Some of this money comes from the federal government. But tribes also develop their own sources of income. Economic development means making money now; it also means investing part of this money in ways that keep generating more money in the future. Yet, as important as money is to tribes, they do not want earning money to harm their social, cultural, or political values or to ruin their environment.

To achieve these goals—which sometimes conflict with one another—a government needs help from teams of experts in business, energy production, environmental protection, and other fields. But rare is the tribe that can afford to hire, train, and support such teams full-time by itself. That usually requires funding from several tribes, coordinated through an intertribal organization.

That is why several tribes joined together to form CERT, a not-for-profit intertribal organization based in Denver, Colorado. CERT is governed directly by the elected leaders (for instance, the tribal chairman) of roughly sixty member tribes in the United States and Alberta, Canada.

CERT started off by helping tribes make money from natural resources that can be used to produce electricity, heat, and other forms of energy. Heat can be used directly, for instance to warm homes, or it can be used to produce electricity. Fuels like coal, oil, natural gas, and wood can be burned to produce heat. Or heat can be obtained from volcanic activity underground (geothermal energy). Heat can be used to boil water and produce steam. Steam can be used to turn a turbine to produce electricity. A windmill is one kind of turbine. Turbines can be turned by wind, steam, or water flowing over a dam. Water-generated electricity is called "hydro" electricity. CERT helped the Blackfeet and Cheyenne tribes with oil and gas, the Paiute tribe with geothermal energy, and the Ute Mountain Ute tribe with coal—to list but a few examples. Energy can also be produced from nuclear reactions, but this is one energy source that CERT does not promote.

Some of the energy produced on a reservation can be sold for use off-reservation, and some can be kept for use on the reservation. CERT helps Native people obtain the electricity and heat energy that they need at reasonable cost and helps them avoid wasting energy. When a home is built tightly so that the wind doesn't blow through it and so that heat doesn't leak out, the people who live there don't need as much heat energy to stay warm and they don't have to pay as much money for heating their home. This is called "energy conservation."

For a tribal government to meet the needs of its people, it sometimes has to obtain goods or services from state and federal governments. For example, when the Blackfeet needed repairs to their roads, they had to bargain with the state of Montana over how much state-controlled money would be spent on the reservation and how much of the labor would be done by tribal members. Such bargaining is called "lobbying." CERT helps tribes lobby for their members.

CERT also keeps an eye on federal agencies such as the Bureau of Indian Affairs (BIA) to make sure that they adequately serve Native peoples. Of particular concern to CERT is BIA's Office of Trust Funds Management (OTFM). OTFM is responsible for collecting, investing, accounting for, and distributing funds from the sale of tribal resources, such as minerals and timber, or the lease of resources such as grazing.

In the modern world, information can be as valuable as money. CERT helps assure that government agencies share their latest, best information with Native people. (For example, what are the most profitable and safest methods and equipment for mining coal or drilling for oil and natural gas?) Sharing such information is called "technology transfer."

There are many other ways of making money, and CERT helps tribes in all of the following ways. Tribes can set up their own businesses—making products as ancient as pottery or as modern as computer components. The Blackfeet tribe, for instance, has made nationally known brands of pens and pencils, as well as calendars and notebooks. CERT helps tribes set up businesses by providing advice on planning, obtaining loans, making products, and finding buyers for the products (marketing).

Another way of making money is to obtain grants from federal and state governments; CERT helps with that. When a state government taxes lands or businesses on a reservation, tribes argue that at least part of the tax money should be sent back to the reservation to meet the needs of the people living there—an argument that the Cheyenne River Sioux won with CERT's help. Tribes can also directly tax businesses or charge special fees for activities such as gaming (gambling).

CERT also raises money by sponsoring fundraising events. These events include a golf tournament, which raised money for the Tribal Resource Institute in Business, Engineering, and Science (TRIBES), a summer college-transition program. CERT has also raised money for Indian scholars through its annual American Spirit Award dinner and through donations by CERT employees.

Transfer of technologies from government agencies to tribes has been promoted through internships with the U.S. Department of Energy and the U.S. Environmental Protection Agency (EPA). Native interns are usually young adults with a college degree. They spend a year with EPA, participating for approximately three months in such EPA program areas as water quality, air quality, solid waste disposal, and toxins. Internships are also available with industry hosts, including the Public Service Company of Colorado and the National Renewable Energy Laboratories.

CERT helps tribes avoid new environmental damage and correct for past damage arising from their own economic development or from that of surrounding communities or government facilities. Of particular concern are pollutants released from military or nuclear energy programs. CERT discourages placement in Indian country of nuclear power plants or sites for disposal of nuclear wastes.

— S. F. Stringham

A man of Micmac and Iroquois descent in traditional clothing at a powwow in Connecticut. The lines on the horse represent coups counted—victories scored against an enemy in battle by touching him lightly with a coup stick.

COUP STICKS, OR COUNTING COUP

To the Plains Indians, war was not just a series of battles conducted to kill enemy warriors or obtain their property. It was the opportunity for individual acts of daring and heroism. Because Plains Indians traveled in small hunting bands, losing even a single man in battle was a loss they could not afford, so relatively few warriors actually died in battle. War, therefore, became a ceremonial affair, full of ritual. Men carried protective medicine bundles and at times painted lightning designs on their horses to symbolize personal power in battle. The main

object of a battle, and a way to gain honor, was a symbolic death they called "counting coup."

Coup is a word taken from the French, meaning a sudden, surprising, and successful stroke or attack. Counting coup was symbolically killing a foe by touching him on the head or any other part of the body with a coup stick—without getting hurt. A special coup stick was used for this purpose, although a war club, ax, bow, or even the warrior's hand would do. Simply touching the enemy in battle, without hurting him, was considered an act of bravery that deserved to be honored. Killing a man from an ambush was no coup because it was too easy. Even a coward could do it. There were also other ways to count coup. Stealing horses right out from under an armed enemy's nose, for example, was considered a fine coup. Coups had to be witnessed in order to be recognized, and tribes developed complex coup systems to keep track of these war honors.

For each successful coup, some tribes awarded a black-tipped eagle tail feather that was notched, split, or dotted with paint to indicate what kind of coup had been counted. If, after counting coup on an armed enemy, the warrior managed to kill and scalp him, he received three coup feathers. The feathers were attached to a skullcap of buffalo hide or deerskin to create a feather headdress. A headdress also had smaller feathers tied to the base of the eagle feathers and tufts of dyed horsehair tied to the tips. Often, the brow band was decorated with quillwork or beadwork and dangling strips of fur or ribbons. Only a few men wore headdresses, those who had earned the privilege to do so. War chiefs usually had the longest headdresses. Capturing an enemy's eagle feathers was considered a major coup.

Heroic coups stories were told around campfires over and over again. Many of these tales also describe the courageous feats of women warriors, who were just as honored as their male counterparts.

Most young Plains Indian men belonged to one of their tribe's warrior societies. Each society had its own insignia, dress, medicine bundles, songs, dances, and code of behavior. In some of these societies, a man automatically became a member when he reached a certain age. Others were more exclusive; a man could only join if and when he was invited, based on his deeds in battle. Some societies were even intertribal. The most famous soldier societies, for example the Sioux Kit Foxes or the Cheyenne Dog Soldiers, were respected and feared all over the Plains.

Many men did die in battle, of course, but on the battlefield even death was ritualized. If Plains Indians tortured their captives until they died, it was not out of cruelty but respect. It was a way to give their victims a chance to display bravery and thereby achieve honor in death.

Coup systems and soldier societies were concepts brought to the Plains from Indian cultures in the East, but it was the Plains Indians who developed these concepts to such an elaborate degree.

SEE ALSO:
Siouan Nations.

COURTING FLUTE

The American Indian courting flute has long been an instrument of Indian music. The flute was once an integral part of Plains, Plateau, Woodland, Eastern, and Southwestern tribal cultures and served important sociological functions that were connected with courtship and entertainment. Its history can be easily traced in historical documents as part of the Plains Indian culture during the past 150 years. Indian oral tradition provides ample evidence that indigenous people have always had some type of blowing instrument like the flute or whistle.

The Plains Indian flute was originally intended to be played by young Indian men as they attempted to court a young Indian woman. The courting flute was a woodwind instrument used many times as love magic, as well as for entertainment. It was played solo, however, not used to accompany the voice; nor was it accompanied by other musical instruments. No formal instruction or training was given to a young man when he began to play it. He simply learned on his own and by listening to other flute players.

Although the popularity of the flute has increased in the last two decades, the number of knowledgeable flute players is still somewhat small. Today, Indian flutists play both traditional love songs and newly written courting songs. The Indian flute is a distinctive musical instrument tuned to F sharp major. Flutes are crafted mostly from red cedar wood and tuned with great care. The recent revival has been promoted with much enthusiasm by both Indian and non-Indian players, makers, and scholars. To play well requires a long time of study and practice, as well as a cultural knowledge of Indian music.

Traditionally, courting flutes were designed in accord with visions of the flute maker. Some flutes resemble birds, horses, turtles, reptiles, or chipmunks. Plains flutes are cherished as a valued personal possession and are buried along with other prized artifacts following the death of the owner.

Near the turn of the century, United States government policy discouraged the continuation of Indian culture by separating Indian young people from their families and their culture. Many young Indians were placed in distant government boarding schools, where they were punished for speaking their Native language or clinging to their culture in other ways. This government policy continued throughout the first half of the twentieth century. During this period, Indian music, as well as other expressions of Indian culture, was repressed.

The past two decades have seen a renaissance of the courting flute. Today, an increasing number of accomplished Indian flutists are continuing this ancient art. They are sharing and teaching Indian young people the beauty of this distinctive instrument for all to enjoy.

COURTS OF INDIAN OFFENSES

Toward the end of the nineteenth century, as the United States continued its westward expansion, reservations began to be thought of less as a means of keeping Indians and non-Indians separate and more as a means of forcing Indians to become assimilated into mainstream American culture. Administration of the reservations was put in the hands of non-Indians—nevertheless referred to as "Indian agents"—who were appointed by the government. These agents often were military personnel, and they had the duty of supervising the adaptation of Indians to non-Indian ways.

In 1883, the Department of the Interior created the Courts of Indian Offenses. Native judges (as well as police) were appointed by, and served under the direction of, Indian agents and had the authority to administer justice for all but the most major crimes. The main purpose of the courts was supposed to be maintenance of law and order; how-

The flute, like the drum, is an ancient musical instrument in the Americas. Today, the art of flute making and flute playing is undergoing a renaissance in many American Indian tribes.

ever, many of the laws punishable by the courts were actually designed to prevent traditional practices that the government wanted ended.

For example, such customs as ceremonial dances, polygamous marriages, the practices of medicine men, and the customary distribution and/or disposal of property after an Indian's death were outlawed. In addition, the regulations regarding judicial appointees showed preference to Indians who could read and write English, who wore non-Indian clothing, and who engaged in "civilized" practices.

The Courts of Indian Offenses served the purpose of filling the vacuum created by the waning of traditional tribal authority. At the same time, they were a competing source of power that helped keep traditional leaders from maintaining or regaining their power and influence.

The courts operated primarily under Bureau of Indian Affairs control until Commissioner John Collier instituted a set of reforms in 1935. Collier published a revised Code of Indian Offenses, which promoted a policy that returned power to tribes and respected their right to self-government. The revised code gave tribes the authority to create their own laws and judicial procedures. With minor changes, this code is still in use and is published in Title 25 of the U.S. Code of Federal Regulations.

Today, most tribes operate their own court systems, complete with their own written laws. However, some tribes still resolve judicial matters through Courts of Indian Offenses using the updated regulations. In addition, while Indians have been able to preserve or return to some ancient traditions, such is not the case with justice. Few tribes operate judicial systems based on tribal tradition. Instead, most tribes have used Bureau of Indian Affairs codes as a basis for their own codes and practices. Contemporary Indian tribal courts have jurisdiction throughout Indian country except for limits imposed by treaty or statute.

SEE ALSO:
Bureau of Indian Affairs; Collier, John; Governments, Native; Tribal Legal Systems.

COVENANT CHAIN

The Covenant Chain was a diplomatic metaphor used by the British as they sought to ally with the Iroquois against the French in the mid-eighteenth century. The alliance was said to represent a chain. When diplomacy was cordial, the chain was being "shined." If the two sides fell out in disagreement, the chain was said to be "rusting."

This chain of alliance saved the New York region, and probably all of New England, from the French in the initial stages of what in Europe was known as the Seven Years' War. (In North America, it was called the French and Indian War.) The Mohawk leader Hendrick, also known as Tiyanoga, was perhaps the most important individual link in the chain. Hendrick died maintaining the Covenant Chain at the Battle of Lake George in 1755, where Sir William Johnson defeated Baron Dieskau.

Early in his diplomatic career, Benjamin Franklin described the diplomatic images evoked by the Covenant Chain after he attended a treaty council at Carlisle, Pennsylvania. The participants in this council were Iroquois and Ohio Indians (Twightees, Delawares, Shawnees, and Wyandots). At the council, Franklin watched the Oneida chief, Scarrooyady, and a Mohawk, Cayanguileguoa, offer condolences to the Ohio Indians for their losses against the French. Franklin listened while Scarrooyady recounted the origins of the Great Law to the Ohio Indians: "We must let you know, that there was a friendship established by our and your Grandfathers, and a mutual Council fire was kindled. In this friendship all those then under the ground, who had not yet obtained eyes or faces [that is, those unborn] were included; and it was then mutually promised to tell the same to their children and children's children."

Having thus offered condolences to the Ohio Indians, Scarrooyady urged all assembled to "preserve this Union and Friendship, which has so long and happy continued among us. Let us keep the chain from rusting. . . ."

Franklin later used the Covenant Chain image in designs for early U.S. coins.

SEE ALSO:
Franklin, Benjamin; Hendrick (Tiyanoga); Iroquois Confederacy.

COYOTE STORIES

Stories about the many-faceted figure Coyote have a long tradition in the Native cultures of western North America, Mexico, and Central America. Today, Coyote has as much to teach us in all his fantastic tales as he did ancestors hundreds of years ago.

Trickster, changer, healer, wise teacher, foolish example, and great presenter of challenges, Coyote is called many names and is known in many forms. His complexity is part of his power as a giver and taker of reality. To the people along the 'Nchi-awana (Columbia River) in the Pacific Northwest, Coyote shaped the valley, fought monsters, and taught people how to fish and share with each other. With a great sense of humor, Coyote placed the stars by scattering them for the Navajo. Coyote stories are told by many tribes in the Americas, which shows how broadly Coyote is dispersed.

Coyote is not supposed to die unless the tip of his tail and the end of his nose are destroyed. This enables him to survive the most horrible accidents and stupid mistakes. We are always amazed at how Coyote pulls himself together after each of his self-created disasters. This side of Coyote helps us to handle our own catastrophes. The wisdom side of Coyote is known among the Sahaptin speakers of the Columbia Basin as *Speel-yi Mi*. This is the challenge: to figure out how to live among all the other beings on this circle of the earth. As we accept Coyote's challenge, we become a deeper part of all things.

The Lakota spider Iktomi, the Northwest Coast trickster-shaper Raven, and the Southeast trickster Rabbit are often compared to Coyote. The ideas behind all the stories are these: If Coyote or another trickster can survive by its wits, so can we human beings. If Coyote can learn from its mistakes, we can too. If Coyote can become a mythical being in stories that give meanings to events and names to all the beasts, then we can be part of these stories.

SEE ALSO:
Storytelling; Tricksters.

CRABB, BARBARA (1939–)

United States Federal District Judge Barbara Bran-driff Crabb (who is a non-Indian) was born in Green Bay, Wisconsin. From 1951 to 1962, she studied at the University of Wisconsin-Madison. After receiving her law degree in 1962, she became a practicing lawyer. She was appointed to the position of federal judge in 1979 by President Jimmy Carter. She was the first woman to serve in this role. Since her appointment, she has made a number of important decisions concerning tribal rights in Wisconsin.

In 1990, Judge Crabb made a significant ruling in a sixteen-year legal dispute concerning Chippewa (Ojibwe) treaty rights. The dispute originated in 1975, when the Lac Court Oreilles Chippewas sued the state of Wisconsin in federal court after some tribal members were arrested for spearing fish. The Chippewas were angry at being punished for practicing a traditional hunting method, which they believed was guaranteed to them by treaty rights.

The conflict between the tribe and the state centered on an agreement that was signed by the Chippewas in the early nineteenth century. During the early 1800s, the Chippewas had sold their land to the federal government. The Chippewas were unhappy because they believed that the treaty guaranteed them the exclusive right to use all of the natural resources on this land. This included timber for logging, and fish, which were still hunted by using the traditional spearing method.

When Judge Crabb listened to this argument in 1989, she agreed with the Chippewas' interpretation of their treaty rights. She ruled that the tribe did have the right to practice off-reservation spearing. Many treaty opponents were unhappy with Crabb's decision. They argued that the Chippewas' hunting methods were draining too many fish from the river. These protesters, led by a group known as "Stop Treaty Abuse," organized ugly demonstrations on the northern lakes. Racial slurs were often used by angry protesters.

Judge Crabb's final decision in 1990 equally divided the public resources between Chippewa and non-Chippewa hunters. She based her judgment on the nineteenth-century treaty. She ruled that when it was signed, the Chippewas were not given an exclusive right to hunt. Neither the state government nor the tribe was completely happy with the decision. However, the six Chippewa tribal chairmen agreed to accept her ruling. At the end of the sixteen-year battle, the Chippewas had succeeded in drawing attention to their treaty rights, and they had won an important decision in court. Judge Crabb continued to support their spearing tradition by barring opponents from interfering with tribal fishing.

(InSeptember 1996, in a similar Wisconsin case, Judge Crabb ruled against a Menominee claim that the tribe should have exclusive hunting right to about 10 million acres (4 million hectares) of non-

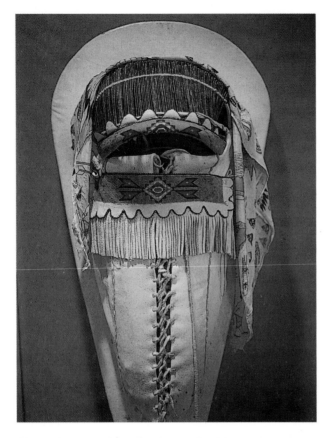

Above: Fine beadwork adorns this Ute cradleboard, located in Colorado's Southern Ute Indian Museum.

reservation land. Although sympathetic to their claim, she said the Menominees had failed to demonstrate that the lack of clarity in an 1831 treaty entitled the tribe to reclaim its exclusive land rights.)

In 1991, Judge Crabb ruled that a 1987 voter-approved constitutional amendment to legalize a state lottery also allowed for all forms of gambling on tribal reservations. When Milwaukee city officials tried to close down the Potawatomi Casino, Judge Crabb ruled that they had no right to do so.

In addition to the state's constitutional amendment, the Federal Indian Gaming Regulatory Act also allowed for gambling on Native land. Despite state and city opposition, and numerous appeals, Judge Crabb's ruling still stands. Her decision allowed all twelve Wisconsin tribes to operate casino games in the state.

SEE ALSO:
Bresette, Walter; Self-determination; Wisconsin.

CRADLEBOARDS

For centuries, American Indian women have used handcrafted items to carry infant children on their backs. In some areas, especially among California tribes, baskets were used for this purpose. Many tribes, however, used cradleboards.

Cradleboards have differed in design slightly from tribe to tribe, but they traditionally consisted of a wooden frame with supports to keep the baby in place on a mother's back. Because the device was secured to her back by straps, she had free use of her hands and could carry her baby with her while she worked.

Babies were generally wrapped firmly in soft furs or tanned hides before being placed in the wooden frame. Some women from the Plains tribes used buffalo hair for padding. It was thought that the baby would develop better posture and strength if it was bound tightly. Some tribes in the Pacific Northwest and elsewhere also used cradleboards to flatten part of babies' heads because such purpose-

Left: This Ute child is tending a baby in a cradleboard on the west slope of the Wasatch Mountains in Utah.

ful physical shaping was seen as a desirable and attractive feature. Ironically, the Flathead tribe was not one of these groups.

Members of some tribes would pack the bottom of the cradleboard with bits of soft moss, which absorbed moisture and could be easily replaced. The moss served, in effect, as one of the world's first disposable "diapers."

With typical motherly pride, women spent much time decorating their babies' cradleboards. Some would not only carve the wood but make elaborate coverings out of beaded designs and porcupine quills.

This American Indian invention is still popular today, but it has undergone several changes. Today, women and men alike of all races and ethnic groups carry babies on frames—usually made of aluminum—that support brightly colored pouches, which are usually made of nylon.

CRAZY HORSE (1842–1877)

Crazy Horse, who was also known as Tashunka Witko, was one of the greatest and most courageous of the Oglala Lakota war leaders and by far one of the most legendary and heroic. He was born east of the sacred Black Hills in what is now South Dakota. As a young boy, he was called Curly; people remarked often about his curly hair, pale skin, and spiritual ways. His father was a medicine man of the Oglalas, and his mother was the daughter of a chief of the Brulé band.

Before the age of twelve, Crazy Horse underwent a difficult rite of passage on the path to becoming a warrior by killing his first buffalo. He then received his own horse. After witnessing him in battle with another tribe, his father gave him the name by which he himself was known—Crazy Horse. About that same time, Crazy Horse experienced a vivid dream while undergoing a vision quest. After fasting for four days and nights, praying for a vision that would guide him through his life, Crazy Horse received a vision of a rider on horseback going through a heavy storm. His father interpreted the vision as a sign of Crazy Horse's future greatness as a warrior and as a brave leader of his people.

By the time Crazy Horse was seventeen, he had achieved full warrior status among the tribe by riding in a raid on the Crows. Riding into battle, Crazy Horse always stood out from the other riders because he dressed as the warrior he had seen in his vision. He wore a stone behind one ear, his cheek was adorned with a lightning bolt, and his body was painted with hailstone spots. His long, unbraided hair streamed out behind him as he rode.

In 1864, fighting broke out throughout Indian country when whites attacked the Cheyennes and Arapahos at Sand Creek, Colorado. It was after this Sand Creek Massacre that the Oglalas, with Crazy Horse among them, were drawn into battles with the United States Army and with white settlers and miners who were advancing deeply into Indian lands.

Crazy Horse joined with Red Cloud and other prominent leaders in the 1866–1968 war over the Bozeman Trail, which was the route to recently opened gold mining areas in Montana. During this war, he participated in many raids and skirmishes against white settlements and forts. He soon distinguished himself as a skilled military planner, employing shrewd decoying tactics and earning respect as a commander of the other warriors. In time, the U.S. government finally gave in to the Lakota pressure. Government officials agreed to abandon the military forts that were strung along the Bozeman Trail on the condition that the raids be stopped.

It was then, in 1868, that the Treaty of Fort Laramie was signed. This treaty guaranteed the Indians that no white persons were to be permitted to settle upon or occupy any portion of the territory around the Bozeman trail or pass through without the consent of the Indians. The treaty also made the territory into a reservation. This forced the Indians to live within its boundaries and to receive annuities and goods from the government. This was unacceptable to Crazy Horse. He preferred living in open country in the traditional homeland of his people, and he did not want to take the white people's handouts. Along with many other Indians, he fled to continue living their traditional way of life.

The discovery of gold in the Black Hills in 1874 brought about more conflict, ending whatever peace had been gained through the 1868 Treaty of Fort

Laramie. The Black Hills, referred to by the Indians as Paha-Sapa and considered sacred, or *wakan*, is a holy place where the gods are thought to dwell. The treaty of Fort Laramie promised that the Black Hills were to belong to the Indians forever. The treaty was broken, however, when in 1874 it was overrun by whites. Ten troops of the Seventh Cavalry (commanded by Lieutenant Colonel George Armstrong Custer), two infantry companies, a photographer, a herd of cattle, and over one hundred wagons marched into the Black Hills for the stated purpose of a "scientific expedition."

What this expedition was actually doing was verifying the presence of gold in the Black Hills. Soon after, hoards of prospectors swarmed into the area, triggering a rush of attacks and raids on them by the Indians. The government offered to buy the Black Hills, an offer that immediately created a sharp division among Indians. Red Cloud was willing to negotiate to ensure peace, but Crazy Horse and Sitting Bull, who had never lived on the reservations or accepted annuities from the government, firmly refused. To them, no Indian land was for sale, no matter what the price. "One does not sell the earth upon which the people walk," Crazy Horse was known to say.

The United States government, seeing that no agreement would be reached, sent out an order that all the tribes within the territory had to go to the reservations or otherwise be considered hostile and a target for army retaliation. In the spring of 1876, after Crazy Horse and Sitting Bull ignored the order, the government sent a large military force into Sioux territory, planning to defeat the Indians permanently.

This declared war, begun in June 1876, was later to be known as the Battle of the Little Bighorn, or Custer's Last Stand. It ended with the spectacular victory of the Lakotas, Cheyennes, and Arapahos. Crazy Horse and Sitting Bull led the resistance, although Sitting Bull did not take part in the actual battle.

This battle was the last great success for the Lakotas. However, it also led to the final, voluntary surrender of Crazy Horse and eight hundred followers at Fort Robinson in May 1877. Even though the Indians had won the battle of Little Bighorn, they were unable to win the war. The following September, Crazy Horse was bayoneted at Fort Robinson during an attempt to confine him to a guardhouse. According to legend, he is buried in his homeland near Wounded Knee, South Dakota, the site of the famous massacre thirteen years later.

SEE ALSO:

Black Hills; Bozeman Trail and the Battle of a Hundred Slain; Fort Laramie Treaty of 1868; Little Bighorn, Battle of the; Sand Creek Massacre; Sitting Bull; Wounded Knee (1890).

SUGGESTED READINGS:

Champagne, Duane. *Native America: Portrait of the Peoples*. Detroit: Visible Ink Press, 1994.

Nabokov, Peter. *Native American Testimony*. New York: Viking Penguin, 1978.

Neihardt, John G. *Black Elk Speaks*. Lincoln: University of Nebraska Press, 1932.

CRAZY HORSE MEMORIAL

In South Dakota's Black Hills, a few miles west of Rapid City, a colossal sculpture, carved in the likeness of the famous Lakota (Sioux) warrior and chief Crazy Horse, is in progress. It stands on top of the 563-foot- (171-meter-) high Thunderbird Mountain, seventeen miles (twenty-seven kilometers) from the Mount Rushmore monument.

Although uncompleted, the Crazy Horse Memorial draws thousands of tourists each year. The finished statue will show Crazy Horse mounted on a horse, his left arm outstretched, pointing to the east. In this pose, Crazy Horse is shown responding to a white trader who asked him, "Where are your lands?" Crazy Horse responded, pointing toward the east, "My lands are where my dead lie buried."

It is estimated that the face of Crazy Horse will be completed by the year 2000. When it is finished, the Crazy Horse monument will be one of the largest three-dimensional sculptures in the world, larger even than Mount Rushmore. The size of the opening between the rider's arm and the horse's withers gives a clue to the size of this sculpture. The space will be large enough for a ten-story building to fit inside.

This model depicts what the Crazy Horse Memorial will look like, on the mountaintop in the background, when it is completed.

Construction of the Crazy Horse statue began in 1948 by Korczak Ziolkowski, an assistant working on the Mount Rushmore monument. Since then, the project has become the life's work not only of Korczak but of many members of his family. Its slow progress and the enormous expenditures of time, money, and labor on the project have become almost as big a story as the monument itself. It was Ziolkowski's intention that the statue reflect another side of U.S. history, to serve as a symbol of and memorial to all North American Indians. Today, South Dakota's most extensive Indian museum lies near the Crazy Horse statue along with a touring facility financed entirely through admission fees and contributions.

SEE ALSO:
Black Hills; Crazy Horse; Siouan Nations.

CRAZY SNAKE

Crazy Snake's English name is derived from the Creek name Chitto Harjo. *Chitto* means "snake" in Creek. *Harjo* is a warrior title that can be rendered as "recklessly brave." Therefore, Crazy Snake is a bit of a mistranslation of Chitto Harjo's name.

Chitto Harjo was leader of a faction of full-blood Creeks who opposed the 1899 tribal election of Pleasant Porter. Porter advocated compromise with the Dawes Commision, which was the government agency that would dissolve the tribes and allot tribal lands to individual landholders. Chitto Harjo had a following of loyal full-bloods who became known as the Snake faction. The Snakes, as they were also called, met at Hickory Ground, Harjo's home ceremonial ground. The Snakes attempted to set up a separate government, insisting on the authority of the treaty of 1832, which guaranteed the Creeks their lands in Indian Territory (present-day Oklahoma) forever. The treaty also granted the Creeks the right to establish their own Native police force, known as lighthorsemen, thereby also granting them the right to carry out and enforce their own laws.

In January 1901, the Snakes passed laws punishing Creeks who cooperated with the Dawes Commission, and they sent out their lighthorsemen to confront Indians who had accepted land allotments, leased lands to white farmers and ranchers, or hired white laborers, thus contributing to the large numbers of whites who were taking over the territory. The Snakes only issued stern warnings to their fellow tribespeople, but a panic ensued among non-Indian ranchers and farmers, and federal marshals

In the Iroquois creation story, the earth was created on a turtle's back, as depicted above. Today, many Native people refer to the earth as Turtle Island, preferring to use an indigenous conception of the world.

and the cavalry were called out. Chitto Harjo and one hundred of his followers were arrested and put in the federal jail at Muskogee, Indian Territory, where their hair was cut and two-thirds of them remained for several weeks without trial. Eventually, they were given suspended sentences and paroled, only to be arrested again in early 1902 after assembling once more at Hickory Ground, this time to discuss their failed corn crop. The same scenario ensued in which they were taken to Muskogee, but this time Chitto Harjo and a few of his followers were given jail terms.

Later in 1902, after spending several months in federal prison at Leavenworth, Kansas, Harjo was again meeting with his followers at Hickory Ground. Then and now, he has served Indians and non-Indians alike as a great example of the spirit of resistance that has sustained Native people, even when it has not met with favorable results.

SEE ALSO:
Creek; Dawes Commission; General Allotment Act.

CREATION STORIES

Almost every culture on earth has an explanation for the beginning of the world and for the beginning of life. Creation stories explain the original ordering of the universe: how something comes from nothing; how thoughts can lead to creations; how the first creatures emerge from inside the earth. Sacred and historic, a creation story also contains symbolic elements that indicate what is important in a society. The narrative may thus also become a model for the world, setting forth the spiritual, religious, philosophical, and even legal principles of a people.

Each Native American culture has a creation story that is unique and sacred to that society. These narratives underpin their society and inform their lifestyle. Although each story is unique, there are several story complexes that contain similar elements. Here are some of the more common ones.

In creation-by-thought stories, the world is a projection of a Creator's thoughts. This is a common theme shared by many people, including the Winnebagos and Omahas. A being, such as Earthmaker, sits in space. He begins to cry, and soon he notices that waters have formed. He begins to wish for light, and there is light. He thinks about the earth, and the earth comes into existence.

Creation-by-emergence stories are important in many Native American cultures of the Southwest. According to these stories, the people are living in another world underground. Because of some impending disaster—or simply a desire for a better place—the people choose to ascend into the current world. This is accomplished by climbing a vine, plant, tree, or mountain. After a scout is sent ahead into the new world, the people arrive through a hole in the ground.

The earth-diver complex is widespread throughout North America. It contains elements of creation by word and creation by clay. Usually some animals are on a raft on the sea in a world containing only water. Feeling the need for land, they dive one by one to see if they can bring up earth from the bottom of the ocean. Many arrive at the surface dead. Finally, a small animal makes the attempt and rises to the surface with dirt in its mouth and ears. This dirt expands and the earth is formed. Often it may be a single animal that dives multiple times in order to bring dirt to the surface.

All creation stories occur in a past time when the world is different. Animals may talk, and people can understand them and communicate with them. The world is filled with extremes (the sun shines all the time or it is always winter) and easy transformations (people are changed into animals or turned into stone). In spite of settings that may seem surreal in comparison to things as they are today, most of the creation stories contain guidance and prescriptions for daily life.

For example, in an Iroquois version of an earth-diver story, a chief living in the sky dreams that he sees the destruction of everything. After the dream, he is compelled to hurl a tree of lights and his wife down through a hole in the sky. From this, it can be concluded that dreams are important and require that the dreamer act on them in order to fulfill them.

Common themes like this abound in creation stories, as do common characters. There are culture heroes, for example, often in the form of twins, such as the Monster Slayers, who save their people. Coyote, the trickster, acts as the transformer (reducing the size of monstrous animals, for example) and, in some stories, is a creator figure as well. Two other

Because of high levels of mercury poisoning caused by the James Bay hydroelectric project, it is no longer safe for this Cree fisherman to eat the fish he catches.

SEE ALSO:
Coyote Stories; Storytelling; Tricksters.

CREE INDIANS AND THE JAMES BAY II PROJECT

The Cree homeland extends through large parts of what are now the Canadian provinces of Quebec and Ontario, a region inhabited by Native people since 4000 B.C.E. or earlier. For many years after Europeans began to colonize North America, the Crees had little contact with them.

Because of its harsh climate and inhospitality to agriculture, Cree land did not attract many immigrants. In the late twentieth century, however, the Crees were fighting the world's largest earth-moving project, which would have ruined large areas of their homeland. After several years of political activism and legal challenges involving the aid of environmental groups around the world, the Crees in 1994 convinced the utility company Hydro-Quebec to shelve the second phase of a major hydroelectric power project.

Before challenges from the outside forced them to convene a central council, the Crees had no centralized political organization that was comparable with those of the Iroquois and Huron peoples to the south. Even individual Cree bands and hunting parties had little or no organized political structure. Such a lack of structure is sometimes called *atomistic* by scholars. Instead of a formal council, Cree bands informally selected a wise elderly man, usually the head of a family, as a source of advice. This man exercised informal, limited influence.

figures that often appear in creation stories are Sky Father and Earth Mother or some variation of these. These figures are both human and supernatural, and they often instigate acts of creation.

Creation stories, the sacred stories of the people, are as different and unique as each culture. Even within a cultural group, different versions of the story may exist, further enriching and enlivening that culture's worldview and organizing principles.

— M. A. Stout

A Cree woman instructs her grandson in the art of making a snowshoe. The tenacity of Cree women in maintaining their culture, under the threat of the James Bay project, is vividly depicted by Chickasaw writer Linda Hogan in her 1995 novel *Solar Storms*.

As with the sachems (chiefs) of the more organized farming and hunting peoples to the south, the informal Cree leaders usually did not relish the exercise of power, probably because most of the people who sought their advice would have resented being dictated to. According to John J. Honigmann, who studied the Cree social structure, "Too great evidence of power is resented and feared by those whom it affects."

Cree life was marked only rarely by multifamily celebrations or rituals. Social life and social control were usually functions of the extended family instead. Outside the family, a Cree might appear ambivalent or reticent, usually out of respect for others' autonomy. People who violated social norms of interpersonal behavior became targets of gossip or sorcery, of a type that was widely used across the continent. Although their society was family based, the Crees recognized no clan or other kinship system between different bands. The society thus did not have the interconnections between settlements offered by the clans of the Iroquois, Hurons, and Cherokees.

Hydro-Quebec's James Bay II project (the first phase had been called James Bay I) proposed to dam eight major rivers that flow into James Bay in northern Quebec, at a cost of up to $170 billion. The purpose was to provide electricity for urban Canada and several states in the northeastern United States. The area is virtually unknown to most Euro-Americans but has been home for thousands of years to roughly ten thousand Crees, many of whom would be forced from their homeland by flooding and contamination. The Crees maintained that James Bay II should be shelved, based on hardships they had encountered as a result of James Bay I, completed in 1985 at a cost of $20 billion.

James Bay I had dammed or diverted five large rivers and flooded 4,000 square miles (10,400 square kilometers) of forest. By 1990, rotting vegetation had released about 184 million tons (167 million metric tons) of carbon dioxide and methane gas into the atmosphere, possibly accelerating global warming. Rotting vegetation also caused an acceleration in the microbial conversion of elemental mercury in submerged glacial rock to toxic methyl mercury, which was rapidly spreading through the food chain. Methyl mercury poisoning can cause loss of vision, numbness of limbs, uncontrollable shaking, and chronic neurological disease. By 1990, some Cree elders had twenty times the level of methyl mercury in their bodies that the World Health Organization considers safe.

A 1984 survey of people residing in Chisasibi on James Bay showed that 64 percent had elevated levels of this toxin in their bodies. The Quebec government responded to these findings by telling the Crees not to eat fish, one of their main sources of protein, just as the Mohawks of Akwesasne had been told to quit eating fish from the rivers of their polluted homeland.

The problems resulting from James Bay I were not limited to the flooding of forestland and the production of toxins. The large-scale construction in the area (including road building) brought in large numbers of non-Indians, a situation that is linked by Cree leaders with rising levels of alcoholism, abuse of other drugs, violence, and suicide in their communities. Traditional family patterns and ways of making a living have been breaking down as well; for example, one-fourth of the Crees' caribou herds—about twelve thousand animals—drowned as a result of James Bay I.

Personal stories illustrate just how pervasive environmental pollution has become in Cree country. The following anecdote, published in *Akwe:kon Journal*, is from Cree Glen Cooper:

"I have a story to tell about my father and the situation that occurred when he killed a moose . . . I remember this very vividly because it struck me very hard and personally. This was the first time that I had ever realized the direct impact that the hydroelectric development and the massive environmental destruction had on me.

"I went out to visit my parents in the woods. Early that day, my father went moose hunting. He was gone all day. Usually, he comes home around 5:00 P.M., when the sun begins to set. That evening, he came home around 9:30 P.M. Everybody was gone; my brother Alan and I were the only ones there. My father walked through the door, totally silent. I was standing in the kitchen, and I asked him if he had killed a moose. He did not respond to my question right away. I could tell my Dad was hurt. He gave my brother a hug and said, 'We can't eat it.' He said that he had killed a moose, but as he cut it open, he saw that the insides were full of mucus, the pancreas had white spots, the kidneys were very small, and the heart had water on it.

"He had tears in his eyes, although he did not cry bitterly. I remember a story I was told that says an elderly man never cries because he must stay strong for the young. My father, who was going to be sixty, wept before my eyes because he had killed a moose that he could not eat and feed his family with. This is one of the social impacts that hydroelectric development has on the Cree people and the Cree way of life."

— B. E. Johansen

SEE ALSO:
Akwesasne (St. Regis Reservation), Pollution of; James Bay Hydro-Electric Project.

CREEK

Contrary to what might be implied by *The Road to Disappearance*, the title of one of the most comprehensive books about Creek history, the Creeks have anything but disappeared.

As of 1994, members of the Oklahoma Creek Nation number 36,695 and comprise a sovereign nation existing within the borders of the United States that covers ten counties in East Central Oklahoma. Their Alabama kinfolk around Poarch, Alabama, also a federally recognized tribe, are descendants of Creeks who escaped removal from their homelands to Indian Territory (today Oklahoma) in the 1830s and number 2,106. In addition, there are a number of state-recognized Creek bands in Alabama.

Because of their larger numbers and the correspondingly larger Creek community in Oklahoma, Oklahoma Creeks have remained more traditional than their Alabama relatives. Oklahoma Creeks still maintain about eighteen ceremonial grounds where they continue to practice the stomp dance religion and retain the Creek language, which many Creek adults still speak. In recent years, however, there has been much contact between Oklahoma and Alabama Creeks, with Oklahomans making trips to Alabama to teach their relatives traditional stories, language, stickball, and stomp dancing.

According to traditional Creek storytelling, the nation was born when the earth opened up in the West near the Continental Divide and spit the people up from below its surface out into the broader landscape. The people journeyed eastward on a quest to discover the origin of the sun until they reached the Atlantic and could travel no more. Turning back, they decided to settle in the area of the Chattahoochee River in Alabama.

One of the most stirring tellings of this powerful story is a contemporary one that Creek elder Louis Littlecoon Oliver includes in his book *Chasers of the Sun: Creek Indian Thoughts*. Mr. Oliver, in poetic language and with a good measure of what can only be called Indian humor, recounts the ancient journey as if he were on it himself, employing the first-person plural "we" throughout: "We came pouring out of the backbone of this continent like ants."

Recalling the story through living memory as a result of his upbringing in the oral tradition, Oliver tells of the Creeks' experience as they head off toward the dawn: They follow an arrow for direction and encounter prophets who come down from the sun and instruct them in their most important rituals. These rituals include the maintenance of the ceremonial grounds and the Creek religion, which culminates in the annual Green Corn ceremony in late July or early August, the layout of the arbors and the proper seating of the clans, the correct use of medicines during the ceremonies, and instruction for the stickball game, at which Creeks excel.

It is important to note, as does Oliver, that this knowledge is contemporary, ongoing, and relevant, not a remnant of some vanishing culture. Stomp dancing, one of the religious rituals learned during the ancient migration, is still very popular among Creeks today.

According to the eighteenth-century writer and trader James Adair, the word *Creek* derives from the many streams and rivers in Creek country along which the Creeks settled. The Creeks' name for themselves is *Muskogee*, and they are part of the Muskogean language family, which includes the Seminoles, Choctaws, Chickasaws, and some other smaller southeastern tribes. A particular historical characteristic of the Creek confederacy was its tendency to incorporate smaller tribes that were con-

William McIntosh, an early nineteenth-century leader of the Lower Creeks, could not prevent the disastrous Creek civil war. This occurred during the War of 1812, when a faction of the nation, known as the Red Sticks, joined Tecumseh's pan-Indian alliance and plunged the Creek Confederation into civil war.

quered or forced into its area because of pressures from non-Native settlement. Even today, this tendency to bring smaller nations into the confederacy accounts for some of the differences in the Creek language from town to town in eastern Oklahoma.

The first contact of Creeks with Europeans occurred in March of 1540, when Hernando de Soto's men encountered the Lower Creek towns in southwest Georgia. In the latter quarter of the seventeenth century, the Creeks evolved from a loosely held confederacy to one of the most formidable groups of warriors on the continent. After the Yamasee War from 1716–1733, the Creeks tried to maintain a policy of neutrality in struggles between the French, Spanish, and English. The policy did not always hold, however, and the Creeks ended up involved in the Spanish Border War of 1739–1748, French-English hostilities from

1745–1748, war with the Cherokees from 1750–1752, and many other skirmishes, including involvement in the American Revolution, which split the Creek Nation into opposing parties.

The most far-reaching changes for the Creeks occurred in the nineteenth century, when, during the Andrew Jackson administration, they were illegally removed from their homelands in Alabama and western Georgia in the forced exodus to Oklahoma in the 1830s that resulted in tremendous losses. The historian Grant Foreman records the results of the genocidal policies of the Jackson administration in his book *Indian Removal* with statistics showing that the Creeks were in 1859 half in number—13,537—what they had been in 1832, and this was even after they had had more than twenty years to recover from removal. (Today, the size of the nation has tripled compared to its size after removal and is even double the size it was before the Creeks were forced into Alabama.)

The U.S. Civil War affected the Creeks just as dramatically as had removal. The Lower Town Creeks, who numbered many more mixed-blood citizens, had a few slaveholders, were more southern in their sympathies, and sided with the Confederacy. The Upper Town Creeks, many of whom were fullbloods with small farms and had no involvement in slavery, sided with the Union. The Civil War destroyed the majority of towns in Indian Territory (Oklahoma), and the population losses were as devastating as those during removal. There is historical speculation that tribes were purposefully stirred up against one another by the federal government in order to wipe out the Indian population of Oklahoma and open up the territory for white settlement.

In exchange for giving up their homelands in the 1830s, the Creeks had been promised lands in Oklahoma in perpetuity (forever), but after a short interlude of less than sixty years, beginning in the 1890s, the United States government illegally forced the Creeks and other Indian nations to accept individual land allotments, dissolve their nations, and become citizens of Oklahoma. This left millions of acres (hectares) open to the "sooners," settlers trying to get into Oklahoma. Their appropriation of Indian lands was in fact an act of theft committed in flagrant violation of agreements forged between the government and Indian nations. In the name

of the "settlement" of Oklahoma, the state continues to this day its celebration of this encroachment on Native lands. As Angie Debo, in her book *And Still the Waters Run*, and many other historians have documented, almost every single member of the Dawes Commission, the congressional body responsible for dissolving the tribes, was involved in Oklahoma land scandals.

Today, in the twentieth century, Creeks and other Indian people are trying to reassert their treaty status as sovereign nations. It is important to note that, contrary to most historical texts on Creeks, Creek culture did not end in 1907 at Oklahoma statehood and is vibrant in Oklahoma today. About eighteen stomp grounds are still active where Creeks practice the stomp dance religion, which culminates in the Green Corn Ceremony that occurs in late July or early August. The purpose of the Green Corn Ceremony is to renew the relationship of members of a particular ground (site) to earth and kin. The members take medicine, fast, dance, and play stickball. Green Corn lasts from Thursday until Sunday, though many grounds members camp in all week in preparation. An excellent description of the Green Corn Ceremony and stomp dancing is contained in Willie Lena's book *Oklahoma Seminoles: Medicine, Magic and Religion*.

One of the best ways to understand Creek history and culture, rather than reading only books by non-Natives that are biased toward the "disappearing Creek" point of view, is to read Creek writers' accounts of themselves. Creeks have produced a number of fine historians, fiction writers, and poets.

Of all the Creek writers, one of the most extraordinary is Louis Oliver, who passed away in recent years. Unfortunately, Oliver did not begin to write until he was well up in age, so the world will never know his full potential. The section entitled "Creek Indian Humor" in Oliver's book *Chasers of the Sun: Creek Indian Thoughts* conveys much of the same comic spirit embodied by *choffee*, the Creek trickster, Rabbit. These comic elements include the use of *'sticati* (literally, "Red Person," or Indian) English and depictions of Creek fullbloods in humorous encounters with each other and the larger outside white world. Oliver's work is more informative in regard to Indian humor than some recent critical studies that fail to recognize the strong roots of humor in the oral tradition and use, instead, Euro-American models to analyze indigenous humor.

Oliver was born in 1904, three years before Oklahoma statehood, when the land in Indian Territory still belonged to its rightful Native owners. He was a member of the Raccoon clan, and his Indian name was Little Coon. As Oliver explains in various autobiographical statements, a drunken Indian agent gave him the name Louis Oliver when Louis's mother refused to reveal his name to a member of the Dawes Commission attempting to enroll the family for allotments that would break up Indian Territory. In Little Coon's own work, he puts to use elements of Native and Euro-American cultures. In two of his works, *The Horned Snake* and *Estiyut Omayat*, he writes a Creek and English bilingual text. Today, Indian writers from many tribes remember and discuss Louis Oliver, grieving the tremendous loss his death brought to Indian people.

In addition to literature and storytelling, the Creeks have kept their culture viable in other ways. In eastern Oklahoma, towns with large Creek populations have Creek community centers with a variety of educational and recreational programs for young people. These programs range from cultural activities to sporting events. Some of these programs address a major concern of members of the Creek Nation—the preservation of the Creek language. In addition to programs that aim to maintain the Native language of the Creeks, many other institutions further the use of the language among Creek people. For example, many Creek Baptist and Methodist churches still conduct services in Creek with their own Creek hymnals and Bibles still in use. Like many other tribes, Creeks have also begun exercising their tribal sovereignty by establishing smoke shops and bingo parlors, both of which provide sources of revenue to the community.

— C. S. Womack

SEE ALSO:
Alabama; De Soto Expedition; Five Civilized Tribes; Gaming; General Allotment Act; Green Corn Ceremony; McIntosh, William; Oklahoma; Oliver, Louis Littlecoon; Removal Act, Indian; Tobacco.

SUGGESTED READINGS:
Corkran, David. *The Creek Frontier, 1540–1783*. Norman: University of Oklahoma Press, 1967.

Debo, Angie. *The Road to Disappearance*. Norman: University of Oklahoma Press, 1941.

Debo, Angie. *And Still the Waters Run*. New York: Gordian Press, 1966.

Lena, Willie, and James H. Howard. *Oklahoma Seminoles: Medicines, Magic, and Religion*. Norman: University of Oklahoma Press, 1984.

Littlefield, Daniel F. *Africans and Creeks: From the Colonial Period to the Civil War*. Westport, CT: Greenwood Press, 1979.

CREEK LITERATURE, CONTEMPORARY

Contemporary Creek (or Muscogee) literature owes much to Creek poet, journalist, and humorist Alexander Posey (1873–1908). Posey was the son of a Scotch-Irish father and a Creek mother. After being raised in Creek culture by his mother near Eufaula, Creek Nation, Indian Territory (later the state of Oklahoma), Posey attended Bacone Indian University during its early years when the school was located in Tahlequah, capital of the Cherokee Nation, Indian Territory. (The school later moved to Muskogee, Oklahoma, where it is still located.) At Bacone, Posey honed a love of writing and literature under the tutelage of a young Euro-American teacher from Indiana named Anna Lewis (no relation to the noted Choctaw historian of the same name). He also learned how to set type.

Much of Posey's writing, especially his humor, appeared in the *Indian Journal*, an Oklahoma Indian newspaper. Posey was a gifted Indian humorist, a satirist who used a sort of pidgin English to poke fun at American cultural values, especially its emphasis on materialism. His writing is full of puns and inside jokes. These jokes, which would have had little effect on non-Native people, were understood and greatly appreciated by Indians. They are credited with helping Oklahoma Indians maintain their sense of identity at a time when their nations were under siege by the U.S. Congress, which was attempting to terminate tribal political sovereignty by allotting Indian lands and extinguishing Indian culture by forcing Indians to assimilate into the dominant culture.

Above: In 1995, Creek poet Joy Harjo became the fourth recipient of the Lifetime Achievement Award from the Native Writers' Circle of the Americas.

Posey was also a prolific poet, but his poetry is not highly regarded today by academics, partly because its forms differ from the contemporary unrhymed and unstructured forms that are the fashion among many college faculties. Posey might have contributed to the literature of the novel, had not his career been cut short by his accidental drowning in flood waters at the age of thirty-four. During his short life, Posey contributed significantly to the education of his people, including serving as superintendent of public instruction of the Creek Nation. For a detailed study of Posey's life and work, see *Alex Posey: Creek Poet, Journalist, and Humorist,* by Professor Daniel F. Littlefield, Jr., of the University of Arkansas at Little Rock (University of Nebraska Press, 1992).

The recently deceased Louis Littlecoon Oliver (1904–1991), who late in life became one of the most influential contemporary Native American writers, was a Creek poet who was deeply influenced by the work of Alexander Posey. Oliver's appreciation of Posey is evident in his poem "Salute to Alexander Posey," which appears in Oliver's collection of his poetry and prose, *Chasers of the Sun: Creek Indian Thoughts* (Greenfield Review Press, 1990). Oliver, a full-blood Creek of the Alabama tribe of the Muscogee Confederation, was born in Koweta Town, in the Creek Nation, in 1904, three years before Oklahoma statehood. Orphaned as a child, he was raised by his grandmother and aunts. The federal government put him through the fifth grade, and then on his own he entered the high school at Bacone College, where he graduated in 1926. He studied the work of American and English writers, and the work of Posey, but he did no publishing until he was nearly eighty years old. Past the age of seventy, he was unaware of the idiom of contemporary Native American poetic expression (which is unrhymed free verse). Under the influence of Posey and non-Native poets, Oliver for many years attempted poetic expression in iambic pentameter and other such formal poetic constructions, but mostly as a hobby, not seeking to have the work published.

Left: Native writer Craig Womack characterizes his cultural heritage as that of "a Creekified Cherokee," referring to his Cherokee grandfather marrying into the Creek Nation, with his descendants being raised in the Creek culture.

Finally, he was given an opportunity to study the forms of contemporary Native American poetry (by attending a workshop for Native writers where he met some contemporary Native poets and acquired some of their books). He then began writing in the contemporary modes of expression and quickly gained the attention of the community of Native poets throughout the continent when his work began appearing in journals such as *The Greenfield Review, Vintage, The Beloit Poetry Journal, Stone Country,* and *Coyote's Journal.*

Oliver soon published a chapbook (a small book or booklet) of poems entitled *The Horned Snake* (Cross-Cultural Communications, 1982), which was followed shortly by a volume of poetry and prose, *Caught in a Willow Net* (Greenfield Review Press, 1983). In 1990, he published the previously mentioned *Chasers of the Sun.*

The esteem in which Oliver is held by his peers was apparent in 1992, when the First Books Awards (a publication prize competition) was inaugurated at an historic conference of nearly four hundred Native literary writers at the University of Oklahoma, a conference called "Returning the Gift." The First Book Award in prose was designated "The Louis Littlecoon Oliver Memorial Prose Award," a testimony to the late Mr. Oliver that is now continued in the annual First Book Awards competition.

At that 1992 Returning the Gift conference, a lifetime achievement award was also inaugurated for living Native writers, to be decided by annual vote of the membership of the Native Writers' Circle of the Americas. In 1995, the fourth annual recipient of the lifetime achievement award was Creek poet Joy Harjo.

Harjo was born in 1951 in Tulsa, Oklahoma. She graduated from the Institute of American Indian Arts, in Santa Fe, New Mexico, in 1968, received a bachelor's degree from the University of New Mexico in 1976, and a master of fine arts degree from the Writers' Workshop of the University of Iowa in 1978. Like Alexander Posey and Louis Littlecoon Oliver before her, she has become a writer whose influence extends far beyond her Creek people.

Her books of poetry include *She Had Some Horses* (Thunder's Mouth Press, 1983), *In Mad Love and War* (Wesleyan University Press, 1990), and *The Woman Who Fell from the Sky* (W. W. Norton, 1994). *Secrets from the Center of the World* (University of Arizona Press, 1989) is her collaboration with photographer and astronomer Stephen Strom. She has a number of books forthcoming, including a children's book entitled *The Goodluck Cat* (from Harcourt Brace), and she is editing an anthology of writing by Native women for the University of Arizona Press, titled *Reinventing the Enemy's Language.*

Harjo has been the recipient of many awards, including the William Carlos Williams Award from the Poetry Society of America, the Delmore Schwartz Award, and the American Indian Distinguished Achievement in the Arts Award. She has also received two National Endowment for the Arts Creative Writing Fellowships and a Witter Bynner Grant for Poetry.

She travels nationally and internationally giving poetry readings, and she plays saxophone with her band, Poetic Justice. She also teaches writing at the University of New Mexico.

There are a number of recently emerging Creek writers who have gained the attention of the Native literary community. Craig Womack is a Cherokee-Creek writer, enrolled in the Cherokee Nation but raised in Creek culture. His Cherokee grandfather moved to the Creek Nation, where he intermarried and adopted the culture of the Creeks. Womack took a bachelor's degree in agricultural economics at the University of Tennessee and, in 1995, a Ph.D in English at the University of Oklahoma. He presently teaches at the University of Nebraska at Omaha.

Womack's short story "Lucy, Oklahoma, 1911," in *Earth Song, Sky Spirit: Short Stories of the Contemporary Native American Experience,* edited by Clifford Trafzer (Doubleday, 1993), could easily appear in the appendix of Angie Debo's exposé of fraud and deceit in the government's dealings with Native people in Oklahoma, called *And Still the Waters Run* (Princeton University Press, 1940). Debo revealed, with scholarly precision, the monumental legal frauds in eastern Oklahoma earlier this century, in which Indians, as wards of the courts, lost their allotted lands, often through the mechanism of guardianship. The frauds were so pervasive that the Eastern District Court in Muscogee, Oklahoma, became the second-busiest federal district court in the United States, second only to the District of Manhattan in New York City.

In "Lucy, Oklahoma, 1911," Womack brings alive the human side of that period in a way that no historian can match. His story vividly depicts the misery of a young Creek boy whose court-appointed guardian is an abusive white farmer who is both ignorant of Native culture and contemptuous of it. In Womack's story, however, members of the local Native community exact justice in a manner that brings this cleverly written, well-paced story to a swift and fiery conclusion.

Womack is also an essayist and a poet whose essays and reviews have appeared in the *American Indian Culture and Research Journal* (University of California at Los Angeles) and whose poetry has appeared in *The Raven Chronicles: A Multicultural Journal of Literature, Art, and the Spoken Word* (Seattle, Washington). He has now turned his attention to book-length fiction, with a novel in progress.

Vincent Mendoza is a recently emerging Creek and Choctaw literary writer from McAlester, Oklahoma, whose book-length nonfiction manuscript, *Son of Two Bloods*, won the 1994 North American Indian Prose Award and is currently being published by the University of Nebraska Press. In *Son of Two Bloods*, Mendoza recounts his experiences as a Marine Corps postmaster in Vietnam.

The North American Indian Prose Award is an annual publication prize competition. It is sponsored by the University of Nebraska Press and the Native American Studies programs at the University of California at Berkeley and the University of California at Santa Cruz. The award was inaugurated in 1990 and is awarded in the spring of each year in ceremonies at the University of California at Santa Cruz. Mendoza is the fourth recipient of the award. Mendoza has now turned his attention to working in novel-length fiction.

— D. L. Birchfield

SEE ALSO:
General Allotment Act; Returning the Gift.

CREEK WAR (1813-1814)

SEE Creek; Jackson, Andrew; Tecumseh.

CREOLES

Creoles are people of European descent born in the West Indies, Latin America, or the southern United States. The term *creole* is derived from the Portuguese word *crioulo*, which means "home-raised" or "domestic." The term was first used during the sixteenth century to distinguish people born in the Western Hemisphere to parents of European birth from residents of the Western Hemisphere who had been born in Europe.

The meaning of *creole* varies from region to region. In Latin America, especially in Mexico, the term usually refers to people of pure Spanish ancestry. In the West Indies, the term applies generally to descendants of any European settlers. In Louisiana in the United States, the term refers primarily to French-speaking white descendants of early French or Spanish settlers or to people of mixed French or Spanish and African descent.

As French and Spanish immigrants settled along the various waterways of the Gulf Coast and the Mississippi delta in the present-day United States from 1699 onward, they interacted frequently with Native American tribes, most often the Caddos, Choctaws, Houmas, Chitimachas, and Atakapas. Native American traders and trappers helped the settlers survive the early years of colonization by supplying them with food, trade goods, and invaluable knowledge. Native Americans knew the country and its resources. They taught the settlers how to hunt, trap, cook, and build homes in a way that made the best use of what was available. This knowledge was essential to the first settlers' survival and was eventually incorporated into subsequent Creole generations. The move to experiment with old traditions and create new hardier habits that would benefit life in a new environment eventually became known as *creolization*.

When colonists brought slaves from Africa to the Americas, the Africans came with a deep knowledge of tropical environments and tropical agriculture. As slaves, they managed, in spite of the cruel and dehumanizing system under which they lived, to contribute substantially to the cultural mix. African influences were especially strong in music, dance, language, art, and religion. The Africans also brought valuable knowledge about exotic tropical fruits and vegetables as well as storytelling skills. These African influences quickly became an integral part of the developing Creole culture.

The term *creole*, then, refers to people, products, and an overall attitude toward life. Peppery Creole seasonings are indicative of the hardy, high-spirited people who grow and package them; home-grown Creole vegetables are fresh and tasty, Creole architecture can withstand the various stresses of the subtropical environment, and the Creole dialect reflects the daily life and diverse cultures of the Louisiana population.

The Creole population developed and dominated the cultural life of Louisiana through French and Spanish rule, the Acadian migration from Nova Scotia in the 1760s, and the Louisiana Purchase in 1803. It continued to flourish through later immigrations of German, Irish, English, and Scottish settlers. These varied peoples contributed the best parts of their original cultures to the regional melting pot of the Creole culture. Although many aspects of this eclectic identity have been lost to mainstream American culture, some Creole customs survive, and others are being resurrected in an attempt to retain the best of the traditions.

A Creole girl in Belize. Most Central American people of mixed European and Native descent consider themselves to be a part of the indigenous American culture into which they were born.

SEE ALSO:
African-Americans; Colonialism.

CROOK, GEORGE (1829–1890)

George Crook was raised on a farm in Ohio. In 1852, he graduated from the United States Military Academy at West Point near the bottom of his class. Yet he became a brigadier general in 1873 and a major general in 1888. General William T. Sherman praised him for his campaigns in the West and for his managerial abilities. Crook first served in the Northwest, where Native people were attempting to resist the intrusion of miners and colonizers onto their lands. In 1862, Crook was commissioned into the Union Army, where he gained distinction in combat during the Civil War, commanding a regiment of Ohio volunteers as a colonel.

After the war, Crook returned to the Northwest, where his application of U.S. military power helped bring an end to resistance by Native people to the occupation of their homelands. After receiving a commendation, he was sent to Arizona in 1871 to contain the tribes who were resisting U.S. colonization in Arizona, particularly the Apaches. By using "friendly" Indian scouts and applying constant pressure, Crook saw to it that most Apaches were soon confined to reservations.

In 1875, Crook commanded the Department of the Platte, where the discovery of gold in the

Black Hills foretold trouble between the Sioux and Euro-American prospectors. The latter were trespassing on the most sacred land of the Sioux, Paha Sapa (the Black Hills). Crook's first job was to clear the miners out of the Black Hills, which belonged to the Sioux by treaty. Soon, however, the U.S. government decided that it would not abide by its treaty obligations, and Crook was ordered to move against the Sioux. After a punishing campaign, Crook was defeated at the Battle of the Rosebud. This prevented him from connecting with the troops led by Lt. Colonel George Custer and other U.S. Army units, as planned, which may have contributed indirectly to Custer's defeat at Little Bighorn in 1876.

In 1882, Crook was returned to Arizona to deal with the Apaches. After several successes, Crook led an expedition into Mexico to convince Geronimo's Chiricahua Apache people to return to the San Carlos reservation. He returned to Arizona only with Geronimo's promise that they would follow. As months passed, Crook was ridiculed openly, but the Apache people returned later that year, as they had promised.

In general, Crook's principles for dealing with Indians included using negotiation, not just aggression, and attempting to refrain from killing women and children in combat. He gained a reputation for integrity. When Geronimo's band later left the reservation, Crook's methods were rejected in favor of harsher methods. Crook was relieved of command and reassigned to the Department of the Platte. He died in Chicago in 1890.

SEE ALSO:
Black Hills; Custer, George Armstrong; Geronimo.

CROW

The Crows call themselves Absarokas, which might be translated as "Children of the Large-beaked Bird." Other Native peoples have called them "Sparrowhawk," "Bird People," or "Crows," and Euro-Americans also called them Crows.

The Crows are a Siouan-language people. According to their oral traditions, they separated from their Hidatsa tribal relatives when they were living along the Missouri River in the central Great

A Crow party in Montana, traveling in winter, takes a break to prepare a meal.

Crows did not become expert equestrians by accident or by starting late in life. Here, in the splendor of a Montana summer afternoon, young Pretty Beads is as poised on horseback as White Arm.

Plains region, more than three hundred years ago, at about the time of the American Revolution. The people who would come to be known as Crows moved upstream on the Missouri to adopt a northern Plains culture at the edge of the Rocky Mountains in present-day Montana. The Hidatsas remained in their native area and eventually were decimated by a smallpox epidemic.

When the Crows reached the upper Missouri, it was the end of a long migration for them, one that had taken them all the way across the continent. At the time when Europeans first arrived on the North American continent, the Hidatsa ancestors of the Crows had been a sedentary agricultural people living in the northeastern woodlands, 2,500 miles (4,025 kilometers) from the future home of the Crows in Montana. However, when the Iroquois acquired European weapons and began experiencing pressures from European colonization in the Northeast, they pushed the Hidatsas westward. In gradual stages, the Hidatsas moved to the region of the Great Lakes and then onto the Great Plains, where the Crows separated from them.

Once the Crows adopted the use of the horse for hunting buffalo on the northern Plains, they all but abandoned the practice of agriculture, except for the cultivation of tobacco, at which they excel. Tobacco, and Tobacco Society ceremonials, are important in Crow culture, and both men and women participate in the tobacco societies. The Crows raise two kinds of tobacco; one is a medicine tobacco for ceremonials, which is raised with great care, and one is grown for ordinary use.

The Crows have a long tradition of friendly relations with the United States, dating from the hospitality with which they greeted the Lewis and Clark expedition in the first decade of the nineteenth century. In the last half of that century, both the Crows and the United States were sometimes at war with the same nations, especially with the Cheyennes, Arapahos, and Sioux. Thus, the Crows had a closer relationship with the United States than did any other northern Plains tribe. The Crows allowed the Bozeman Trail to pass through their country, along which streams of non-Native immigrants passed, headed for the Oregon country. The neighbors of the Crows, the Sioux, strenuously opposed allowing the Bozeman Trail to pass through their country and, under the leadership of Crazy Horse, succeeded in completely closing the trail for a time, even though several U.S. Army posts had been built along it to try to keep it open.

In 1804, Lewis and Clark estimated the Crow population to be about 3,500, with about 350 lodges. Their population was estimated to be about 4,500 in 1834. By 1890, their numbers had dropped to 2,287, and by 1904, their population had dropped to 1,826. During the last half of the nineteenth century, as contact with Euro-Americans rapidly increased, the Crows had fallen victim to the same European infectious diseases, such as smallpox, that ravaged the populations of other Native peoples. The twentieth century has seen a steady recovery of their numbers.

By a treaty of peace and friendship with the United States in 1825, the Crow homeland was formally recognized as a block of land encompassing 38.5 million acres (15.4 million hectares) in present-day Montana and Wyoming. After the U.S. Civil War, however, the U.S. government sought a drastic reduction in the amount of Crow land. By the treaty of Fort Laramie, in 1868, more than 75 percent of the Crow land was transferred to the United States, leaving the Crows with about 9 million acres (3.6 million hectares).

The size of the Crow Reservation continued to be reduced as the United States repeatedly sought more Crow land near the end of the nineteenth century and early in the twentieth century. In 1882, Crow land was exchanged in return for the construction of some houses for the Crows. In 1890 and 1905, the federal government made outright purchases of Crow land. The 1890 agreement paid the Crows $946,000 and reduced their holdings to about 3 million acres (1.2 million hectares). The United States paid the Crows less than five cents an acre for the land. Further reductions followed, and today the Crows own only about 1.5 million acres (0.6 million hectares), which still leaves them in possession of the largest reservation in Montana.

In the twentieth century, the Crows have struggled economically. Industry has been difficult to attract to the reservation. Some land has been placed in agricultural production. Cattle raising is a more important economic activity, but it had a very slow start. As late as 1953, fifty-four ranches on the Crow Reservation, which were being operated by Indians, had an average of only forty-eight cattle per ranch. Much of the rangeland on the reservation, as is true of most reservations in the northern Plains, have been leased to non-Indian cattle ranchers, an arrangement that brings in much-needed cash but builds nothing for the future. During the winter months, unemployment sometimes reaches 65 percent, and the average annual unemployment rate is nearly 30 percent.

In 1948, the Crows adopted a written constitution that provides for a form of government called a general council, which is similar to a town meeting. In this arrangement, each enrolled adult member of the tribe who is present at a meeting of the general council is entitled to vote. A chairman, vice chairman, secretary, and treasurer are elected every two years.

The Crow Agency is located south of Hardin, Montana, not far from Interstate 90. Custer Battlefield National Monument is located near the Crow Agency and is the scene of an annual reenactment at the site of the battle on Little Bighorn Creek. The most important event during the year is the Crow Fair each August, which is one of the largest Indian gatherings on the continent. Some of the finest beadwork crafted by American Indians is on display at the Crow Fair. The Crows are especially well known for their floral patterns and for their beaded horse gear, which is on display during the parade. A large powwow is also a part of the fair, during which the flattened roach headdresses of the Crows are distinctive as Crow participants dance with American Indians from tribes throughout the continent. Another distinctive feature of the Crow Fair is the large number of tipis that can be seen during the celebration.

— D. L. Birchfield

SEE ALSO:
Bozeman Trail and the Battle of a Hundred Slain; Hidatsa; Lewis and Clark Expedition; Montana; Tobacco.

SUGGESTED READINGS:
Frey, Rodney. *The World of the Crow Indians*. Norman: University of Oklahoma Press, 1987.

Medicine Crow, Joseph. *From the Heart of the Crow Country: The Crow Indians' Own Stories*. New York: Orion Books, 1992.

Yellowtail, Thomas. *Yellowtail, Crow Medicine Man and Sun Dance Chief: An Autobiography*. Norman: University of Oklahoma Press, 1991.

CROW DOG (1835–1910)

Crow Dog (Kangi Sunka) was a leader of the Brulé Sioux. He is regarded by many as a heroic figure: a man who was committed to protecting his people's interests and who kept his tribe together in difficult and challenging times. His name came to him during a vision, in which Crow Dog and his people were warned by a coyote of an impending attack by white settlers and Crow Indian scouts. In the vision, Crow Dog was seriously injured, and after his health was restored by two coyotes, he was shown back to his people by a crow.

Crow Dog was a leader who firmly resisted federal authority. He was associated with Crazy Horse, whom Crow Dog accompanied on the day of Crazy Horse's surrender and brutal slaying at Fort Robinson in 1877. Through his leadership, Crow Dog prevented further bloodshed on that day by riding between the U.S. soldiers and the angry Sioux who were intent on avenging Crazy Horse's murder.

Crow Dog was also responsible for killing a Brulé chief named Spotted Tail. On August 5, 1881, Crow Dog, who was angered over a tribal leadership dispute, assassinated Spotted Tail by shooting him as he rode along a trail on the Rosebud Reservation in present-day South Dakota. Crow Dog was arrested two days later by Hollow Horn Bear, another Brulé chief, and taken to Fort Niobara. Black Crow, who was thought to be a conspirator in the killing, was also arrested. The case was settled by a tribal council meeting that, following Brulé law, ordered peacemakers sent to both Crow Dog's and Spotted Tail's families. Crow Dog's family paid six hundred dollars, eight horses, and one blanket to the family of Spotted Tail, and harmony was restored within the Brulé tribe. However, a year later, Crow Dog was tried in the Dakota territorial court, convicted of murder, and sentenced to death.

Crow Dog's case was appealed. His conviction was overturned in a landmark U.S. Supreme Court decision that ruled that the federal courts had no jurisdiction over crimes committed on reservation treaty lands. Thus, it was recognized that American Indians had sovereignty and were entitled to uphold their own laws. But in 1885, in response to the Crow Dog case, Congress passed the Major Crimes Act, which provided that an Indian who committed a major crime against another Indian, such as murder or burglary, was subject to the laws of the territory or state where the crime was committed. And so, Crow Dog's case played a key role in the expansion of federal jurisdiction over events occurring on Indian land.

Crow Dog was a leader of the Ghost Dance movement and led his people to the Badlands of South Dakota to await their rebirth in 1890. He died in 1910.

SEE ALSO:

Crazy Horse; Ghost Dance Religion; Indian Major Crimes Act; Siouan Nations; Spotted Tail.

CROW DOG, HENRY (1899–1985)

Henry Crow Dog was among the most powerful and respected spiritual leaders of the twentieth century. The father of Indian activist Leonard Crow Dog, Henry Crow Dog greatly helped keep the Lakota language and many of the tribe's traditions alive.

He recalled growing up in a time when his tribe's tipis and abundant game disappeared, leaving behind a sparse diet of muskrats, squirrels, berries, and roots. Through the years, Crow Dog taught his son and others how to hunt and fish in the old ways. For example, Crow Dog would drop burning kindling wood into a rabbit hole, then kill the rabbit by bashing its head with a stick when it popped out of the ground.

In his thirties and forties, Crow Dog made a living as a railroad laborer and migrant worker. But despite much hardship, Crow Dog steadfastly refused to sell his family's land allotment, calling it "Crow Dog's Paradise." It was an important spiritual place in the Indian universe.

According to his wife, Mary (1900–1987), Crow Dog was a master craftsman. He built the house on Crow Dog's Paradise with his own hands and also made feathered bonnets and dance regalia. He made extra money to feed his family and the many visitors by cutting and selling wood.

Crow Dog joined the Native American Church in the 1930s after Catholic Church officials refused to let him bury his son in a cemetery because it was for "good Christians only." He soon developed a

Leonard Crow Dog, a spiritual leader of the American Indian Movement (AIM), is photographed at Wounded Knee, South Dakota, on March 4, 1973, where he has been attempting to negotiate a peaceful settlement to problems on the Pine Ridge Reservation.

strong reputation within the Indian religious movement. Native Americans and others came from around the country to hear Henry and other elders tell of the old ways. They sparked a fire for knowledge in the hearts of many that is burning yet today.

SEE ALSO:

Crow Dog, Leonard; General Allotment Act; Native American Church.

CROW DOG, LEONARD (1942–)

Leonard Crow Dog is a fourth-generation Brulé Lakota spiritual leader who was a key participant in several landmark American Indian protests. In November 1972, Crow Dog was among several hundred protesters who took over the Bureau of Indi-

an Affairs offices in Washington, D.C., for a full week. The takeover came as the culmination of "The Trail of Broken Treaties," a caravan from San Francisco to Washington designed to confront the U.S. government with numerous issues of concern to Native people, including treaty violations. Following an agreement from the Nixon administration to review the issues, the siege ended with U.S. government officials agreeing to give protesters sixty thousand dollars for gas money and bus fare to go home.

Just four months later, Crow Dog revived the illegal Ghost Dance at Wounded Knee, South Dakota, site of the most publicized slaughter of American Indian people in history. Here, in 1890, hundreds of Sioux were killed by U.S. soldiers for participating in a Ghost Dance. Although the Ghost Dance in 1973 was not advertised, about forty Indians from tribes around the country came to South Dakota to participate. It was the first time the drumless dance had been performed in eighty-three years.

The next month, Crow Dog and about three hundred others began the occupation of Wounded Knee, taking over a trading post and holding it for seventy-one days, an event that attracted media attention to the Pine Ridge Reservation in South Dakota.

Over the years since then, Crow Dog has been a road man in the Native American Church. Road men are leaders of the church who are allowed by federal officials to transport peyote buttons used as sacraments during all-night ceremonies. Thousands of Indians and non-Indians have visited the home of the Brulé Lakota spiritual leader over the years to participate in the Sun Dance or various other ceremonies.

In 1995, Crow Dog recounted his life story in a book simply called *Crow Dog*. The book is an outstanding record of Lakota history and traditions. As Crow Dog modestly explains in the book, because he had never learned to read or write, he dictated his story to author Richard Erdoes.

SEE ALSO:
American Indian Movement; Bellecourt, Clyde and
Vernon; Bureau of Indian Affairs; Crow Dog, Henry;
Crow Dog, Mary; Ghost Dance Religion; Longest Walk;
Trail of Broken Treaties; Wounded Knee, Confronta-
tion at (1973).

CROW DOG, MARY (1953–)

Mary Crow Dog brought the 1973 takeover of
Wounded Knee back into the spotlight in the 1990s
through a pair of powerful books. The first, called
Lakota Woman, tells the story of the American Indian Movement protests during the 1970s from a
woman's perspective. The follow-up book, called
Ohitika Woman, was written after Mary had ended
her traditional Indian marriage to Lakota spiritual
leader Leonard Crow Dog and went by her family
name of Brave Bird.

Mary's books, which were cowritten with noted
author Richard Erdoes, received critical acclaim
because of the way they provide new insight into
American Indian cultures and the 1970s protest
movement. In telling her story, she has also managed to chronicle modern Sioux tribal life in a way
that no one else had done up to that point. She
also explains the significance of ceremonies and
customs performed by her former husband, Leonard.

In *Lakota Woman,* Mary also tells of her close
friendship with Anna May Pictou Aquash, a Micmac whose slaying in the 1970s is being reinvesti-
gated in the 1990s, after a long protest by Native
people that the FBI failed to conduct a proper investigation and may have even conspired in her death.
She also provides an intimate portrait of such American Indian Movement leaders as Dennis Banks
and Russell Means, and she describes how she gave
birth to her first child as bullets were flying during
the Wounded Knee takeover.

From the Rosebud reservation in South Dakota, Mary chose to shun the spotlight from her literary success. She made some appearances but
ignored numerous requests for interviews that could
have brought her more renown. Mary's story and
the Wounded Knee saga came to television in 1994,
when TBS created a 110-minute version of *Lakota Woman.*

Mary and Leonard's son, Pedro, has become a
spiritual leader for the Lakota people, running peyote meetings and sweat lodge ceremonies.

SEE ALSO:
American Indian Movement; Aquash, Anna Mae; Pic-
tou; Bellecourt, Clyde and Vernon; Crow Dog, Leonard;
Ghost Dance Religion; Longest Walk; Trail of Broken
Treaties; Wounded Knee, Confrontation at.

CUBA

Cuba is the westernmost and largest island in the
Antilles chain in the Caribbean Sea. The coast of
Florida lies 90 miles (145 kilometers) to the north
across the Straits of Florida. Haiti lies 50 miles (81
kilometers) to the east across the Windward Passage,
and Jamaica lies some 90 miles (145 kilometers) to
the south. The island is long and narrow, running
from the northwest to the southeast, and is approximately 750 miles (1,208 kilometers) in length.

Cuba was a colony of Spain from 1511 until
1898. U.S. troops occupied Cuba until the first
national election in 1902 (and briefly again a few
years later). On January 1, 1959, revolutionaries
under the command of Fidel Castro seized power
and established a socialist state.

Cuba was first encountered by Europeans on
October 27, 1492, when Columbus touched shore
during his first voyage to the Americas. At that
time, there were primarily two Native groups inhabiting the island, the Guanahatabeyes and the Tainos. There is some controversy over the name and
number of the Native peoples of Cuba because the
only record we have remaining of them comes from
the archaeological record left behind by the Indian people and from Spanish writings during the
conquest. The Guanahatabeyes occupied the western end of Cuba, possibly having been pushed there
by the Tainos. It is likely that they were descended from the original inhabitants of the island and
that they lived in caves instead of villages. The
Tainos, more recent occupants of Cuba, lived in
large villages and cultivated fields of tobacco, cotton, corn, and potatoes. Their society had a rec-
ognizable social structure that was headed by a chief,
or cacique.

Diego Velazquez established the first permanent Spanish settlement on Cuba in 1511, founding the town of Baracoa on the northeast shore. The Spanish crown sponsored this occupation, lured as always by the promise of gold and the need for more Indian slaves.

The Tainos greeted the Spanish with a fierce and hostile defense of their homeland. The resistance was led by a chieftain named Hatuey, an exile from the island of Hispaniola, where he had already experienced Spanish conquest. The Tainos had neither the military skills nor the weaponry to defeat the Spanish; when Hatuey was finally captured, tried, and burned at the stake, resistance diminished considerably. Pacification between Spain and the Tainos was aided by the famous Fray (Friar) Bartolomé de Las Casas, who preceded the Spanish into Indian villages and convinced them to cooperate with their conquerors. (Las Casas is probably best known for his illustrations and graphic descriptions of the brutality brought upon Native people by the Spanish invaders.)

Diego Velazquez implemented the *encomienda* system in Cuba. Like the mission system used elsewhere in Spanish colonies, it was a political system designed to give the Spanish control of Indian populations. Under the encomienda system, Natives were assigned to a Spaniard who would extract labor and tribute from them. The Spaniard in turn was obligated to the crown to Christianize the Natives, transforming them into obedient Spanish subjects. This system was no bargain for Cuba's Native population, which declined steadily under Spanish occupation because of disease, maltreatment, and emigration. From an estimated sixty thousand Native Cubans at the time of conquest in 1511, the number had dropped to five thousand by 1550.

After they had decimated the Native populations, the Spanish began to import slaves from Africa as laborers. Indigenous people who survived the sixteenth century in Cuba continued to live under their own cacique into the early 1900s, and they continue to live in Cuba today.

SEE ALSO:
Cacique; Caribbean, Indigenous Cultures of; Columbian Exchange; Columbus, Christopher; Demography, Native; Encomienda; Hispaniola; Las Casas, Bartolomé de; Taino.

CULTURAL OPPRESSION

SEE Acculturation.

CULTURE AREAS OF NORTH AMERICA

Anthropologists have divided the North American continent into several culture areas to help them study how Native cultures have evolved and how they interact with both their environments and with other cultures. The culture areas of North America are usually designated as Arctic, Subarctic, Northwest Coast, Plateau, Great Basin, California, Great Plains, Northeastern Woodlands, Southeastern Woodlands, Southwest, and Mesoamerica.

The location, topography, and climate of a culture area are major factors in how its early inhabitants got food—whether it was by farming, hunting and fishing, gathering and ecological management, or a combination of these methods. The food supply, in turn, was often the deciding factor in whether people built permanent villages or had seasonal locations. The way a culture developed had a lot to do with the environment of its culture area.

Arctic and Subarctic Culture Areas
The Arctic and Subarctic culture areas comprise a region that extends more than five thousand miles (eight thousand kilometers) across the far north, from the Aleutian Islands off the southwestern tip of Alaska all the way to Labrador in Canada. Although most of this region lies in Canada and northern Alaska, it also extends around the northern rim of North America to eastern Greenland and to northern Russia (Siberia).

Linguists have divided the early inhabitants of this region into four language family groups: the Athabascans of the western Subarctic, the Algonquians of the eastern Subarctic, the Aleuts of the Aleutian Islands, and the Inuit (Eskimo) of the Arctic north. Each of these language groups is made up of smaller divisions and tribes.

Athabascan-speaking groups included the Dogrib, Hare, Kutchin, Slavey, Koyukon, Mountain, Slave, Tanaina, Yellow-knife, Dunne-za or Beaver, and others. Most Athabascans now call themselves Tinneh or Dene (or Dena), which means "people" or "humans."

The Algonquian language group includes the Cree, Naskapi, Montagnais, Micmac, Malecite, Ojibwe (who are also known as Chippewa and call themselves Anishinabe), and other nations; northern Algonquian peoples call themselves Innu. Another Algonquian group, the Métis, are the descendants of nineteenth century Dene, Ojibwe, and Cree marriages with French and Scottish fur traders.

Inuit groups include the Mackenzie or Inuvialuit, Copper, Netsilik, Caribou, Iglulik, Ungava, and North Alaskan or Inupiaq, among others. *Innu*, like *Inuit*, is a word meaning "persons" or "human beings."

Early inhabitants of the Arctic had to endure long, bitterly cold winters, with few hours of sunlight each day and land that was almost always frozen solid. Even in summer, it was only the surface ice that thawed. The subsoil remained frozen year-round, creating a treeless environment called tundra, where the only vegetation were lichens, herbs, mosses, and stunted shrubs. To the south, the cold, wet forests of the Subarctic provided a climate only a little less harsh. Heavy rains in the summer, deep snows in the winter, and endless chains of rivers, lakes, swamps, and *muskeg* (waterlogged land) made travel impossible except by canoe, toboggan, dogsled, or snowshoes.

However, most Arctic and Subarctic cultures used the bitter climate to their advantage. Herds of migrating caribou or other game such as moose, bear, and deer were easy to track in the snow. People speared fish through holes they cut in the ice and, where available, hunted sea mammals, such as whales, walruses, seals, and sea lions, in watertight, one-person hunting vessels called kayaks.

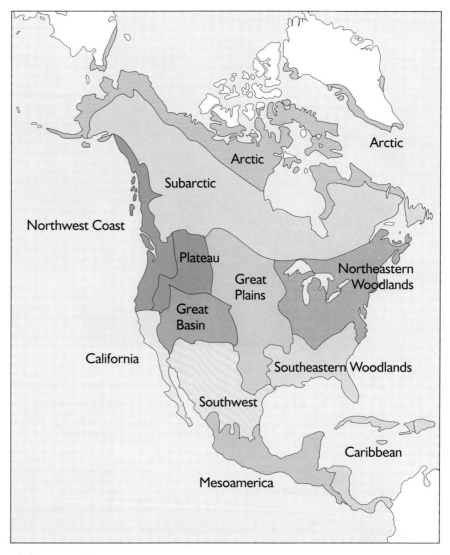

A depiction of the North American continent according to its division by anthropologists into regions of Native culture.

This meant they usually had an abundant supply of food. The hides of the caribou grew dense and thick in the winter and, when sewn together, made clothing so protective that people wearing them could comfortably withstand temperatures of fifty to sixty degrees below zero F. (forty-five to fifty degrees below zero C.) and more.

Even their housing took advantage of the cold. Some groups built domed snow houses; others built homes of stone, whalebone, and sod, which they clustered together in small villages. All were effective at keeping them warm and dry.

The European fur trade of the sixteenth and seventeenth centuries greatly disrupted the Subarctic cultures by introducing disease, alcohol,

A Nenet woman feeds boiled fish to a young reindeer at a camp in Yamal, Siberia, Russia. In addition to including parts of Canada and the United States, the Arctic culture area extends into northern Russia and western Greenland.

trading posts, missions, and other manifestations of Western exploitation of the area and its people.

Northwest Coast Culture Area

The Northwest Coast culture area stretches over 2,000 miles (3,220 kilometers) from southern Alaska to northern California but extends only 150 miles (242 kilometers) from east to west at its widest point. Several mountain ranges (like the Coast and Cascade Ranges) cut the area from north to south, often coming right down to the edge of the ocean where they form steep, rocky cliffs. A large part of this culture area consists of islands that are really the tips of submerged mountains in the Coast Range. These islands include Vancouver Island, the Queen Charlotte Islands, and the Alexander Archipelago.

The climate is surprisingly warm for an area so far north. The Japanese current warms the ocean along the coast and causes moisture-laden winds to blow inland, providing a warm but very wet climate, perfect for the giant evergreen trees that cover the area. Only the mountain tops and steep rock faces are treeless.

Unable to live in the dense, dark forests, Northwest Coast Indians usually lived right at the ocean's edge, building their villages on narrow gravel and sand beaches. For the most part, they lived in large, multifamily, gabled houses made of hand-split red cedar planks. Many people carved their family crests and clan affiliations into the house posts and door poles (sometimes called totem poles).

Northwest Coast cultures are considered remarkable for a number of reasons. They produced a high culture (equal to the Temple Mound peoples of the Southeast or the Pueblo of the Southwest) without the benefit of either agriculture or pottery. Northwest Coast peoples were also the only high culture in the northern Western Hemisphere not affected by the ancient civilizations of Mexico. Instead, there is evidence that they may have been in contact with cultures in northeast Asia.

One reason for their highly developed culture was an abundant food supply. The sea provided sea mammals and saltwater fish. Freshwater streams also carried an abundant supply of fish, particularly salmon. Forests were filled with elk, deer, bears, and mountain goats, and there was always an abundance of roots, berries, nuts, and shellfish to gather. Not only did Northwest Coast inhabitants not have to farm for food, they could do almost all of their hunting and fishing in spring and summer, then smoke or dry the surplus and stockpile it for the rest of the year. This gave them the time to spend the mild winters creating art, holding ceremonial rituals, and carrying out elaborate giveaways called potlatches. Northwest Coast people are particularly known for the fantastic and intricate woodcarvings that decorated their homes, dugout canoes, chests, masks, and food-serving boxes. They also created beautifully decorated blankets, baskets, mats, and jewelry. Both individual and group wealth were considered very important, and social status was measured by the number of possessions a person had and could give away, possessions such as cedar-bark blankets, dentalium shells, dried fish and fish oil, dugout canoes, and slaves.

From north to south, major Northwest coast tribes include the Tlingit, Haida, Tsimshian, Kwakiutl, Nootka, Salish, Coos, Tolowa, Yurok, Karuk, and Hupa.

Plateau Culture Area

The Plateau culture area is the highland area lying between the Rocky, Coastal, and Cascade Mountain Ranges north of the Great Basin. The Columbia River flows through this territory, and the Plateau covers what is today southeastern British Columbia and parts of Washington, Oregon, Montana, Idaho, and northern California.

The mountain ranges that surround the Plateau get enough rain each year to support giant evergreen forests (including some of the tallest trees in the world), but because the mountains trap most of the rain clouds, the flatlands and rolling hills of the Plateau are so dry that they primarily support only grasses and sagebrush. The sparse ground vegetation meant that early inhabitants could hunt very little game. There were some elk, deer, and bears at the edge of the forests, but only antelope and jackrabbits lived out on the dry plains of the Plateau.

While the land could not supply much food, the Plateau's rivers could. The people of the Plateau did not farm along the Columbia and other smaller rivers but lived on many kinds of fish (salmon being the most important) and the berries, roots,

A Yakima engages in an ancient practice of his people, netting chinook salmon in the Klickitat River, a tributary of the Columbia River in Washington.

and bulbs that grew along the river beds. For the most part, Plateau peoples lived in small, independent villages of fifty to one hundred people each, although some villages were much larger. In summer, they abandoned these villages for camps at fishing sites and berry-collecting or root-digging sites.

After 1740, when the use of horses started to spread northward, Plateau peoples used them to participate in the great bison hunts. This improved their standard of living—but not for long. Euro-American and European fur trappers arrived during the early nineteenth century, followed by missionaries and tens of thousands of colonizers. By 1860, severe disruptions, especially those brought by disease, had occurred in the lives of Plateau peoples, who nevertheless continue to endure in the region today.

Some of the best-known Plateau tribes are the Flathead, Kutenai, Nez Perce, Okanogan, Shuswap,

Spokane, Yakima, Coeur d'Alene, Lillooet, Thompson, and Umatilla. The languages of most of these groups are of either the Salishan or the Sahaptian families.

Great Basin Culture Area

The Great Basin refers to a large, bowl-shaped area of desert in the western part of North America, an area that includes practically all of what is today Nevada and Utah, as well as parts of Oregon, Idaho, Wyoming, Colorado, and California. This sunken desert area is surrounded by highlands—the Rocky Mountains to the east, the Sierra Nevada Mountains to the west, the Columbia Plateau to the north, and the Colorado Plateau to the south. Because of the dryness and the basin's extremes of heat and cold, little grows there, just low grasses, sagebrush, and juniper and piñon trees.

Because of this barren environment, few early Great Basin inhabitants practiced any form of agriculture. Instead, they hunted and gathered to survive. They caught desert jackrabbits, rodents (like field mice, kangaroo rats, gophers, and ground squirrels), a few birds, some snakes and lizards, and insects such as grasshoppers. Coyotes were plentiful but were not eaten because people believed they were endowed with supernatural power. Mostly, however, Basin peoples gathered edible wild plants like berries, seeds, and nuts. Because of their food economy, the non-Indian newcomers labeled the Basin Indians "Diggers," a derogatory name that is still sometimes used to refer to Great Basin cultures. Most Indians in this region constantly traveled in search of food, usually in small groups of extended families, living in simple, cone-shaped structures made out of poles and brush, called *wickiups*. Hunting conditions improved somewhat for basin tribes in the eighteenth century when horses were introduced to the area. For a while, the people successfully used horses to hunt bison.

Four of the major tribal groups in this area—the Paiute, Ute, Shoshone, and Bannock—speak Numic (Shoshonean) languages. The only exception is the Washo tribe in the west, which speaks a Hokan dialect.

Tribal leaders were usually respected male elders, and there was very little conflict between tribal groups. The first non-Native colonizers treated the Indians in this region with great cruelty, but the people have endured. Today, Shoshones in the region still practice their traditional round dances.

California Culture Area

The California culture area includes most of the central and coastal areas of the present-day state of California, as well as perhaps the lower California

Eager anticipation and cultural pride can be seen in the face of this woman as she awaits the Grand Entry at a Shoshone/Bannock powwow.

peninsula, called Baja California, that is now part of Mexico. The Sierra Nevada range and another, smaller range further west run north to south; between the two mountain ranges, in the heart of the culture area, is the Great California Valley. The northern end of this huge valley receives enough rain each year to support tall forests, while the southern end, the Mojave Desert, is dry.

Aside from the dry areas, most of the California culture area provided its early inhabitants with plenty of game and plant foods. Crops were grown in various parts of northern California and as far south as Death Valley. Most Native Californians practiced an advanced system of ecological management: "herding" deer and "farming" native grasses and other species of plants. The main staple of their diet was the acorn, which they shelled, dried, and then pounded into flour for meal, bread, and soup. They also ate many other plants, including berries, seeds, nuts, greens, roots, bulbs, and tubers, as well as insects such as caterpillars and grasshoppers. California Indians hunted deer, ducks, geese, and swans with bows and arrows and set snares and traps to catch smaller game like rabbits. Lakes, rivers, and streams offered a plentiful supply of fish. Along the ocean, they used clubs to hunt sea mammals like seals and otters and collected clams, oysters, and mussels from tidal basins.

Because it was relatively easy to find food, California Indians did not have to spend all their time hunting and gathering and therefore had time for leisure pursuits like art and games. They were particularly known for their durable and beautifully decorated basketwork, their wood and bone carvings, their pottery, and for musical instruments such as flutes, clappers, and drums. There was a good deal of trading between tribes, and people often used strings of shells as money.

California tribes were often organized as interrelated villages. A central village would often be surrounded by smaller groups, each an extended family or clan presided over by the clan's headman. Typical houses were cone-shaped pole constructions covered with grass or cattails or domed, bark- or earth-covered pit houses. People traveled by foot and by water.

Religion played a major role in almost all early California cultures. In some villages, a single medicine person had the power to heal illness and invoke spirits. In others, secret societies shared these spiritual powers. Initiation ceremonies and death rites were very important, and some cultures used hallucinatory plants like jimsonweed to produce spiritual visions.

Juan Rodriguez Cabrillo first sailed along the coast of California in 1542, but the Spanish did not establish their first California mission to convert local peoples to Christianity until 1769. The so-called Mission Indians include the Cahuilla, Diegueno, Gabrileno, Luiseno, and Serrano. These Mission Indian peoples have had their populations greatly reduced. The hordes of non-Natives arriving in California during the gold rush of 1849 massacred many California Indians and caused severe disruptions in the lives of Indians throughout the region. Despite great losses and hardships, the Native peoples of California, and their cultures, endure today.

It is estimated that from three hundred thousand to one million people, divided into a large number of independent communities or confederations, lived in the region at the time of European contact. Cultural groups include the Modoc, Pomo, Pit River, Chumash, Ohlone (Costanoan), Maidu, Miwok, Wintun, Yokuts, Yuki, Cahuilla, Kamia, and Luiseno.

Great Plains Culture Area

Anthropologists define the Great Plains (or Plains-Prairie) culture area as the territory extending from the Mississippi River west to the Rocky Mountains and from what are today the provinces of Manitoba, Saskatchewan, and Alberta in Canada south to central Texas. Most of the terrain in this region is one of two different types of grasslands. The Mississippi Valley region is an example of the first type—prairies or tall grass plains. Because these areas get a good deal of rain each year, the grass grows tall. Further west, where the annual rainfall is a lot less, the grasslands are called the high plains and have much shorter grass. Although both regions have occasional stands of trees, hills, plateaus, and even mountain regions, some parts of the high Plains seem to be an enormous ocean of grass stretching as far as the eye can see.

Early Plains hunters found plenty of game here, including antelope, deer, elk, bears, wolves, coyotes, and rabbits, but the grasslands were especially well

Apache dancers perform at a festival on the Casa Grande Reservation in Arizona.

suited to the buffalo. This bulky beast was an essential part of early Plains cultures because it provided meat for food, bones for tools, and hide for clothing and shelter. It also had great spiritual significance. After the Spanish introduced the horse to Mexico and its use spread to Mexican and Plains tribes in the 1600s and 1700s, the buffalo became even more important because it was easier to hunt.

The first dwellers on the high Plains were Apache, but many woodlands nations, such as the Cheyenne, Arapaho, and Sioux, gave up their permanent villages. They gradually became tipi-dwellers in the Plains due to pressures from nations farther east who were, in turn, being driven west by non-Native intrusion. Also moving west were the Blackfeet (Piegan or Pikuni, Blood or Kainah, and Siksika), Nakoda (Assiniboine), Cree, some Ojibwe, and the Crow (Absaroka).

Some groups, such as the Mandan, Hidatsa, Arikara, and Pawnee, never abandoned their villages and farm life entirely. They did, however, set off on long hunting expeditions for part of each year.

Plains tipi-dwellers carried all their possessions with them, dragging them behind their horses on poles laced with buffalo hides. These poles and buffalo hides were also used to set up their tipis when they stopped to make camp. The Plains and Prairie nations shared hunting and warring customs and religious ceremonies and even devised a common sign language for trade and councils.

The horse-based Plains culture reached a peak in its number of horses in the eighteenth and nineteenth centuries. But Plains culture began to decline after the 1820s, as traders and travelers introduced a trading economy and brought diseases. The U.S. and Canadian governments launched concerted campaigns between the 1850s and 1890s to force the nations onto reservations in order to open up vast lands for non-Native colonization and exploitation. Many wars were fought, such as the great Sioux wars and the Cree-Métis uprising in Manitoba and Saskatchewan. But by 1890, Indian resistance ceased, and the buffalo herds were annihilated.

The Plains tribes have all survived, however, and many of them are quite strong today, with growing populations, sovereign tribal governments, and their own radio stations, colleges, and other institutions. The Plains nations captured the imagination of non-Natives as great warriors, but now their image includes writers, artists, teachers, and actors, as well.

Northeastern Woodlands Culture Area

The Northeastern Woodlands culture area extends from the Atlantic Ocean west to the Mississippi River and from southern Canada to the Ohio Valley. The terrain varies greatly from sea coast to mountains and has an enormous number of inland bodies of water, including several major rivers and the five Great Lakes. What all these regions have in common is woodlands, with many prairies cleared originally by the indigenous people.

Forests were the single greatest resource for early inhabitants, providing wood for their houses, boats, tools, and fuel, plus bark they shredded to make clothing, roofing materials, and bedding. The forests, and especially the grasslands managed by the people, provided an environment for abundant game, especially deer, and for some tribes, buffalo as well.

The oceans, lakes, and rivers were a plentiful source of fish, waterfowl, and wild rice. While most woodland Indians were farmers who lived in permanent villages, growing mostly corn, beans, and squash, the growing season in the Northeast was cold and short, especially north of the Great Lakes. Thus, they also had to depend on hunting and gathering vegetable and tree foods to survive. They developed technologies of ecological management to ensure success in their environment.

Anthropologists believe that Northeastern Woodland peoples are descended from ancient settlers who can be traced back ten thousand years and more. More recent woodland peoples include a mound-building culture centered in the Ohio Valley between 100 B.C.E. and 200 C.E. This culture is thought to have been influenced by ancient Mesoamerican civilizations that developed in Mexico. These Mound Builders constructed more than one hundred thousand earthwork mounds (some of which can still be seen today), as well as walled towns of up to thirty thousand inhabitants each. The great Cahokia Mound near St. Louis, Missouri, and the Great Serpent Mound in southern Ohio

are examples of the Ohio Valley culture's spectacular accomplishments. They were a well-organized and religious people.

The "high cultures" of the Ohio Valley region continued to evolve until disease introduced by contact with Europeans seems to have disrupted the region after the 1540s. On an even more speculative note, some scholars have suggested that diseases introduced by the Norse in Greenland, Newfoundland, and Labrador in the eleventh through fifteenth centuries may have had some impact at an earlier date.

The people who built the mounds may have included Siouan-speaking people, such as Ho-Chunk (Winnebago), Quapaw, Osage, and Iowa-Missouri, who later moved west, as well as the Saponi and Catawba, who moved east. At the time of first recorded European contact, Algonquian- and Iroquoian-speaking groups dominated most of the region, organized in numerous confederacies such as the Five Nations, the Illiniwek (Illinois), Miami, Cat Nation (Erie), Wyandot (Huron), and many others.

The Northeastern Woodland area blends imperceptibly into the southeast area, and no sharp distinctions can be made. Groups such as the Shawnee, Yuchi, Cherokee, Powhatan-Renape, and others lived in both areas or moved from one to the other.

The Iroquois groups of New York State shared many "southern" characteristics also. They lived in communal longhouses (made of elm bark) that were so large that twenty or more families lived in them. Their villages were generally governed by a council in which women played a prominent leadership role. Sometime during the sixteenth century or earlier, five tribes (Cayuga, Mohawk, Onondaga, Oneida, and Seneca, later joined by the Tuscarora) united into the powerful Ho-de-no-sau-nee or Five Nations, an important military and political power in North America until the end of the eighteenth century.

Other Algonquian speakers include the Micmac, Maliseet, Abenakis, the Delaware (or Lenape), Fox, Kickapoo, Mahican, Massachuset, Menominee, Mohegan, Ottawa, Pequot, Sauk, Shinnecock, and Wampanoag. They lived along the eastern seaboard and in territory extending north and west from the coast to the Great Lakes. Algonquian towns were usually self-governing but united in confederacies with neighboring villages. Now, many of these Algonquian-speakers live in Oklahoma.

The Powhatan-Renape people of the Virginia area had developed a strong confederacy by 1607. Some Renape and Lenape groups were led by women, called queens by early white visitors.

Although Algonquian tribes were among the first Native North Americans to suffer disruption at the hands of Europeans, they have survived in virtually every region from Nova Scotia south to North Carolina.

Southeastern Woodlands Culture Area

The Southeastern Woodlands culture area is bordered on the east by the Atlantic Ocean; on the west by the Mississippi, Arkansas, and Trinity Rivers; on the north by the region of the Tennessee and Potomac Rivers; and on the south by the Gulf of Mexico. Like the Northeastern Woodland culture area, the Southeast is considered woodlands. Although it has a great variety of terrains—coastal plains, saltwater marshes, stands of cypress trees, the jungle swampland of the Everglades, fertile river valleys, and highlands like the Smoky and Cumberland Mountains—the Southeast was mostly covered with yellow pine forests.

Native American people began practicing agriculture in the Mississippi and Ohio River valleys over two thousand years ago and, by about 400 B.C.E., had developed a thriving culture known for its burial mounds, ceremonial centers, extensive trading, and highly developed art. By 400 C.E., this culture, known as the Hopewell, was on the decline. Several hundred years later, a Temple Mound culture evolved in the same area, influenced by Mexican civilizations that had spread north to the lower Mississippi Valley and from there all the way up to Wisconsin.

This Temple Mound culture, which reached its peak between 1300 and 1500 C.E., developed into a great number of different tribes, each with its own language, customs, and religious beliefs. But all these different peoples did have a number of practices in common. They were all hoe farmers growing the same crops, like corn, beans, sunflowers, squash, and melons. They fished with the same kind of tackle, hunted forest and swampland animals, and gathered wild plant foods to subsidize their diets. They all rode the rivers in the same type of dugout canoe or poled the swamps with the same type of cane raft. Even the village systems were more or less alike, large towns of two hundred to three hundred houses that were sometimes surrounded by a palisade or moat for defense and that acted as a center for smaller surrounding communities.

By the time the Spanish, French, and English began exploring the Southeast, the largest and most powerful of these Indian groups was a loose confederacy of about fifty towns of Muskogee tribes that English traders named the Creek Indians. West of the Creeks were the Chickasaw peoples, and south of the Chickasaws were the Choctaws, both of which were also Muskogean-speaking peoples. The Natchez, Siouan-speaking tribes like the Biloxi and Catawba, Algonquian nations like the Shawnee, Iroquoian peoples like the Tuscarora, and Cherokee were living in the Southeast culture area, along with the Yuchi and numerous nations whose languages are not known today.

The southeastern nations faced a drastic change from the 1520s to the 1540s when Spanish slave raiders and military expeditions ravaged the coasts and even a large part of the interior. During this period, Africans and Mexicans escaping from the Spanish joined the southern tribes. Later, the Spanish, French, and British all attempted to control the region. Large numbers of Natives, especially Choctaw and Florida nations, were enslaved in South Carolina and Louisiana. Many were sold to New England, Barbados, Haiti, and other regions.

In spite of European aggression, most of the larger southeastern tribes have survived. Some still live in Virginia, North Carolina, South Carolina, Florida, Alabama, Mississippi, Louisiana, Tennessee, and Arkansas, while others were forced by the United States to relocate to Oklahoma and Texas. The famous Seminole War and the Five Civilized Tribes are reminders of the importance of this area.

Southwest Culture Area

The Southwest culture area covers the region also known as "Aztlan." This includes Sonora and Chihuahua in northern Mexico, most of Arizona and New Mexico, and small parts of California, Utah, Colorado, and Texas in the U.S. Southwest. The geography of this area varies greatly—from the high

This Navajo family is enjoying a traditional meal of fry bread in their hogan. The construction of a hogan is steeped in tradition. Its doorway always faces east, admitting the first rays of the sun in the morning.

country of the Colorado Plateau in the north to the depths of the enormous Grand Canyon along the Colorado River. There are rugged regions like the Mogollon Mountains of New Mexico and vast deserts like the Sonora Desert in Arizona. What all these landscapes have in common is dryness at lower elevations, except where intersected by major rivers.

This dry terrain made both hunting and farming difficult, yet the early indigenous peoples who lived here were so adept at both that they could produce enough food to support large villages in some areas. Some of these cultures were primarily comprised of farmers who stayed in one place and developed sophisticated irrigation techniques to raise corn, beans, cotton, and pumpkins. Others moved with the seasons; they did not farm but instead managed their resources by hunting game and harvesting nuts, herbs, and berries. Most Southwest cultures were both farmers and ecological resource managers.

Anthropologists divide the ancient Southwest into several traditions. These include the Anasazi, the Mogollon, the Hohokam, the River Pai, and others. The Anasazi, or Puebloan, culture has exist-

ed from before 200 C.E. to the present, with a focus in the area that is today known as Four Corners, the place where the states of Arizona, New Mexico, Colorado, and Utah all meet. The name Anasazi is derived from a Navajo word. The Navajo oral traditions relating to the period of 1000 to 1200 C.E. make mention of meeting and mixing with many Anasazi groups.

Anthropologists call the earliest Anasazi people Basket Makers because of their extraordinary basketwork. They created baskets so expertly and tightly woven they could be used for watertight cooking pots. Until about 800 C.E., they lived in pit houses dug into the ground, then started building houses out of logs, adobe mortar, and stone.

Southwestern architecture and art really came into their own with the rise of the Pueblo culture. The Pueblo peoples built giant community houses of adobe brick or stone, some up to five terraced stories high, with eight hundred rooms that probably housed more than one thousand inhabitants. They created beautifully decorated pottery, feather fabrics, colored cotton cloth, and turquoise jewelry. The present-day Hopi, Zuni, Tewa, Tiwa, Keres, and Tano peoples of the Southwest are all derived from Puebloans, as are the Opata and other peoples of Sonora and, in part, the Navajo and Western Apache.

Another culture group, the Hohokam, flourished to the southwest of the Anasazi in the deserts of what is today south and central Arizona. Anthropologists estimate that the Hohokam peoples settled the area as early as 500 B.C.E. and started growing maize (corn) about 200 B.C.E. The Hohokam peoples, with a Mexicanlike culture, developed a remarkable irrigation system that stretched as long as 150 miles (242 kilometers) in some places. Present-day Hohokam-influenced cultures include O'odham, Pima, and Papago, and the Quechuan peoples of Arizona and California.

A third culture, the Mogollon, lived in southwestern New Mexico and southeastern Arizona, an area that has both deserts and mountains. It is believed that the Mogollon tradition started somewhere between 3000 and 500 B.C.E. They disappeared from the area around 1200 C.E., possibly migrating to the west or to the Chihuahua and Sonora areas of northern Mexico. They lived in multistory adobe dwellings and cliff houses built into caves, growing corn and making pottery, baskets, and woven cloth.

Athabascan groups (known as Apache and Navajo) linguistically related to Athabascan speakers from the North appear in the Southwest between 400 and 1200 C.E. They intermarried with Puebloan, Yuman, and other peoples and developed a wide variety of cultures. The Jicarilla Apache at one time lived in single-story pueblos in northern New Mexico, practicing agriculture. Other Apache used the tipi and lived on the plains as far north as the Black Hills. The Chiricahua, Mescalero, and Western Apache lived in the desert basin and range environment, as did the Navajo. Further south were the Athabascan-speaking Suma, Jano, Jocome, Manso, and Cholone. In the Chiso Mountains of Texas were the Chiso.

Other important peoples of this culture area are the Yuman (River Pai peoples such as the Quechuan and Mohave), Desert Pai groups such as the Yavapai and Walapai-Havasupai, and Gila River Pai such as the Maricopa and Kaveltcadom and many members of the Uto-Aztecan language family (the O'odham or Pima and Papago of Sonora and Arizona, the related Tepehuan of Durango, the relat-

ed Julime of the Rio Grande-Rio Concha junction, the Yaqui and Mayo of southern Sonora, the Taraumara of Chihuahua, and the Opata or Tewi of northern Sonora).

Today, the southwestern region includes millions of descendants of all of the above groups. Some speak only Spanish and are called Mexicans or Chicanos, while others speak their indigenous languages. Today, the Navajo make up the largest Native American group in the United States. Many people believe that they and their Pueblo neighbors, the Hopi, have the best-preserved traditional cultures in North America, but the Taraumara and others in Mexico are also very traditional.

Mesoamerican Culture Area

The Mesoamerican culture area covers the region from Nicaragua and Costa Rica north to central Mexico. In the centuries before the arrival of Europeans, Mesoamerica was the most densely populated area of the Americas. This terrain ranges from cool highland plains ringed by volcanoes to deep sea coasts along the Pacific and Caribbean to tropical rain forests. People have been hunting, fishing, and cultivating maize, beans, squash, tomatoes, and a hundred other edible plants here for thousands of years.

The most famous Mesoamerican cultures were those of the Maya (Yucatec), Olmec, Toltec, and Nahua, but many other groups are also justly famous, including the Huastec, Lenca, Mixtec, Puropacha (Tarascan), Zapotec, Chontal, Chorti, Jicaque, Mixe, Otomi, Totonac, Zacatec, Zoque, and others. Archaeologists divide up the history of this region into three basic eras: the preclassic period from 1500 B.C.E. to 100 C.E., when the Olmec and Olmec-like cultures dominated the area; the classic period from 100 to 900 C.E., when the Teotihuacan, Toltec, and Classic Maya flourished; and the postclassic period from 900 to the arrival of the Spanish in the 1500s, when the other groups, and later the Aztecs, dominated the north, and various Mayan and other states existed in the south.

The remarkable cultural developments of the people called Olmec had a major influence on all of the Mesoamerican cultures that followed them. Centered on the southern Gulf coast of Mexico, these ancient Native peoples had a trading network that extended into the central Mexican highlands and southeast along the Pacific coast to El Salvador and beyond. They practiced slash-and-burn farming (cutting down and then burning areas of forest to create farmland) and built massive public works projects such as clay building platforms, stone pavements, and even drainage systems. The Olmecs are famous for giant, helmeted heads carved from basalt, a type of volcanic rock, and for their jade carvings, often with jaguarlike or babyish features.

The Olmecs may have spoken many languages, including Mixe-Zoque tongues as well as Maya and others. It is not known if the Olmec culture declined because of invading tribes, failing crops, or disease.

The Mayas of the classic period lived in southern Mexico, Belize, Guatemala, El Salvador, and Honduras. Mayan life revolved around one hundred or more ceremonial and economic centers that functioned as city-states and educational centers. These cities had elaborate stone structures, including pyramids with temples built on top, shrines, astronomical observatories, monasteries, palaces, ball courts, and vaulted tombs. Scattered throughout the cities were paved roads, bridges, plazas, causeways, reservoirs, and even aqueducts. Classrooms and public baths were also available.

The Mayas developed a hieroglyphic writing system similar to one used in the Olmec region in 150 to 200 C.E., along with bark-paper books and maps, positional mathematics and the concept of zero (also patterned after the Olmec), a highly accurate calendar, and the ability to predict eclipses. In addition to their magnificent architecture, the Mayas produced wonderful art—jade carvings and masks, ceramic figures, colored pottery, wood carvings, cotton and feather clothing, and intricately designed jewelry.

According to the *Popol Vuh*, the sacred book of the Quiche Maya, Nahua-speaking people also came into the Mayan region. In about 800 to 1000 C.E., the Mayas were joined by the Toltecs coming from central Mexico. The Toltecs did not conquer the Mayas so much as they merged cultures with them, injecting a new lifeblood into the declining Mayan civilization of Yucatán.

The Toltecs have long been famous as great artists, poets, and builders living in the area of the Valley of Mexico. As they became more powerful, the Toltecs built magnificent stone pyramids, palaces, and temples, all decorated with stone murals. They developed or borrowed hieroglyphic writing and new kinds of corn and squash, wove beautiful cotton cloth, and created jewelry. At its height, the Toltec influence stretched from the Gulf of Mexico to the Pacific Ocean. After about 1100 C.E., the Toltecs were plagued by a series of droughts, famines, fires, and, finally, invasions by northern tribes. After a period of tribal rivalries and power struggles, the Aztecs rose to power.

The Aztecs migrated into the Valley of Mexico from the north, arriving in that region about 1168 and fighting local tribes until they finally established the great city of Tenochtitlán. Through alliances and conquest, the Triple Alliance (the Aztec confederacy) eventually came to include five million people. They, too, created remarkable art and architecture, hieroglyphics, calendars, poetry, and historical records and were especially adept at city planning. The Aztecs developed an elaborate social system of councils, judges, nobles, priests, and war chiefs, and an economic system that demanded that conquered subjects pay tribute. According to some interpretations, the Aztecs believed that human blood had to be continually sacrificed to appease Huitzilopochtli, their patron saint; thousands of war captives were said to be ritually sacrificed on top of the stone pyramids. Some scholars believe, however, that these accounts have been exaggerated by enemies of the Aztecs.

In 1519, the Spaniard Hernando Cortés began his attack on the Aztecs and defeated them completely by 1521. A million people still speak Nahuatl, the Aztec-Toltec language, today, and millions of other Mexicans and Chicanos are of Aztec lineage.

SEE ALSO:

Caribbean, Indigenous Cultures of; Central America, Indigenous Peoples of; Central and South Andean Culture Areas.

SUGGESTED READINGS:

Baldwin, Gordon. *America's Buried Past*. New York: Putnam, 1962.

Driver, Harold E. *Indians of North America*. Chicago: University of Chicago Press, 1969.

Eagle/Walking Turtle. *Indian America: A Traveler's Companion*. Santa Fe: John Muir, Publications, 1995.

This 1914 Edward S. Curtis photo, like the thousands of other photos by Curtis, was taken at a time when Native peoples were rapidly losing many of their treasured traditional artifacts to museums, anthropologists, art dealers, and collectors. Many of Curtis's photos depict traditional material culture that is now irretrievably lost.

CURTIS, EDWARD S. (1868–1952)

Edward S. Curtis was a photographer, writer, and filmmaker. He captured the values and images of many Indian nations through his books and camera work. Curtis created a twenty-volume work titled *The North American Indian*, which was an attempt to depict Native peoples just after the turn of the twentieth century. His production was staggering: 40,000 photographs, four additional books and sixteen other volumes, a collection of 350 traditional Native stories, 10,000 recordings of speeches and songs, and one of the first films starring (and produced in collaboration with) Native people.

Most of the photographs taken at that time were still, studio poses of people grimly facing the box camera. In contrast, Curtis took pictures that told stories. For example, when he photographed people from Arikara or Kwakiutl, he encouraged them to either bring out of storage or remake their traditional clothing. Also, the spiritual expression on people's faces in Curtis's pictures often conveyed the emotions of their subjects. This is because Curtis took photos not for postcards or for tourists but to seriously document how life for Native people had recently been and was to be remembered. Some have criticized Curtis's photos because they were intentionally posed, maintaining that this helped to perpetuate a romantic image of Native people. Some have taken issue with the clothing of some of the subjects, saying that sometimes it was not traditional to their region.

Curtis began his work in a Seattle studio in the 1890s, photographing Chief Seattle's daughter Angeline and local tribes fishing or picking hops. During expeditions to Alaska, he began recording more formally, until he had sufficient recognition and enough pictures for his first two collections. After obtaining seventy-five thousand dollars from financier J. Pierpont Morgan, Curtis was able to extend his work through the Oklahoma Territory of the Kiowas, Comanches, and Poncas; into the Southwest to capture Zuni, Navajo, and Havasupai images; and into California and across the American and Canadian Plains to photograph Cheyennes and Piegans.

His Northwest work was capped with a feature film that included, according to its advertisements, such experiences as "vision quest, love, hunting, wars and feasts." Curtis produced the film with Kwakiutl assistant George Hunt, who was also an assistant to anthropologist Franz Boas. *In the Land of the War Canoes*, as the film is now known, was completed in 1914 and never made back a fraction of its costs. Curtis paid Native people at Fort Rupert, British Columbia, a good wage for acting and for reconstructing their villages, canoes, and ceremonies. In return, they added plot line and characters. Even today, people from this area proudly show the place where the sets were struck on Deer Island.

Curtis was able to recreate many scenes as suggested by the Native people he photographed, capturing their dramatic poses of work, prayer, and ritual. He is best known, however, for his portraits, such as those of the Zuni governor, Geronimo, Red Cloud, and Chief Joseph. Because he was so disciplined and focused, we are able to return to his work for reminders of how villages or housing looked during preconquest times. Up into his eighties, Curtis continued to write and take action and still photographs for the early California movie industry. Selections from his works are available today in inexpensive editions, and many museums, which provided little support or recognition during his life, now have extended exhibitions of his Southwest, Northwest, and Plains series.

CUSTER, GEORGE ARMSTRONG (1839–1876)

George Armstrong Custer was born December 5, 1839, in the small town of New Rumley, Ohio. As a boy, he longed to become a soldier, and at eighteen, he entered the military academy at West Point. He was a poor student, however, and barely graduated. Upon his graduation in 1861, the Civil War broke out, and Custer's military career began to accelerate rapidly.

Lieutenant Custer gained a reputation as a courageous cavalry commander. Incredibly, he was promoted from captain to brigadier general early in the Civil War by General George McClellan, his commander. McClellan called Custer a "reckless, gallant boy, undeterred by fatigue, unconscious of fear." By the war's end, at twenty-three, Custer

No single event in Native history has inspired more pictorial representations than the imagined last moments of Lt. Colonel George Armstrong Custer. Custer's reckless, fatal blunder usually becomes transformed, as above, into a feat of heroism.

had become the youngest general to serve in the Union Army.

After the Civil War ended, the size of the U.S. Army was drastically reduced, wartime promotions were being reevaluated, and Custer continued in active service on the western frontier at the rank of lieutenant colonel. There, in the climate of complete disregard for the rights of indigenous peoples, he achieved fame in the eastern press as an Indian fighter and published an autobiography called, *My Life on the Plains*. The book, which told his version of his many battles with Indians, added to his fame. In reality, Custer engaged in unprovoked attacks on Indian villages filled with women and children, such as his attack on Black Kettle's village in 1868 (which has become known as the "Battle" of the Washita).

Custer's version of these events, however, contributed to the widespread belief that his troops always seemed to attack the right place at the right time. Critics also contributed to the myth of Custer's image when they began saying that his victories were due to what they called, "Custer's Luck." Rival officers, on the other hand, called him a glory seeker, and it was said that he often risked the lives of his men by rushing into battle.

In 1874, gold was discovered in the Black Hills of what is now South Dakota, and Custer was ordered to lead an exploring expedition. The expedition violated the 1868 Treaty of Fort Laramie, which had promised the Black Hills and the surrounding region to the Indians forever. The treaty violation gave the Indians no recourse but to attempt to defend the illegal invasion of their homeland. They attacked the camps of the invading miners, and the government sent troops to retaliate. Soon a bloody war had begun.

One of the government troops was the Seventh Cavalry consisting of about six hundred men, commanded by Lt. Colonel George Armstrong Custer. Riding with Custer were several Crow scouts. On the morning of June 25, 1876, the scouts sighted an Indian encampment on the Little Bighorn. It was probably the largest gathering of Indians ever on the Plains. There were at least three thousand

Lt. Colonel George Armstrong Custer, photographed with scouts in Montana Territory in the early 1870s, while Custer was in command of troops guarding crews that surveyed and built the Northern Pacific Railroad.

people from the seven bands of the Lakotas and several families of Cheyennes and Arapahos, with leaders such as Crazy Horse and Gall among them.

Using a masterful series of decoys and strategies, Crazy Horse and the other warriors were able to attack a column from the north and west, while Gall charged Custer and his forces from the south and east. The U.S. troops, hampered by Custer's poor military judgment and brashness, were surrounded and completely annihilated. It was a triumphant victory for the Indians and the first and only defeat for Custer. The Battle of the Little Bighorn Creek is sometimes referred to as "Custer's Last Stand." As part of a campaign of anti-Indian propaganda in white periodicals, this phrase made Custer a sensational hero and legend, forestalling for nearly a century any realistic appraisal of his career in the West. Recently Custer has been presented, in movies such as *Little Big Man* (1970), as one author said, "the psychotic he clearly was."

SEE ALSO:
Black Hills; Crazy Horse; Fort Laramie Treaty of 1868; Little Bighorn, Battle of the; Sitting Bull; Wounded Knee (1890).

D-Q UNIVERSITY

D-Q University is an accredited tribal college located near Davis, California. Founded in 1971, D-Q differs from most other American Indian colleges in that it is not associated with a single tribe or reservation. D-Q strives to bring together the indigenous peoples of North and Middle America in an educational setting that overcomes language barriers, cultural differences, and outside barriers so that Native people can incorporate their own heritage into contemporary education. The university's name, which reflects this effort to bring together Native cultures, comes from Deganawidah and Quetzalcoatl, Iroquois and Aztec figures representing two intellectual traditions of Native America.

The educational philosophy that guides the school is that Indian people of all ages need the benefits of education. D-Q seeks to provide educational opportunities in an environment that honors and preserves the rich heritage of Indian peoples

and respects, values, and understands the unique place of Indians in contemporary American life.

In 1992, D-Q enrolled 1,053 full and part-time students. Seventy percent of the student body are Bureau of Indian Affairs certifiable American Indians. This gives D-Q the highest percentage of Native American students of any California institution of higher learning. More than sixty tribal affiliations from across the United States are represented at D-Q. Courses at D-Q are accepted for transfer to the University of California and the California State Universities and Colleges.

DAKOTA

SEE Siouan Nations.

DANCE, AMERICAN INDIAN

Today, as in the past, dancing plays a significant role in virtually every Native American culture. Indian people dance for a variety of reasons, all of them vital to the continuation of tribal traditions and the survival of ancient customs and beliefs. They dance to celebrate their rich and diverse heritage, as a means of prayer, to reestablish their ties to an old way of life, to promote unity within and among the various nations and tribes, and to express the abundant strength and pride of Indian nations.

Every Indian nation has its own, centuries-old ritual dances and tribal ceremonies that define its specific culture. Some of these include the potlatch celebrations of the Native people of the Northwest Coast, the summer and winter dances of the Pueblos in New Mexico, the False Face dances of the Iroquois in the Northeast United States and Canada, the healing dances of the Pomos of California, the healing dances of the Inuit in the far north, and the Stomp Dances of the Cherokees. These ceremonies and dances provide spiritually empowering experiences to the group as a whole and to individuals within the group.

With the arrival of Europeans on the North American continent, many Native groups were dispersed—through wars, treaties, and political

Colorful powwow regalia is a featured attraction for spectators at the American Indian Exposition at the Crazy Horse Memorial in South Dakota.

Dancers prepare to perform the Eagle Dance at an Intertribal ceremonial at Jemez Pueblo, in New Mexico.

forces—from their original homelands to reservations or cities. Because of this dispersal, many Native rituals, dances, and ceremonies became endangered. Some Native groups' spiritual and traditional ways were made illegal, such as the Sun Dance of the Plains Indians, which was outlawed during the nineteenth century.

In their dealings with Indians, Euro-American colonial governments and churches sought to make Native people look, behave, and think like Europeans. One way of accomplishing this was to send Native children great distances from their families and tribes to live in boarding schools. There they were not allowed to practice any elements of their cultures, not even to speak their own languages. Despite such severe measures, Native American customs, religions, languages, cultures, and dances still thrive today. In fact, Native American dance means more to Indian nations than ever before. For many Native people, dance is a powerful celebration of their nation's endurance and survival.

Native American dances would not be complete without accompaniment by singing and a variety of musical instruments. These instruments include bird-bone whistles, flutes, striking sticks, and deer-hoof rattles. Other rattles are made of turtle shells, animal teeth, animal horns, gourds, and shells. Perhaps the most important instrument of all is the drum. Without the drum, a dance event would not be complete, especially for dance events called powwows. However, not all Native American people dance with the drum. Every Native culture has its own varied and distinctive ways of making music.

Drumming and singing ensembles include leader-chorus songs, unison chorus songs, and multipart songs. A singer must have a strong, wide-ranging voice and the ability to perform with others. Some Native groups sing in a high falsetto voice, pushing the music out from deep within their throats.

For a listener unfamiliar with Native American singing, this music presents a challenge. But to the trained ear, the complex subtleties and melodic flow of Native music can be instantly recognized and appreciated. While some songs use Native languages to carry the melody, others employ vowel sounds such as *ya*, *hey*, *hi*, and *lay*.

Native music is comprised of diverse songs that vary in meaning and purpose. Trick Songs, for example, start and stop suddenly. Slow songs, such as Crow Hop or Sneak Up songs, are reenactments of war tribulations and courageous deeds. Songs range from the very slow to the very fast, and a certain kind of song often represents a particular type of dance.

Although there are many diverse styles of Native American dance, body movements are usually restrained and conservative. These movements allow the dancer's body to stay close to the earth. Sometimes a dance may last all day or night, so it is important for a dancer to conserve energy. In some dances, the participants act out the movements of animals or the experience of a hunt, fishing expedition, or war exploit. Some dances are very elaborate, with a pronounced sense of drama. Dancers who mimic certain animals or birds also must have a talent for acting. When a dancer has fully studied a particular animal, his movements and expressions can be a dynamic work of art and quite visually compelling. In the Eagle Dance, for example, the dancer imitates the soaring of an eagle.

Many dances are patterned in a circle, with the dancers moving clockwise or counterclockwise depending upon the group's worldview. Another type is line dancing, with participants moving either forward or backward, dancing in place, or moving in a procession. The pattern of a dance is closely

The Hoop Dance is but one of many dances performed at the Native American Exposition at the Crazy Horse Memorial.

linked to a particular tribal belief system. The words and music, sets of repetitions, types of instruments, costumes, and interactions of the performers are all symbolic of a tribe's spiritual beliefs.

Today, the most widely known dance events are powwows, but not all dancing exists within this type of gathering. Many dances are centuries old and performed as traditional ceremonies. Ancient songs and dances contain spiritual and supernatural forces and are practiced as part of seasonal or life cycle events, such as to celebrate a harvest or the coming of spring. Life cycle events might include

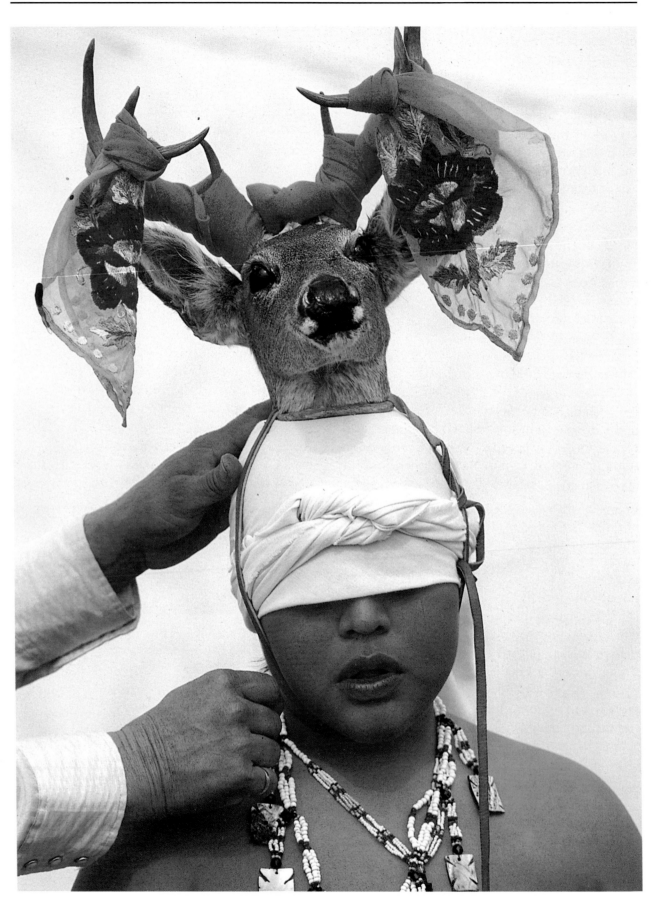

At a celebration in Casa Grande, Arizona, the Pascua Yaquis maintain traditions that have sustained them for generations. Here, Narciso Blue prepares his eleven year old son, Angelo Blue, to participate in the Deer Dance.

the passage of a young woman into adulthood or the birth of a baby. Other dances and ceremonies are practiced for healing, storytelling, playing games, hunting, praying, offering thanks, and initiation. Native American people recognize that being alive guarantees movement and constant change, and they have honored and respected life transitions through dance and song.

In the twentieth century, many changes have taken place in the lives of Native Americans. These changes have had a profound effect on Native music and dance. Celebrations and dance events that were once performed only by Native people and for Native people have expanded to include people of non-Native descent, and they take place in nontraditional settings. Today, American Indian dance is performed at public receptions, country fairs, conferences, tourist attractions, museums, political demonstrations, urban parades, and American Indian education programs. Widening the formats has created opportunities for Native dance and tradition to be appreciated by a larger audience. Non-Native people can gain a better understanding and insight into Native American issues and concerns. Through dance, American Indian

people are relaying a strong message: "We are a living culture, we are proud, our traditions have survived."

While traditional dances remain intact, actively practiced, and deeply valued, Native American singers and dancers are also reinventing and creating dances and songs, ones that reflect a changing world and a growing culture. These new dances and songs provide continuity for Native people. Some members of the Kiowa Nation, for instance, have "scored" song and dance to represent the 1991 Operation Desert Storm. Innovations in "standard" dance categories are changing all the time. Some of these changes have revived wider participation and allow Indian dance to remain fresh and exciting.

As Native dance styles and music have continued to develop creatively, so too have Native dance costumes. With every season, dance costumes, particularly costumes worn in powwow events, seem to get bolder and brighter. Feather bustles grow larger, and beaded capes and side drops get more intricate and elaborate. Where long ago dancers adorned their costumes with rattling shells and teeth to create a tempo with their movements,

Apache women dancing at a Sunrise Dance at Fort Apache Reservation, Whiteriver, Arizona. This puberty dance requires up to six months of preparation and is a public event, proudly and vigorously advertised by the tribe.

Exquisite beadwork and other features of the regalia for the Men's Fancy Dance can cost thousands of dollars. This Fancy Dancer is performing at a Shoshone/Bannock powwow.

and beautiful, sometimes costing upward of two thousand dollars. Because powwow dances and celebrations often include competition for prize money, a dancer wants to ensure being noticed.

Not all dances are performed within the context of the powwow, and in many cases, dance and ritual are synonymous. One such example is the Great Feather Dance, practiced by peoples within the culture of the People of the Longhouse (Iroquois). The Great Feather Dance is a ceremony that observes the abundant gifts of life given by the Creator and expresses the people's gratitude. Young people are instructed by their elders to dance hard and shout out their joy and happiness so that the Creator will know of their thanks and continue the blessings upon the people.

today's dancers use more modern accessories. Chiming bells, for example, are used to accentuate the presentation of a Fancy Dance; tobacco can lids are sewn on the dresses of jingle dancers. When the Northern Plains Grass Dance first originated in the nineteenth century, dancers wore braids of sweet grass woven in feather bustles. Today grass dancers opt for brightly colored yarn hanging in varying lengths from their costumes.

Certain costumes reflect fads or trends that have spread from tribe to tribe. A style that might have its origins in Oklahoma can quickly become a new fashion in Montana. Dance outfits can be dazzling

A ceremony among the White Mountain Apaches is the Sunrise Dance. Performed to mark the passing of a young woman into adulthood, it takes place the summer after her first menstrual cycle. The dance is performed to call upon the spiritual presence of Changing Woman. The Changing Woman spirit will help transform the young woman by giving her the strength and blessings needed to live a long and healthy life. The Sunrise Dance itself is a four-day affair, but the actual preparation usually begins six months or more before the ceremony. The preparations include ritual procedures such as collecting and making objects to be used in the dance, blessings and rites of purification, prayers, and songs. A week before the dance, activities include feasting, social dancing, and vis-

This Corn Dance, though a colorful spectacle, is not performed for the benefit of tourists at Santa Clara Pueblo in New Mexico. The dance has deep significance in the life cycle of the pueblo.

iting. The Sunrise Dance is practiced to honor a particular young woman through the presence of Changing Woman, although the dance is also performed to enrich the entire community. Often during the Sunrise Dance, healing takes place.

Among the Tewa Pueblo Indians in the southwestern United States, dance and ritual performances are a rich and diverse celebration of their millennia-old agricultural culture. Because agriculture is based on seasons, each dance relates to a part of the growth cycle. For instance, the late winter and early spring dances mark the beginning of planting. Summer and fall dances offer prayers for fertility and a bountiful harvest. Corn, squash blossoms, butterflies, rain, and cloud symbols are featured in the costuming, movements, and songs. Among the dances are the Blue Corn Dance, the Butterfly Dance, and the Rain Dance.

For the Southern Plains people, dance and music are tightly woven within the fabric of their cultural life. Their dances range from the very sacred and private to the highly visible and public. There are dances of the Black Leggings Society of the Kiowas and the Gourd Dances of the Comanches. Comanche Gourd Dances are mostly line-type dances performed by men's societies. Many dances of the Southern Plains take place within powwow

events and may include the Round Dance, Buffalo Dance, Hoop Dance, Eagle Dance, and Spear-and-Shield Dance.

Among the Northern Plains tribes are the Shoshones, Flatheads, Blackfeet, Crows, and Sioux. Dance, costume, and song styles of the Northern Plains cultures are similar to those of the Southern Plains styles but with slight differences. Both regions have regular powwow celebrations, and both have warrior and men's societies. Popular dances of the Northern Plains tribes include the Men's Fancy Dance, Women's Fancy Shawl, Men's and Women's Traditional, Men's Northern-style Grass Dance, and Women's Jingle-Dress. These dances are categories for powwow contests, and people from the very young to the very old compete for big prizes.

Ceremonies are also prevalent among the Northern Plains people. Perhaps the most solemn ritual is the Sun Dance, which is thought to be the center of a tribe's existence and is practiced to bring good to the people. The ceremony, which is not itself a dance but usually includes several dances, is held during the midsummer, lasts for four days, and traditionally includes the participation of several different Plains groups who gather for the event. The most compelling aspect of the Sun Dance is the piercing of the dancer's flesh and the "tearing

Many hours of precise and skillful work have been invested in the creation of this jingle dress, shown here in a performance of the Jingle Dance at a Shoshone/Bannock powwow.

Haidas, and Tsimshians gather for a celebration lasting for four days. This event began in 1982 for the education and revitalization of clan songs, dances, and cultural values.

In the last century, Native American dance has entered a new theatrical arena, the stage. One high point of this outreach is the American Indian Dance Theater, formed in 1987. This company consists of some of the country's best Native dancers; they tour and perform tribal dances such as the Zuni Buffalo Dance, Eagle Dance, Apache Crown Dance, and Hoop Dance.

American Indian dance reaffirms tribal strength and unity and helps provide the means by which Native customs, religions, traditions, and values carry through into the next century. American Indian dance has survived for countless generations and will undoubtedly survive for generations to come.
— T. Midge

themselves free." A Sun Dancer will undergo great pain for the enrichment of the tribe.

Dances and ceremonies of the Native peoples of Alaska are varied and complex. For many years, traditional dances and ceremonies were suppressed by the Christian missionaries. It has only been because the Alaskan Native peoples persevered and clung to their culture that the ceremonies have survived. Today, their dances and ceremonial practices are thriving; young people are actively learning the traditions, songs, dances, and languages of their ancestors. Every two years, the Tlingits,

SUGGESTED READINGS:

Collier, John. *American Indian Ceremonial Dances*. New York: Alfred A. Knopf, 1972.

Erdoes, Richard. *Crying for a Dream*. Sante Fe: Bear and Company Publishing, 1989.

Heth, Charlotte. *Native American Dance: Ceremonies and Social Traditions*. Washington, D.C.: Fulcrum/Smithsonian, 1992.

Horse-Capture, George P. *Powwow*. Wyoming: Buffalo Bill Historical Center, 1989.

Scholl, Jane D. "Dancing in Honor of Their People." *Smithsonian*, February 1993, pp. 90-97.

DANCING RABBIT CREEK, TREATY OF

Better known as the Treaty of Dancing Rabbit Creek, the "Treaty with the Choctaw, 1830," was signed on September 27, 1830, between the United States and the Choctaw Nation. Signed at Dancing Rabbit Creek in the Choctaw Nation (present-day Mississippi), the treaty was ratified by Congress and proclaimed on February 24, 1831.

The Treaty of Dancing Rabbit Creek was the climax of a generation of effort on the part of the United States to remove eastern Indians to the West. The policy was first suggested by President Thomas Jefferson and presented to the Choctaws at the negotiations for the Treaty of Mount Dexter in 1805. The Choctaws rejected it. Repeated efforts by the United States resulted in the Choctaws agreeing to exchange a portion of their Mississippi lands in 1820 for lands in the West, but the Choctaws again refused to move. After the deaths of two of the three Choctaw district chiefs in 1824, Pushmataha and Puckshenubbe, and after the election of Andrew Jackson as president in 1828, the Choctaws found themselves unable to resist removal, a policy that Jackson pursued vigorously.

By this treaty, which was negotiated in the face of vigorous opposition within the Choctaw Nation, the United States forced the Choctaws to cede their remaining lands in Mississippi, the core of their ancient homeland. The Choctaws were to be removed as a nation to land west of the Mississippi River, land that the Choctaws had purchased from the United States by the treaty of 1820. By that earlier treaty, the Choctaws held title from the United States to an immense territory in the West. It reached from present-day central Arkansas on the east to the headwaters of the Canadian River in the west, which are in the front range of the Rocky Mountains in the northeastern section of present-day New Mexico. This Choctaw land included present-day southwestern Arkansas, the southern half of Oklahoma, the area now known as the Texas Panhandle, and a large portion of northeastern New Mexico.

But there were other claims to this land. The western half of this region was the very core of the Comanche heartland; neither the United States nor the Choctaws paid any attention to this. Plus, the extreme far western portion of this land lay within the Republic of Mexico in 1820. But in 1830, a treaty modified the western boundary to

An eighteenth-century French artist produced this drawing of Choctaws. Being situated near French Louisiana, Spanish Florida, and the English Carolinas, the Choctaws gained skill in diplomacy that enabled them to secure title from the United States to a huge track of land west of the Mississippi, to which they were removed by the Treaty of Dancing Rabbit Creek.

exclude Mexican territory from the grant. By a treaty in 1825, the grant was modified to exclude territory that is now within Arkansas. These changes left the Choctaws holding title, in 1830, to what now constitutes the southern half of Oklahoma. In subsequent treaties, the Choctaws leased the western half of this area to the United States, which used it for a reserve for the Comanches, thus making the Comanches the tenants of the Choctaws in their own homeland.

By the terms of the treaty of 1830, the Choctaws were given a choice of removing to the West or accepting individual allotments of land in Mississippi and becoming citizens of that state. Many Choctaws attempted to receive allotments, but they found that government officials refused to enroll them for the plots. Fraud and corruption, as well as indifference to their plight and to their rights under the agreement, resulted in very few Choctaws actually receiving any Mississippi land. The United States was also obligated to sell the Choctaw Mississippi land and then pay to the Choctaws the net proceeds from the sale. The federal government sold the land but then refused to pay the money to the Choctaws. This "net proceeds" fund became a subject of lawsuits and repeated Choctaw appeals to Congress for decades before payment was finally made. Unfortunately, by this time, attorneys' fees had consumed a huge portion of it.

Having experienced the attempts of the state of Mississippi to interfere in Choctaw national affairs after Mississippi Territory gained statehood in 1817, the Choctaws demanded guarantees of their sovereignty in the West in the 1830 treaty. The treaty read: "The Government and people of the United States are hereby obliged to secure to the said Choctaw Nation of Red People the jurisdiction and government of all the persons and property that may be within their limits west, so that no Territory or State shall ever have a right to pass laws for the government of the Choctaw Nation of Red People and their descendants; and that no part of the land granted them shall ever be embraced in any Territory or State."

By this treaty, the Choctaws became the first Indian nation to be removed to the West by the United States as an entire nation. The removal, conducted in installments during the winter months between 1831 and 1834, killed twenty-five hundred Choctaws. They arrived in the West impoverished and traumatized, forced to abandon centuries of improvements to the farmland in their ancient homeland. They also suffered from the death of most of their elderly people, who had possessed irreplaceable cultural, medicinal, and spiritual knowledge. The Choctaws were removed to the extreme eastern portion of their land in the West, which now constitutes a ten and one-half county area of Oklahoma. The guarantees to the sovereignty of their nation in the West proved hollow when the United States admitted Oklahoma to statehood in 1907 and proclaimed that the Indian nations within the new state had been abolished, a contention that is vigorously contested by Choctaws and other Indian nations to this day.

— D. L. Birchfield

SEE ALSO:
Choctaw; General Allotment Act; Jackson, Andrew; Oklahoma; Removal Act, Indian.

SUGGESTED READINGS:
Debo, Angie. *The Rise and Fall of the Choctaw Republic.* Norman: University of Oklahoma Press, 1934.
Gipson, Arrell, ed. *America's Exiles: Indian Colonization in Oklahoma.* Oklahoma City: Oklahoma Historical Society, 1976.
Kappler, Charles, comp. *Indian Affairs, Laws and Treaties,* Vol. II. Washington, D.C.: U.S. Government Printing Office, 1904.

DANN SISTERS

Carrie and Mary Dann are members of the Western Shoshones and live in Nevada, where they work as ranchers. The sisters have become well known for their fight for land rights for the Western Shoshones. In 1993, in honor of their lifelong commitment to Native rights, they won the Right Livelihood Award, an award given for outstanding international contributions in situations of conflict.

At issue in the land-rights fight in which the Dann sisters are active are the Western Shoshone Nation's rights to self-government and land use, based on the Treaty of Ruby Valley signed by the

Western Shoshones and the U.S. government in 1863. The treaty, one of peace and friendship, entitles the United States to rights of passage and trade, but it does not give land.

For the past twenty years, the Dann Ranch has released its livestock onto Shoshone land to graze. The U.S. government, however, claims that the land belongs to the United States. The Bureau of Land Management has rounded up Dann livestock for "unauthorized" grazing on "public land." The Dann sisters have refused to get a permit to graze their cattle, stating the land belongs to the Western Shoshones.

In 1979, the United States government made a payment of $26 million to the Shoshones in damages for land taken by gradual encroachment. Viewing the issue as one of land and not of money, the Western Shoshones refused to accept the money, so the Secretary of the Interior acted as trustee for the Shoshones and accepted the money in their behalf. The payment, which sits in a U.S. Treasury account, has grown to more than $60 million. The Western Shoshones continue to refuse to accept the money, claiming that the land still belongs to the Shoshones.

In 1992, the Dann sisters' livestock was rounded up and impounded. In an effort to stop Bureau of Land Management authorities, Clifford Dann, Carrie and Mary's brother, doused himself with gasoline and threatened to set himself on fire. He was charged and convicted for assaulting federal officers and was sentenced to nine months in prison.

The struggle has continued and has brought international attention to the Dann Ranch and the struggle of the Western Shoshones to maintain their land.

SEE ALSO:
Bureau of Land Management.

DAWES COMMISSION

In March 1893, the U.S. Congress passed into law an act that gave the U.S. government increased authority over Native lands. With the passage of the Dawes Severalty Act, the president of the United States became authorized to appoint three commissioners to make agreements with Indians for allotting communal Indian lands to individual Indians and selling the remaining Indian land to whites.

Henry L. Dawes, a former senator from Massachusetts, became chairman of the commission. Meredith H. Kidd of Indiana and Archibald S. McKennon of Arkansas were appointed by President Grover Cleveland as the other members of the commission. The commission was officially designated as the Commission to the Five Civilized Tribes, but because of the fame of its chairman, it became known as the Dawes Commission.

Henry Laurens Dawes (1816–1903), author of the so-called Dawes Act of 1887, which caused Indian nations in present-day Oklahoma to lose their last remaining tribal lands.

Part of the commission's responsibility was to divide land up into equal values, so it ended up appraising the land, as well as making agreements with the different Indian nations. These agreements were extracted under duress, with the Indians being told that they would get less land if they did not agree to the allotment process and that the commission would go ahead with the allotment with or without the consent of the Indians.

To accomplish allotment, it became necessary for the commission to formally enroll tribal members. Tribal rolls had been kept, but the commission found that the rolls and census were neither accurate nor up-to-date. So commission employees began enrolling tribal members.

The commission ended up going to every remote village and town in the lands of the so-called Five Civilized Tribes (Cherokees, Creeks, Chickasaws, Choctaws, and Seminoles), in present-day eastern Oklahoma, seeking out Native people for enrollment. Being listed on the rolls was the only way a tribal member could obtain an allotment of land.

These rolls, known as the Dawes Rolls, eventually became a way of tracing Native ancestry. It has also become a way for the government to determine the amount of Indian blood a person has. The Dawes Rolls are among the few rolls in which blood quantum—the amount of Indian blood—is registered. For some Indian nations, this figure can be very important when people apply for tribal membership, and it sometimes has a bearing on government benefits for which one may be eligible. In the eyes of the U.S. government and various Indian groups alike, the Dawes Rolls have become a way of measuring one's "Indianness," or the extent to which a person is Indian.

Several court cases have relied on the integrity of the Dawes Rolls after people have tried to claim Indian lands for themselves. The courts have ruled that the Dawes Commission so thoroughly and precisely enrolled people that the Dawes Rolls should stand as the final word among the Five Civilized Tribes.

Despite the heavy authority that has been given the Dawes Rolls, their accuracy may be questioned for the simple reason that many people refused to sign the rolls. Even though these people were Indi-

an, they disagreed with the breaking up of communally held tribal lands and would not sign the rolls or accept the allotments. Although these people believed they were doing the right thing, because their names do not appear on the rolls, their children and grandchildren are considered "non-Indian" by the federal government. Those who do not have ancestors on the Dawes Rolls are not allowed to enroll in certain nations.

Because of this difficulty, these Indians are not allowed their rights as Indian people with the protections granted those who are enrolled in nations recognized by the federal government. The Dawes rolls totaled only 101,506 names of men, women, and children. Based on this figure, the Indian land was allotted to individual Indians.

Land not allotted to individual Indians was opened to white settlement, resulting in the loss of millions of acres of Indian land. The breaking up of the tribal land estate was a devastating blow to Indian tribal sovereignty and the traditional Indian way of life. Today, the work of the Dawes Commission is seen as one of the strongest tools used by the United States in its attempt to extinguish Native American culture.

SEE ALSO:
General Allotment Act; Nonrecognized Communities.

DEBO, ANGIE (1890–1988)

Angie Debo, a non-Native historian from Marshall, Oklahoma, devoted much of her life to writing about American Indian history. She was born on January 30, 1890, the year after Oklahoma (formerly Indian Territory) opened for non-Indian settlement.

Debo came from a pioneer family that settled in Oklahoma and farmed for a living. She studied at the University of Chicago and obtained her M.A. in international relations. She received a Ph.D. degree in history from the University of Oklahoma, and her doctoral dissertation was published in 1934 by the University of Oklahoma Press under the title *The Rise and Fall of the Choctaw Republic*.

While Debo wrote more general works about

Indian history, the history of the Oklahoma Indians was a special interest. Her writings reveal how the Indian Territory, which had been guaranteed by treaties to the so-called Five Civilized Tribes of the Southeast (Choctaws, Chickasaws, Cherokees, Seminoles, and Creeks), was systematically stolen by the United States government from the Indians.

Putting herself at great personal risk, in one of her books she implicated prominent Oklahoma politicians in conspiracies to defraud Native people of their allotments (portions of once-tribal lands now open to individual settlement). The University of Oklahoma Press refused to publish the book, saying in its rejection letter that one of its chapters was "dangerous." Debo's work was later published in 1940 by Princeton University Press under the title *And Still the Waters Run*. To this day, this book is considered a major source of information concerning the history and treatment of Native people in Indian Territory (later Oklahoma).

Debo wrote about how the Dawes Commission, established by the United States government, lied and defrauded the Five Civilized Tribes to get them to go along with the government's policy of dividing their communally owned lands into individual allotments. Once the land was allotted, it was easy for non-Indians to force the Indians to sell their plot or to otherwise acquire the land. With the discovery of oil on Indian land, the pace of non-Native acquisition accelerated. Twenty years after the allotment system was put in place, only 20 percent of the land remained in Indian hands.

In addition to working as an author, Angie Debo was a high school teacher, maps librarian, and pastor. In an interview shortly before her death (February 2, 1988), which was later broadcast as a PBS television special, she stated that her philosophy about life was to dedicate that life to service, integrity, and creative use. She was devoted to seeking knowledge and to telling the truth.

SEE ALSO:
Cherokee; Chickasaw; Choctaw; Creek; Dawes Commission; Five Civilized Tribes; General Allotment Act; Oklahoma; Seminole.

DECLARATION OF INDEPENDENCE, U.S.

Native Americans and their societies figured into conceptions of life, liberty, and happiness in the minds of Thomas Jefferson, who wrote the Declaration of Independence, and Benjamin Franklin, who operated in many ways as Jefferson's revolutionary mentor. A major debate at the time resulted in the phrase "happiness" being substituted for "property," in which the two founders' description of American Indian societies played a provocative role.

Both sought to create a society that operated as much as possible on consensus and public opinion, while citing the same qualities in Native societies. Both described Native people's passion for liberty while making it a patriotic rallying cry for the American colonists. And both Jefferson and Franklin admired Indians' notions of happiness while seeking a definition that would suit the new nation.

Franklin wrote: "All the Indians of North America not under the dominion of the Spaniards are in that natural state, being restrained by no Laws, having no Courts, or Ministers of Justice, no Suits, no prisons, no governors vested with any Legal Authority. The persuasion of Men distinguished by Reputation of Wisdom is the only Means by which others are govern'd, or rather led—and the State of the Indians was probably the first State of all Nations."

Jefferson said much the same in his *Notes on Virginia*. This wording was inserted into the 1787 edition, as the Constitutional Convention was meeting: "The native Americans," wrote Jefferson, had never "submitted themselves to any laws, any coercive power and shadow of government. Their only controls are their manners, and the moral sense of right and wrong . . . An offence against these is punished by contempt, by exclusion from society, or, where the cause is serious, as that of murder, by the individuals whom it concerns. Imperfect as this species of control may seem, crimes are very rare among them."

The lesson here seemed clear to Jefferson: "Insomuch that it were made a question, whether no law, as among the savage Americans, or too much law, as among the civilized Europeans, submits man to

427

the greater evil, one who has seen both conditions of existence would pronounce it to be the last."

As they decried and turned their backs on contemporary Europe, architects of the new nation such as Franklin, Jefferson, and Thomas Paine described American Indian societies in ways strikingly similar to their visions of the state they hoped to erect, modified to suit a people of European ancestry. Jefferson wrote: "The only condition on earth to be compared with ours, in my opinion, is that of the Indian, where they have still less law than we." When Paine wrote that "government, like dress is the badge of lost innocence" and Jefferson said that the best government governs least, they were summing up their observations of Native American societies, either directly, or through the eyes of European philosophers such as Locke and Rousseau.

Writing to Edward Carrington in 1787, Jefferson linked freedom of expression with public opinion as well as happiness, citing American Indian societies as an example: "The basis of our government being the opinion of the people, our very first object should be to keep that right; and were it left to me to decide whether we should have a government without newspapers or newspapers without a government, I should not hesitate for a moment to prefer the latter. . . . I am convinced that those societies [as the Indians'] . . . enjoy in their general mass an infinitely greater degree of happiness than those who live under European governments."

— B. E. Johansen

SEE ALSO:
American Revolution; Constitution, United States; Franklin, Benjamin; Jefferson, Thomas.

DEER, ADA B. (1935–)

Ada B. Deer is an enrolled member and former chair of the Menominee Nation of Wisconsin. She was nominated by President Bill Clinton on May 11, 1993, to be Assistant Secretary-Indian Affairs in the U.S. Department of the Interior. Following her confirmation before the Senate Committee on Indian Affairs, she was sworn into office on July 16, 1993.

Ada Deer became the first woman and sixth person to hold the office since it was created in 1977. Just prior to her appointment, she had served as a senior lecturer at the School of Social Work and American Indian Studies Program at the University of Wisconsin-Madison. She was also a candidate for the U.S. House of Representatives in 1992.

At her Senate confirmation hearings, Deer stated that her life as a Menominee, as a social worker, and as a human being had contributed to her having dedicated herself to being an agent of change. "You should know that forty years ago my tribe, the Menominee, was terminated; twenty years ago we were restored; and today I come before you as a true survivor of Indian policy," she told the committee.

Deer also told the committee that her vision for the Bureau of Indian Affairs was to create a federal-tribal partnership in which long-held promises would be fulfilled and long-overdue injustices would be addressed. In her view, federal Indian policy must be dedicated to the growth of tribal sovereignty, and the role of the federal government should be "to support and to implement tribally inspired solutions to tribally defined problems." According to Deer, "The days of federal paternalism are over."

Deer was born on the Menominee reservation, where thirty years later she led the struggle to restore federal recognition to her tribe after it was terminated by what she describes as "the misguided and now-discredited . . . policies of the 1950s." She has led a long and distinguished career of involvement in Indian causes ever since.

Deer is a founding director of Americans for Indian Opportunity and the American Indian Graduate Program. She was appointed by the U.S. Senate to the American Indian Policy Review Commission in 1974 and has been a client, a staff member, a board member, board chair, and finally chair of the National Support Committee of the Native American Rights Fund. She has also served on the boards of the Girl Scouts, Common Cause, Independent Sector, National Association of Social Work, and other organizations. She was appointed by both Presidents Carter and Reagan to the President's Commission on White House Fellowships.

On July 16, 1993, Ada Deer, a Menominee, became the first woman to serve in the U.S. Department of the Interior as assistant secretary for Indian Affairs.

Deer was the first member of her tribe to graduate from the University of Wisconsin (1957) and the first American Indian to receive a master's degree from the School of Social Work at Columbia University (1961). She was a fellow at the Harvard Institute of Politics, John F. Kennedy School of Government, in 1977. In addition, her academic honors include Doctor of Humane Letters from the University of Wisconsin-Madison. Among numerous other honors, Deer was presented a National Distinguished Achievement Award by the American Indian Resources Institute in 1991 and was named Woman of the Year by the Girl Scouts of America in 1982.

SEE ALSO:
Bureau of Indian Affairs.

DEGANAWIDAH

The Iroquois Confederacy was founded by the prophet Deganawidah, who is called "the Peacemaker" in oral discourse among many Iroquois. Deganawidah enlisted the aid of a speaker, Aionwantha (sometimes called Hiawatha), to spread his vision of a united Iroquois confederacy.

Deganawidah needed a spokesman in the oral culture of the Iroquois because he stuttered so badly he could hardly speak, a condition that Iroquois oral history attributes to a double row of teeth. The confederacy was founded before first European contact in the area, possibly as early as 900 C.E. or as late as 1500 C.E. Deganawidah sought to replace blood feuds, which had devastated the Iroquois, with peaceful modes of decision making. The result was the Great Law of Peace (sometimes called the Great Binding Law) of the Iroquois, which endures to this day as one of the oldest forms of participatory democracy on earth. The Iroquois Confederacy originally included the Mohawks, Oneidas, Onondagas, Cayugas, and Senecas. The sixth nation, the Tuscaroras, migrated into Iroquois country in the early eighteenth century.

According to Iroquois oral history, the visionary Hiawatha tried to call councils to eliminate the blood feud, but they were always thwarted by an evil and twisted person, Tadadaho, an Onondaga who used magic and spies to rule by fear and intimidation. Failing to defeat Tadadaho, Hiawatha traveled to Mohawk, Oneida, and Cayuga villages with his message of peace and brotherhood. Everywhere he went, his message was accepted with the condition that he persuade the formidable Tadadaho and the Onondagas to agree to peace.

Just as Hiawatha was despairing, the prophet Deganawidah entered his life. Together, the two men developed a powerful message of peace. Deganawidah's vision gave substance to Hiawatha's words. Through Deganawidah's vision, the constitution of the Iroquois was formulated. In his vision, Deganawidah saw a giant white pine reaching to the sky and gaining strength from three counterbalancing principles of life. The first principle was that a stable mind and healthy body should be in balance so that peace between individuals and groups could occur. Secondly, Deganawidah stated that compassionate, humane conduct, thought, and speech were a requirement for equity and justice among peoples. Finally, he foresaw a society in which physical strength and civil authority would reinforce the power of the clan system.

With such a powerful vision, Deganawidah and Hiawatha were able to subdue the evil Tadadaho and transform his mind. Deganawidah removed evil feelings and thoughts from the head of Tadadaho and said ". . . thou shalt strive . . . to make reason and the peaceful mind prevail." Tadadaho became reborn into a humane person charged with carrying out the message of Deganawidah. After Tadadaho had submitted to the redemption, Onondaga became the central fire of the Iroquois and the Onondagas became the "firekeepers" of the new confederacy.

SEE ALSO:
Hiawatha; Iroquois Confederacy; Mohawk; Oneida; Onondaga; Tuscarora.

DELAWARE (STATE)

Delaware became a U.S. state in 1787 when it was the first of the former colonies to ratify the U.S. Constitution. Delaware is named for Thomas West, Baron De La Warr, who was the first governor of Virginia from 1609 to 1618.

Barton Cartwright, a Delaware, displays traditional dance regalia.

The first European contact in Delaware occurred in 1609 when Henry Hudson explored the area. The first European settlement in Delaware was established in 1631 by the Dutch West Indian Company, which founded a tobacco growing and whaling company at Zwaanendeal, the site of present-day Lewes. The settlement lasted just one year and was abandoned because of strong Native resistance.

A Swedish settlement was established at Fort Christina, present-day Wilmington, in 1638 as part of the colony of New Sweden. In 1655, the Dutch gained control of the colony, but they surrendered it to the British in 1664.

Along with the European invasion, the Lenapes also faced pressure from the Iroquois League. By 1720, the Lenapes had been pushed from Delaware into eastern Ohio, where they resisted American expansion until 1795, when they ceded their Ohio lands. After 1795, the Lenapes lived in widely dispersed bands in Ohio, Missouri, Arkansas, Texas, and Ontario, Canada. Many Lenape men served as U.S. Army scouts during Indian wars on the Plains and in the Pacific Northwest.

No federal reservations exist in Delaware, but the 1990 U.S. Census lists 2,019 Indians as Delaware residents, placing Delaware forty-eighth among U.S. states in Native American population. The Lenape, or Delaware tribe, lists members throughout the United States and in Canada.

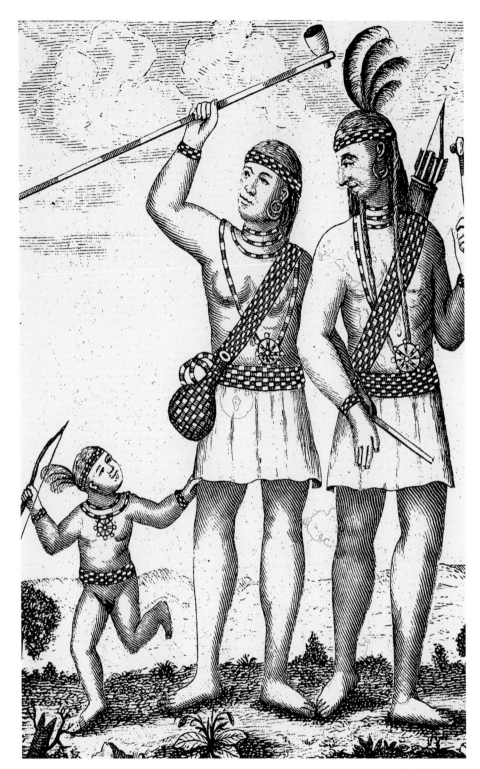

A depiction of Delawares from a drawing titled "New Sweden," by Campanius.

One major Indian group lived in the Delaware area. This group was called "the Delaware" by Europeans, but they called themselves the Lenape. The Lenapes were a confederated group made up of the Munsees, the Unalachtigos, and the Unamis.

SEE ALSO:
Lenape.